CORUŇA TO SEVASTOPOL.

FROM CORUNA TO SEVASTOPOL

THE HISTORY

OF

'C' BATTERY, 'A' BRIGADE

(LATE 'C' TROOP),

ROYAL HORSE ARTILLERY

WITH SUCCESSION OF OFFICERS FROM
ITS FORMATION TO THE PRESENT TIME

BY
COLONEL F. A. WHINYATES
LATE ROYAL HORSE ARTILLERY,
FORMERLY COMMANDING THE BATTERY

The Naval & Military Press Ltd

published in association with

FIREPOWER
The Royal Artillery Museum
Woolwich

Published by
The Naval & Military Press Ltd
Unit 10 Ridgewood Industrial Park,
Uckfield, East Sussex,
TN22 5QE England
Tel: +44 (0) 1825 749494
Fax: +44 (0) 1825 765701
www.naval-military-press.com

in association with

FIREPOWER
The Royal Artillery Museum, Woolwich
www.firepower.org.uk

In reprinting in facsimile from the original, any imperfections are inevitably reproduced and the quality may fall short of modern type and cartographic standards.

PREFACE.

In compiling this History, the following sources of information have been consulted, namely, Mobility of Field Artillery Past and Present, by Lieut. H. W. L. Hime. R.A., Institution Papers. Manuscript Notes, from an officer of the War Academy, Berlin. Modern Artillery, by Lieut.-Colonel Owen, R.A., Murray, London, 1871. Records of the Horse Brigade, by Colonel J. E. Michell, Royal Horse Artillery, Boddy and Co., Woolwich, 1874. England's Artillerymen, by J. A. Browne, R.A., Hall, Smart and Allan, London, 1865. Journal of Waterloo Campaign, by General C. Mercer, R.A., Blackwood, Edinburgh, 1870. Letters of Lieut.-Colonel Sir Augustus Frazer, R.H.A., edited by Major-General Sabine, R.A., Longman and Roberts, London, 1859. The Royal Artillery Record Office. Kane's List of Officers of the Royal Artillery, Delahoy, Greenwich, 1815. The Record Tower, Dublin Castle; History of the Irish Rebellion, 1798, by Maxwell, Bailey

Brothers, Cornhill, 1845. Annual Registers. Private Letters of Sir Edward Whinyates. Campaign of the British Army in Spain under Lieut.-General Sir John Moore, by J. Moore, London, 1809. Napier's History of the Peninsular War, Murray, London, 1827. Despatches of the Duke of Wellington. History of the 52nd Light Infantry, by Rev. W. Leeke, Hatchard and Co., London, 1866. History of the King's German Legion, by Beamish, Boone, London, 1832. History of the Royal Artillery, by Captain Duncan, R.A., Murray, London, 1872. Souvenirs de General Mathieu Dumas. Paris, Grosselin, 1839. Vie de General Pajol, General in chef, Paris, 1874. Conquête de l'Andalousie, par Col. Lapéne. Histoire de la Guerre de la Péninsule, par le Général Foy, Paris, 1827.

The writer has aimed at producing a trustworthy as well as an interesting work. Nothing, therefore, has been stated but what rests on a sound and authentic basis. He takes this opportunity to offer his sincere thanks to all those who have rendered him assistance, especially to the writer of the Crimean Narrative, to whom he feels deeply indebted.

UNITED SERVICE CLUB,
London, 1st November, 1883.

CONTENTS.

	PAGE
CHAPTER I.—INTRODUCTION	1
,, II.—FORMATION OF 'C' TROOP.—TWO GUNS DETACHED TO IRELAND, 1798.—CHANGES OF QUARTERS.—EXPEDITION TO SPAIN, 1808	24
,, III.—DIARY OF CORUÑA CAMPAIGN.—REMARKS ON CAMPAIGN.—RETURN HOME.—FROM 1809 TO 1815 ...	32
,, IV.—PENINSULAR SERVICE OF 'D' TROOP, ROYAL HORSE ARTILLERY.—REDUCTIONS IN HORSE ARTILLERY.—CHANGES OF QUARTERS.—AUGMENTATIONS PREVIOUS TO CRIMEAN WAR	55
,, V.—EMBARKATION FOR TURKEY.—BULGARIA.—INVASION OF CRIMEA.—BULGANAK	73
,, VI.—BATTLE OF ALMA.—FLANK MARCH.—CAPTURE OF BALACLAVA.—PLATEAU OF SEVASTOPOL	92
,, VII.—BATTLE OF BALACLAVA	124
,, VIII.—REMARKS ON, AND FURTHER RECOLLECTIONS OF, THE BATTLE OF BALACLAVA	149
,, IX.—CAMP AT THE COL.—INKERMAN.—WINTER, SPRING, AND SUMMER AT BALACLAVA	203
,, X.—EXPEDITION TO EUPATORIA	239
,, XI.—RETURN TO ENGLAND.—CHANGE OF QUARTERS.—EMBARKATION FOR INDIA.—INDIAN SERVICE.—RETURN HOME.—IRELAND.—CONCLUSION	260
APPENDIXES	279
GENERAL INDEX	301

ERRATA.

Page 5. Fourteenth line from top, after 1621 there should be a comma.
,, 6. Last line, *for* Trantenau *read* Trautenau.
,, 7. Fifth line from bottom, ditto.
,, 9. Third line from bottom, *for* pounders *read* pounds.
,, 24. Second line from bottom, *for* Griffith *read* Griffiths.
,, 28. Twelfth line from bottom, ditto.
,, 38. Eighth line from bottom, *for* Allen *read* Alten.
,, 41. Eighth line from bottom, *for* Quinton *read* Quintin.
,, 58. Eleventh line from top, *after* Peninsula *read* " with Lord Wellington."
,, 62. Twelfth line from bottom, *for* a mitraile *read* à metraille.
,, 70. Fifth line from bottom, *after* August *read* 1837.
,, 94. Thirteenth line from bottom, *for* Badderly *read* Baddeley.
,, 272. Twelfth line from bottom, *for* J. Burnett *read* T. Burnett.

CORUÑA TO SEVASTOPOL.

CHAPTER I.

INTRODUCTION.

THE strong regimental feeling which has always existed in the English Army, and which has been its great source of strength, is represented in the Artillery by an equally deep attachment to the Batteries to which the officer or the man belongs. Thus the past history of any Battery cannot be a matter of indifference to any one who has served with it. As also the whole regiment of Royal Artillery prides itself on the achievements of each of its parts, the records of a Battery which has a long and glorious history may be read by a wider circle than that actually personally interested in its deeds. In the case of the Battery whose history this work attempts to recount, the fact of its formation at the first introduction of Horse Artillery into England, and of its participation in the longest and hardest-fought campaigns which have since added fresh glories to the British arms, may make the tale acceptable to the general reader, and all the more so as the writer has been successful in obtaining original accounts of both the Peninsular and of the Crimean Wars, which are worthy of comparison with the more generally circulated histories.

Every year the survivors of the Crimea and of other campaigns drop off, as well as the older officers who remember the traditions of the Peninsular recounted by their former comrades. Many an interesting and valuable story has thus already been lost, and the unused mine of anecdote is farther from our reach every day. The author thus hopes that his history of the Battery with which he was most intimately connected may be met with sympathy. In writing it, the records of other Batteries have to be alluded to, and common misconceptions as to their history have to be rectified. Each of these Batteries has its own history, and it is only by collecting their experiences that the ground for a worthy record of the whole Horse Artillery can be prepared.

It has been hoped that this work may interest the general reader, and therefore, before commencing the history of the Battery itself, it will be best to give a short description of the nature of the force and of its origin, progress, and development.

The military reader must pardon the lingering over details well known to him; while the general reader must be asked to remember that details of marches, etc., dry to him, have an interest to the military man: in peace as the record of the life of the Battery; in war as giving interesting means of checking the accounts of the general historians.

In Europe the invention of cannon may be considered nearly coincident with the discovery of gunpowder, or at least its application to military purposes about 1320. Cannon were probably first used in the attack of towns and castles, but gradually they superseded the ballistæ and other military machines of the period, and formed an adjunct to armies in the field. Unwieldy and mounted on ill-constructed carriages, they appear in early days to have been an impediment rather than a service to the armies to which they belonged. They could seldom be brought up for sudden action, nor could they change their positions in a pitched battle; and if the army were forced to retire, the guns, being unable to accompany it, generally fell into the enemies' hands. The then simple character of battles, and the almost entire absence of manœuvres by contending armies, prevented much advance being made in the mobility of field artillery during the first three centuries of its existence. It was then organized into what were called "Trains," the size and the armament of which varied according to the undertaking for which they were formed: the heavy guns for siege purposes, and the lighter pieces intended for the field, together with the ammunition waggons, vehicles for the conveyance of implements and stores, etc., being massed together in one body without any distinct organization or equipment. When a warlike expedition was decided upon, and the size of the train fixed, in England the Master-General of the Ordnance was called upon to arrange its details, and to appoint to it the officers and attendants, whose services however, with the exception of a small permanent staff, ceased when the expedition was concluded.

As an example of the composition of these Trains, it may be stated that the one with which Marlborough in 1702 began his campaign against the French consisted of thirty-four pieces of ordnance, including fourteen sakers or guns for field service, sixteen three-pounders, and four howitzers or pieces firing shells (hollow iron spheres filled with powder), and was attended by two companies of gunners, one of pioneers, and one of pontoon men, besides a number of artificers, and the staff. A Train of Artillery formed part of a camp held in Hyde

Park in 1723; this Train was composed of twenty guns of different sizes, and had seventy-six horses for its transport, with a personnel of three officers, six non-commissioned officers, and sixty gunners and matrosses. The latter were soldiers in the Train who assisted the gunners in working the guns; they carried firelocks and marched with the store-waggons, both as a guard, and to give assistance should a waggon break down. Lastly, in 1727, a Train of Artillery for field service in Flanders was prepared of the following proportions. Twenty-four guns and six mortars or short pieces of ordnance used in sieges for throwing large shells and carcasses (shells filled with a highly inflammatory composition), manned by a complete company of artillery, twelve artificers, and twenty-two pontoon men, a total of 140 of all ranks, with a staff of twelve officers, including one kettle-drummer and his coachman. In camp a particular position was assigned to the Train, the transport of which on the march was effected either by horses or bullocks. They, with their drivers, were hired in the country the army was operating in: a system which obtained till the beginning of the present century; but any attempted movement of guns on the field of battle was carried out by hand. For the protection of the Train on the march, it was preceded by a body of light cavalry; they were followed by the carriages loaded with gyns, capstans, levers, and other machines; next came the guns of various sizes, followed by the ammunition waggons, by the pontoons and their attendants, by the artillery artificers, and lastly by the baggage. The whole moved under the direction of the Chief of Artillery. As the Train was not subdivided in any way into distinct units, the mass was an unwieldy one; and the difficulty of extricating any particular guns from it for sudden action, or of attempting any manœuvres for the whole in the field, can be imagined.

During the fourteenth, fifteenth, and sixteenth centuries, attempts at progress in Artillery were principally confined to improvements of accuracy of fire, till at length successful efforts were made by Gustavus Adolphus, King of Sweden, who may justly be considered the father of modern field artillery, to form a distinct body of that arm, by introducing alterations which enabled it to co-operate with other troops in their movements, and to thus perform its proper duties on the field of battle. Perceiving during his early campaigns the great disadvantages of his cumbrous field artillery, he determined to increase its mobility at all risks, and accordingly during his war against Poland, brought into the field about 1621 very light pieces called "Kalter" guns, made of copper and strengthened with leather and coiled rope, the superior mobility of which more than compensated for their inferiority of precision as compared with the iron guns of the time. But before commencing his German campaigns he was able to replace these leather guns by light iron four-pounders of about five cwt., which were each drawn by two horses, and their rapidity of fire was increased by the use in loading of cartridges, that is, placing the powder, already weighed, in a flannel bag, instead of weighing out on the spot a charge of powder suited for the exact range intended to attain, and placing it in the bore of the gun by means of a long ladle, as had hitherto been the custom. Fully appreciating the importance of Artillery, he also largely added to the number of guns with his army. The battle of Leipsic against the Imperialists under Tilly, in September, 1631, was won through the effective manœuvring of these light iron guns by Gustavus Adolphus. On the death of the King, who was before his age in artillery tactics, improvement ceased, and Artillery for some time may be said to have rather retrograded than advanced.

At the beginning of the eighteenth century Artillery was still in a very backward condition. That belonging to Austria was the most efficient and best handled in Europe; and it was in consequence of the heavy losses experienced by the Prussian Infantry from the fire of the Austrian guns in the early part of the "Seven Years' War," that Frederick the Great, who till then had set little value on the ordnance of his own army, turned his attention to its improvement.

Furthermore, Frederick found that the Prussian Cavalry had been drilled to deliver its fire at a halt. He quickly discerned the defects of this system, and abolished it. But, having deprived his cavalry of its fire, it was necessary to find a substitute.

With the object of meeting these difficulties he adopted for the field some light guns, mounted on carriages constructed of the best materials, combining strength with lightness, and carrying a large amount of ammunition per gun. The new guns were formed into a small manageable group or unit, called a Battery. They were drawn by horses driven postilionwise; and the gunners were mounted men. This artillery could thus manœuvre with cavalry, change position, and protect the deployment of columns in a manner hitherto impossible. The germ of mobility is traceable to the Swedish Artillery of Gustavus Adolphus, but the art of manœuvring in the face of an enemy cannot be said to have had any existence till towards the close of the "Seven Years' War," or about 120 years ago. Frederick had devised the above-mentioned improvements in 1758, but it was not till the following year (see Appendix I.) that four light six-pounders of the newly-organized artillery were ready, and formed a part of the King's column, with which, on the 29th and 30th June, 1759, he made his raid from Lanshut to Trantenau. The Battery was organized as follows (and it is curious to note how similar the Batteries of Horse Artillery of the present day are in the main to the original model, of which, moreover, the King undertook the drill and instruction, daily directing its movements). The Battery consisted of six six-pounder guns; each piece had six draught horses with three drivers, and a detachment of seven or eight mounted gunners, one of whom acted as horse-holder when the others dismounted to serve the gun. The riding horses of the teams and of the detachment carried dragoon saddles, behind each of which were fastened a corn sack, a forage cord, a bundle of hay, and a picketing peg. The off-horses of the teams carried pads, and the officers and men were dressed much the same as the rest of the artillery. Each division (two guns) of the Battery was commanded by an under officer, and the whole by an officer. The drivers and horses were entrusted to a Commissary of Horse—a faulty arrangement, tending to withdraw them from the care of the officers; furthermore, the drivers were at first taken from the scum of the army, till the destruction of the Prussian Horse Artillery at the battles of "Kunersdorf" and "Maxen," through the misconduct of these men, led on each occasion to its reconstruction, and eventually to the drivers becoming an integral part of the Battery. A waggon-master and an artificer were responsible for the completeness of the carriages, on which, in the limbers, were carried a large amount of ammunition, eighty rounds of shot and twenty of canister per gun. So successful was the performance of the four guns of this Horse Artillery in the Trantenau Expedition that its organization was approved, and a similar Battery was raised at Pretsch by Prince Henry of Prussia, 29th October, 1759. A unit of artillery was thus established as capable of individual control in the field as cavalry and infantry regiments.

Some thirty years after Horse Artillery had been established by Frederick the Great, "Light Artillery," as it was also then called, was adopted by the Austrians, but with an inferior organization. In France in 1791, at the instigation of General De La Fayette, two *Divisions* of Horse Artillery were formed, each of eight guns, reduced soon to six, the original number being found too many for a company of men, and they did such good service that the number was increased, and in 1794 France possessed nine regiments of Horse Artillery. The rest of Europe by degrees, like the French, selected the Prussian or mounted detachment system. The question of this arm forming part of the English army was brought before the authorities in 1788; but a definite organization was not decided upon till the virtual rupture with France in 1792. In January, 1793, orders were issued for the formation of two bodies of Horse Artillery, each with four guns, called a "Troop," the term "Battery" being substituted in 1859. It has been asserted that Horse Artillery was employed in India as early as 1756, but the letter in Appendix II., from Colonel A. Wellesley (afterwards Duke of Wellington) to Major-General St. Leger, would certainly lead to the belief that no such force existed in that country as early as 1797.

As Horse Artillery has usually to keep pace with the Cavalry, all the gunners to work the gun, except two carried on each limber and hence called "limber gunners," are mounted men, and are equipped and armed as such. They are called the "detachment," and can accompany the guns at any pace, dismounting to work their pieces, and when mounted they can on an emergency act as a protection to their Battery. As an instance of what can be done by mounted gunners of Horse Artillery, over and above their ordinary duty, it is worth relating that in the Indian Mutiny, on 5th January, 1858, the detachments of 'E' Troop (now F Battery A Brigade) served independently as cavalry with a force without any of that arm, at Munseta near Allahabad, to which latter place their guns had been previously sent on. During the operations of the day the detachments made a gallant charge, placing a considerable number, between 200 and 300, of the rebels *hors de combat*.

Horse Artillery has to support the advance, to cover the retreat, and to help to gather the fruits of the victory of the cavalry. Further, its rapidity of movement makes it also suited for the reserve, where, armed with heavier guns, waiting till required, it can at the moment of need be moved very quickly to the weak point of the army, or of the enemy. Thus some of Napoleon's most successful attacks were prepared and covered by his Horse Artillery. At Wagram, at a critical moment, the Emperor rallied the broken troops of Massena by himself bringing up the Horse Artillery of the Imperial Guard with a body of Cuirassiers, and gained time to organize his famous attack on the enemies' position, covered by 100 guns, which resulted in the retreat of the Austrians. This function of being quickly moved to a threatened point would appear to be one that will at least be as much required in these days, when forces of cavalry and of mounted infantry are thrown in advance of the army to stop a retreating or advancing enemy, as the French army under Bazaine retreating towards Verdun, 16th August, 1870, was held fast by the Prussian Horse Artillery and Cavalry at Vionville, till the arrival of their infantry compelled the French to fall back into Metz.

It may here be remarked that the weight of the projectile of Horse Artillery guns has never varied very much, ranging from six to twelve or thirteen-pounders. It can easily be understood that the weight of the piece to be used in the field is limited by two considerations—

the power of moving rapidly and the amount of ammunition that can be carried with the Battery. Thus not only would a heavy gun have to move slowly, but very few rounds of ammunition could be carried with it, the latter being a very important point, as Horse Artillery guns cannot always be closely followed by their waggons. Experience shows that six horses cannot move a greater weight at speed or over bad ground than about thirty cwt., and this fixes the weight suitable to an ordinary Horse Artillery gun and limber, with ammunition and stores complete. In the Peninsula the light six-pounder with fifty rounds of ammunition and two limber gunners of about twelve stone each, the whole in marching order, weighed about thirty-one cwt. The present Horse Artillery rifled muzzle-loading nine-pounder, with forty rounds of ammunition under similar conditions, weighs about thirty-seven cwt.; thus the weight behind the team has increased, whilst the quantity of ammunition carried with the gun has decreased. The extra weight of the present equipment is mainly due to the wrought-iron carriage used now in place of the wooden ones of former days. If accounts of recent operations in Egypt be correct, the weight of the Horse Artillery equipment, though extra horses were added to the regular teams, told against its mobility in some movements of the campaign. Teams of eight horses are used with Horse Artillery when armed with a heavier gun: four troops at Waterloo and two troops in the Crimea had nine-pounders, and were so horsed; but these large teams are more difficult to manage and to obtain from the horses their full power of draft than with the ordinary six-horse teams.

It has been sometimes urged that Horse Artillery is valueless and costly, and that it performs no duties that could not as easily be carried out by the less expensive and more heavily armed Field Batteries. Those who take this view forget that it is in the long-continued movement at a rapid pace in conjunction with cavalry that one of the most important duties of Horse Artillery consists. The rapid retreat on the 17th June, 1815, of the English Horse Artillery and Cavalry before Napoleon from Quatre Bras to Mont St. Jean, a distance of upwards of fourteen miles, over a wet and heavy country, is a fair instance of what may be required in this respect. The march of "C" Troop from the Plateau before Sevastopol to the Plain of Balaclava on the morning of the 25th October, 1854, hereafter to be detailed, may also be instanced.

Having briefly described the composition and duties of Horse Artillery, it is necessary to explain that there are other descriptions of Batteries which accompany and form an important part of armies in the field; these are called "Field Batteries." They generally accompany the Infantry, those with heavier guns being for the most part with the reserve or corps artillery. As Field Batteries are not intended to maintain a rapid pace for long, the men required to work the guns accompany the Battery on foot when on the march, being carried on the limbers, axletree-box seats, and waggons, when the Battery is to move quickly. When a Field Battery approaches the enemy, the waggons are generally left at some distance, so as to bring as few men and horses as possible under fire; thus the full strength of the detachment cannot be brought up very rapidly, but only enough men to work the guns for a short time. Though the duties in the field of the two branches of "Field Artillery" are very different, yet in their interior economy, system of equipment, and in many other particulars, they are similar.

Civilian readers must bear in mind that as the squadron

and battalion are the units of cavalry and of infantry, the battery is the unit of artillery, and the details are arranged to make it complete in all its parts, having with it "camp equipage," which includes tents, picket ropes and posts, lanterns, camp kettles, reaping and bill hooks, leather buckets, blankets, and felling axes. "Intrenching and artificers' tools," such as pickaxes, shovels, spades, hand-saws, hammers, pincers, and tool chests complete for the farrier and shoeing smiths, the saddlers or collar makers, and for the carpenter or wheeler. The "Miscellaneous stores" comprise water brushes, tarred rope, oil, grease for wheels, clasp knives, needles, worsted, scissors, and string. "Stable necessaries" include corn sacks and corn bags, hoof-pickers, sponges, scissors, curry combs, horse brushes, harness brushes, and nose-bags. There are also in possession swords and carbines, havresacks, water-bottles, etc. In addition to all of which there are the "Ordnance stores" especially appertaining to the guns, ammunition, and carriages. These are very numerous, far too much so to give a complete list, but some of the principal items are as follows: cartridges, common and shrapnel shells, case shot, time and percussion fuses, and a number of implements for fixing and setting them, friction tubes, portfires, slow match, spikes, spare tangent sights, besides hand-spikes, drag-ropes, lifting jacks, spare sponges, spare shafts, spare drag washers, spare wheels, swingletrees, a portable forge, etc., all of which articles a battery carries with it. Thus a battery on the march can halt and encamp at any spot, requiring only supplies of food and forage, and not being dependent on any other branch for its materiel. It has always been a special care in the Artillery to maintain this completeness, and to take as much pride in the appearance of the stores of all sorts as in the more ordinary and showy details.

Organization of a Battery.

Batteries of Horse and of Field Artillery on service consist of six guns, each of which, with its men, horses, ammunition, carriages, camp equipage, stores, etc., is called a subdivision. The six subdivisions are numbered from right to left, and are always known and called by their respective numbers. Batteries are organized in three "divisions," called 'right,' 'centre,' and 'left,' of two "subdivisions" each. A division is commanded by a lieutenant, a subdivision by a sergeant or a corporal, called the "No. 1." A subdivision is an important charge and is complete in itself, having a fixed proportion of the stores, etc., already enumerated ; the men occupy the same rooms and stables in quarters ; they are messed and paid by the "No. 1," who is responsible for the good order and completeness of their kits and clothing, and who musters and inspects his men before all parades, and to whom they look in all matters as their immediate superior, and as the channel of communication with their officers. The duties in stables are not the least onerous part of a "No. 1's" work. He draws and issues the forage for the horses of his subdivision, or anything that may be required for their use ; he is responsible they are properly groomed, watered, fed, and punctually shod, that any sickness or injuries are at once reported, and that the harness and appointments belonging to them are kept clean, in repair, and always fit for use.

The "No. 1" has constantly to visit the gun-park, and satisfy himself that the limber-gunners, whose special duties are with the carriages of the subdivision, keep them, with their fittings, etc., clean and in good order, that the ammunition and stores are serviceable, and that everything is kept neat and in its proper place. There are other duties, especially the care and instruction of young soldiers, and the beneficial influence a No. 1 may exert towards making his men steady, contented, and zealous, that need not be gone into here; but it may fairly be said that when he has conscientiously and actively performed his various duties, he has done a hard and a good day's work. Considerable rivalry usually exists between the different subdivisions of a Battery; each strives to turn out the cleanest horses and harness, to have the neatest barrack-rooms and stables, and to be smartest and quickest in the field. The "No. 1" on whose zeal and tact mainly depend the good order and esprit of a subdivision is responsible for his charge, with its numerous belongings, to the Lieutenant who commands the division, who, in his turn, is directly responsible to the officer commanding the Battery. It will be seen from this how complete a Battery is in all particulars. It can be broken up into half-batteries under the Major and the Captain, or into divisions under their Lieutenants, or subdivisions under their "Nos. 1," and still each body is a perfect whole. It will easily be understood that even in peace the command of such an important unit involves on the Commanding Officer great responsibilities connected with the pay, clothing, and food of his men, which in foreign armies are taken by a distinct body. In addition, the welfare of his horses requires constant attention, and the care of the numerous stores in charge is no light duty. In regiments of cavalry and infantry these duties are divided among the Regimental Staff, an Adjutant, Paymaster, and Quartermaster.

Without attempting any invidious comparisons, the commander of a Battery of Horse or Field Artillery in action has a most difficult task. Infantry and cavalry can await the approach of the enemy with the knowledge that even if the position is reached and lost, and however much the men may be dispersed, there is still the possibility of eventually rallying. The artilleryman knows almost with certainty that the enemy reaching his guns means the loss of them. On the other hand, his last discharge may be effectual, and his premature retirement may dishearten the troops alongside of him; thus Mercer at Waterloo disobeyed his orders, believing that to withdraw his gunners into the squares from their guns, however temporarily, would cause the flight of the battalions of Brunswick troops between which he was placed on that memorable day. Not to lose a gun is a proud boast, but the credit of the Battery must sometimes be sacrificed for the sake of the Army. Thus Todleben compares favourably the action of the English Artillery at Inkermann with that of his own army. The English moved with their infantry as was necessary in those days of short ranges, coming into close quarters with their foes and overwhelming them with case; while the Russians, certainly not for want of personal bravery, but apparently from fear of losing their pieces, retained their first positions to a great extent, and thus failed to fully support their own troops in their advances. Probably for the same reason, their cavalry attack at Balaclava was unsupported by artillery. The English guns at Inkermann that for a moment fell into the enemy's hands were recovered; and if it had not been so, there would have been no dishonour in the loss of the pieces that had thus been necessarily sacrificed in the performance of their duty. Thus, also, the brave Austrian Artillery devoted themselves at Sadowa to cover the retreat of their infantry. To die by the side of a captured gun brings no disgrace to the gunner, but no honour is gained when flag or gun is saved by premature flight from its proper place—the centre of the struggle.

As this history deals especially with a Battery of

Horse Artillery, some space must be devoted to an account of the drivers, gunners, and non-commissioned officers composing the personnel of that branch of Field Artillery, and of the duties they have to perform. These latter, and those of drivers especially, are very arduous; it is therefore important they should be undertaken by willing men, who from their previous occupation and physique are capable of easily acquiring a knowledge of the necessary work and of carrying it out. For the above reasons the men of the Horse Artillery are selected volunteers from the recruits enlisted for the Royal Artillery at large.

Before touching on the duties of drivers at the present time, it will be as well to refer to the system originally pursued for the transport of Artillery. The men and horses employed for this purpose were then obtained by contract. The drivers, called 'waggoners,' were peasants in smock frocks, who, on foot, long whip in hand, drove three hired horses in single file. This system, as it may be supposed, did not furnish satisfactory results, as the flight of the 'waggoners' with their horses on more than one occasion from the field of battle resulted in the capture of their guns by the enemy.

The non-military peasants employed on these duties being untrustworthy under fire, obliged any changes of position attempted for the guns when in action to be performed by hand, either by the gunners or by infantry soldiers. The formation of the Horse Artillery showed how the evil could be remedied, and in 1794 the Driver Corps was raised as an additional branch of the regiment, and from it the Field Batteries, whose mobility was thus established, received its drivers. In 1817 this corps was placed under Artillery officers, and in 1822 the men were enlisted into the Artillery as "gunners and drivers," or, in reality, drivers ceased to exist (except in the Horse

Artillery), until the 1st of April, 1858, when special drivers were re-introduced, the Crimean and Indian Mutiny campaigns having shown the defects of the "Gunner and Driver System."

There are no soldiers in the army who have harder work or more trying duties than drivers of the Artillery in general, and of the Horse Artillery in particular. A driver has at all times two horses and two sets of harness to look after, besides taking his share of the numerous duties and fatigues common to all the men of the Battery. His work, which usually begins before daylight, is rarely finished till late in the day, and is pretty constant throughout the year: a late field day will often keep him in stables till 8 or 9 P.M., as he is expected, if necessary, to turn out his horses and harness next day as usual. It is found, as a rule, that farm labourers make the best drivers. Men of this class, from 5ft. 4in. to 5ft. 5½in., are preferred, and some of the best of these excellent soldiers come from among the labourers of the agricultural counties. The gun drivers of Horse Artillery are picked men, and it is considered a distinction to be one. Of those in a gun team, the lead and wheel drivers fill the most important places. The former must have a good knowledge of field drill, being often entirely responsible for the gun when the detachment becomes separated from it by bad ground; he needs quickness and intelligence at once to comprehend the orders given, the course to pursue in an emergency, or the most suitable spot at which to surmount an obstacle; while on the wheel driver, the strongest man, with the most powerful horses in the team, depends the accurate movement of the gun at all times, whether starting from a halt, pulling up when at speed, coming in or out of action, or crossing a difficult obstacle. The centre driver is usually a smart young soldier, who aspires to fill a vacancy in time, in the lead or wheel of a gun team, and meanwhile benefits by the example of the older drivers of his Battery. An old lead driver is often as much looked up to among the drivers of a subdivision as a non-commissioned officer, and practically obeyed as such. Drivers, as will be seen hereafter, are liable to ugly falls and serious and unavoidable accidents at drill or at exercise. To move a gun with a team of six or eight horses at full speed over rough or unknown ground, and to bring it safely and accurately into position, requires both nerve and good horsemanship; and to extricate one from such a difficulty as encountered Mercer's two guns in a narrow *cul-de-sac* during the retreat through Genappe on the 17th June, 1815, requires presence of mind and skill. Gun drivers, who are unarmed, are placed in a very trying position when the Battery is in action. They require to be steady and cool when the guns are close pressed and must be fought to the last moment possible. Unlike gunners, who have occupation and excitement in serving the gun, they must sit passively to be shot at, content with being sometimes able to observe the effect of the fire of their own Battery, or the damage caused in it by that of the enemy. Yet in the Horse Artillery such is the prestige attached to the position of a gun driver, that it is a punishment to be removed to a waggon or spare carriage. There is consequently no need to urge how absolutely necessary matured and disciplined drivers are for the thorough efficiency of a Battery of Horse Artillery. The status and prospects of these valuable soldiers have been much improved in the last twenty-five years. They are now eligible to become non-commissioned officers, and in each Battery a selected number of the most efficient and deserving annually receive badges with a gratuity; formerly nothing but a pension on discharge was within their reach.

The gunners of the Horse Artillery require sufficient height and length of limb to mount and dismount rapidly, and to work the gun with ease; while it is desirable they should not be too heavy for their horses. For these reasons active well-made men, from 5ft. 8in. to 5ft. 11in., are most suitable, and though through necessity smaller men at times are taken, this has always been considered disadvantageous since the earliest days of the Horse Artillery.

Ten non-commissioned officers and gunners are required to work the ordinary Horse Artillery gun. Of these, three non-commissioned officers and five gunners are mounted and compose the "detachment," and two gunners are carried on the limber. In action, to man the gun, the limber gunners and five of the detachment dismount, the remaining men acting as horse holders. The limber gunners, who are picked men, their duties requiring extra strength and activity, are the most powerful of the gun's crew : having charge of the carriages, stores, and ammunition of their subdivisions, and being employed on many other important duties, they need also to be steady and trustworthy. No special notice is necessary of the functions of the other gunners of the detachment; but it may be remarked that while the failure of a single private or of a trooper does not much affect a regiment of Cavalry or Infantry, the mistake of a gunner or driver may ruin the whole action of his gun; hence the necessity in the Artillery for the most careful and intelligent individual training. For this reason much time and attention is paid to the instruction of the gunners and young non-commissioned officers by the officers and senior non-commissioned officers in theoretical and practical gunnery, and in drill. An examination in these subjects is held before the annual practice, and only a limited number, those who have passed the best examination, are eligible to compete for the badges with gratuity given at the competitive practice. Thus, though the gunners may have less actual hard work than the drivers, still, as will be seen from the above, their time is fully occupied.

The non-commissioned officers, a class forming an important link between the officers and the rank and file, are selected from among the gunners and drivers of their Battery, intelligence, scholarship, zeal, and steady conduct being necessary to obtain first appointment. Their promotion up to sergeant goes on in their own Battery. There is some difficulty at present in obtaining suitable men; those educationally qualified have often not sufficient experience of their duties, and the older soldiers who have the practical knowledge are frequently deficient in scholarship.

Of the duties of non-commissioned officers in the field it may be briefly explained that in each detachment there are three, the senior being the "No. 1" of the subdivision, and, as has been already shown, the commander at all times of it. In action No. 1 lays his gun, and sees the duties of the other men about it are correctly performed. When manœuvring he gives the necessary words of command, and is responsible for the dressing, distance, and accurate movement of his charge. To do this, he is so placed that while the leading driver of his gun is immediately on his right hand, his detachment in two ranks is close to his left; the waggons do not closely accompany the guns, but are kept in charge of an officer at a safe and convenient distance. The second senior non-commissioned officer is called the "Coverer"; he gives general assistance to his "No. 1," when in action, holds his horse, and takes charge of the led horses and gun team of the subdivision, which are then separated some distance from the gun. At drill, or when manœuvring, he acts as a marker—*i.e.* shows where the subdivision is to move on. The duties of the third non-commissioned officer are chiefly when the gun is in action; he has then charge of the limber-boxes and their contents, and is responsible that the proper ammunition and fuses required at the gun are sent up to it.

The men of the Horse Artillery being constantly required to mount and dismount as rapidly as possible to serve the guns, their dress has to be suited to the work; and at present, while the rest of the Army has adopted the tunic, they alone retain the jacket. Their uniform, indeed, has not altered very much since its first introduction, a former difference in that of the drivers being assimilated in 1823.

To make plainer the difference between the ancient and the modern organization and mobility of Field Artillery, let the reader try to picture to himself two such scenes as the following. It is the year 1709. An English army under Marlborough is serving on the Continent against the French, and an English general with a column on the march suddenly sees that the enemy is about to attack, and that a neighbouring hill must be at once occupied by guns. His train is slowly toiling on its way below, and he sends off to the "Chief of Artillery" to detach some suitable pieces. The whole long column of carriages has to halt while the best guns for the service required are picked out, and the selected carriages then commence to painfully force their way up the slope, the hired drivers becoming more and more nervous and frightened as they get within view of the enemy. When near the top, the horses and bullocks have to be removed, and the man-harness hooked on to the carriages. Some infantry have to be brought up to help the gunners, who are wearily straining at the dragropes, and manning the spokes of the wheels. When the guns are at last in position, all but the very lightest have to be shifted on their carriages from the travelling to the firing position, the stores have to be searched for, the powder has to be weighed out and ladled into the gun, and the favourable moment is probably passed before fire can be begun.

On the other hand, let us pass over 100 years, to the year 1811, when an English army under Wellington in the Peninsula is again fighting against the French, and turn to what may be seen there, or viewed often enough now in mimic or real warfare. The staff have just reached the crest of a hill when the commander sees the enemy below and exposed to his fire. An aide-de-camp shoots down to a little hollow where a Battery of Horse Artillery is lying concealed. Out of the valley at once rises a cloud of dust, from which, as it comes rapidly nearer, shine out gleams of colour and dim forms of men and of horses and of guns. The Staff scatter as at full gallop the Battery breasts the slope, taking at a rapid pace what you yourself have ridden up with some little care. Every horse is at full stretch, and each team is winding its way round the obstacles. One gun goes with a crash into a hollow, while another seems all but over as it crosses a hillock; but the drivers have true eyes, and good nerves, and each piece is being guided by its No. 1 to what seems the most advantageous spot for effective fire at, and concealment from, the enemy. A shrill "Halt!" tells that the position is reached. Another word of command, and the Battery is broken up into little groups of men and horses apparently hopelessly intermixed; here the men are spinning a gun round, there the horses and limbers are winding their way to the rear, while a few men are running from the limbers to the gun with the ammunition. In a moment the apparent confusion ceases as if by magic, the guns, each as much under cover as possible, are firing steadily, while limbers and horses are well protected in rear. What you have seen is an every-day occurrence, but one that is only possible by years of training and drill of the men, and by long preparation and selection of the material, and by every man and horse knowing his work and being anxious to do it.

The foregoing details will perhaps enable the reader to understand the immense difference between the old unmanageable train of Artillery moving slowly along, with the drivers on foot, and the present organization of a Battery of Horse Artillery, such as that with which Norman Ramsay with 'I' Troop (now 'I' Battery 'A' Brigade) cut his way at full gallop through the French Cavalry at Fuentes D'Onore in May, 1811, his mounted detachments, sword in hand, protecting the drivers and their teams.

CHAPTER II.

FORMATION OF 'C' TROOP.—TWO GUNS DETACHED TO
IRELAND, 1798.—CHANGES OF QUARTERS.—EXPEDITION TO SPAIN, 1808.

WE have now to record the birth of the Troop whose history we are going to narrate. Soon after the first two troops of Royal Horse Artillery were raised in January, 1793, as already described, it was decided to add to their strength, both by raising new troops and by increasing the number of guns in each from four to six. With this view 'C' (see Appendix III.) and 'D' Troops were formed at Woolwich on the 1st November, 1793, and were by degrees brought up to an establishment of six guns, five officers, fourteen non-commissioned officers, eighty-five gunners, forty-five drivers, and one hundred and eighty-seven horses. The strength and armament of 'C' Troop have varied considerably at different periods of its history, and these alterations will be given as far as possible in their chronological order; but it may be stated here once for all that the number of combatant officers has always been five, and that those first appointed were Captain (afterwards Sir Edward) Howorth, second Captain G. Cookson, and Lieutenants W. Millar, F. Griffith, and second Lieutenant T. Fenwick. An Assistant Surgeon and a Veterinary Surgeon have at times been attached to the Troop; an Assistant Surgeon between 1859 and 1873 formed part of the establishment.

In November, 1794, the Troop marched to Canterbury, and during the year the number of its guns was increased to eight, for which the personnel was fixed at fifteen non-commissioned officers, ninety-seven gunners, seventy-one drivers, and 246 horses; this was, however, reduced the following year by twelve gunners, twenty drivers, and seventy-six horses. In June, 1796, it was moved to Lavant (a small town in Sussex), where it remained till ordered to Brightelmstone (Brighton) in January, 1797. Whilst quartered at the latter place 'C' Troop detached a division of two guns for service in Ireland, the disturbed state of which country and the fear of foreign invasion having caused reinforcements to be asked for. Three other Troops, 'A,' 'B,' and 'F,' each detached a similar number of guns, and the whole, under Captain and Brevet-Major E. Howorth, embarked at Woolwich on the 27th November, 1797 (see Appendix IV.). Shortly after arrival in Ireland the detachments of 'A,' 'B,' and 'C' Troops were employed in quelling the insurrection that broke out the following summer, and which may be mainly traced to the machinations of "The United Irishmen," a secret organized Society, who, encouraged by the successful revolt of the American Colonies, and the victories of the French Republicans, in 1796 entered into a correspondence with the French Directory, which resulted in a force of 15,000 French troops being embarked for Ireland under General Hoche. The expedition reached Bantry Bay, but, owing to bad weather and mismanagement, returned to Brest on the 1st January, 1797, having effected nothing. The Dutch Republicans also fitted out an expedition, which was to have sailed on the 9th July, 1797, but it was so long delayed in the Texel through foul winds that the design was eventually abandoned. Despairing of help from abroad, and believing the Government were acquainted with their intentions through the arrest on the 12th March, 1798, of the Committee of United Irishmen for the county of Leinster, the leaders of the conspiracy appointed the 25th May for a general rising throughout Ireland. The Government, however, being fully prepared, issued instructions to meet the outbreak. The attempt on Dublin signally failed, but the large gatherings of rebels at various parts of the country took some time to disperse. The principal of these were at Carrickbyrne, near Ross, and at Vinegar Hill, at both of which places the detachments of the Royal Horse Artillery were employed.

The town of Ross was occupied by about 1400 troops under Major-General Johnson. Early on the morning of the 5th June, 1798, the rebels, some 20,000 strong, under the command of Bagenal Harvey and Father Roche, attacked the place, and so determined was the assault that the Troops were driven into and through the town. But for the rebels giving themselves up to drink and plunder, the King's troops must have suffered a serious defeat. General Johnson however rallied his men, and renewing the contest, eventually succeeded in driving the rebels with great slaughter out of the town. This engagement, the most sanguinary of the rebellion, lasted from 5 A.M. till 3 P.M. The despatches of Major-General Johnson, and the return of killed and wounded, will be found in Appendix V.

After the victory at Ross, it was decided to capture the rebel camp on Vinegar Hill, and by this means relieve Wexford and Enniscorthy, which places had been for some time in their hands. A combined assault was accordingly arranged by General Lake to take place on the morning of the 21st June, 1798. The operation was successful, but one of the attacking columns, owing to unforeseen circumstances, being unable to reach its position in time, the bulk of the rebels escaped, leaving all their arms, guns, and plunder behind them. The brunt of the action and the greatest proportion of the loss fell on the Brigade of Major-General Johnson. General Moore's Brigade not reaching the heights above Wexford till 5 P.M. on the 21st June, the town of Wexford was only recovered on that day, after having been in possession of the rebels for twenty-three days, during which time the most horrible atrocities had been committed. Had the troops but arrived a day sooner, they would have saved ninety-seven Protestants who were cruelly butchered on the bridge. In comparison with the results attained, the casualties at Vinegar Hill were insignificant, viz. two officers and eighteen rank and file killed; six officers and sixty-nine rank and file wounded. The rebels lost between three hundred and four hundred men, and thirteen guns of various calibre were captured. Lieut.-General Lake in his despatch of 21st June, 1798, says: " To the rapid and well-directed fire of the Royal Artillery, and the gallantry of their officers and men, for which they have ever been distinguished, I consider myself this day highly indebted, and am happy in expressing my obligations to Captain Bloomfield commanding the British, and Captain Crawford commanding the Irish Artillery, and the officers and men under their command." With these decisive engagements open insurrection may be said to have been suppressed, but the tranquillity of the country was far from being established. The detachments of the different troops of Horse Artillery were therefore retained for service in Ireland, and in September, 1801, they were amalgamated and became a new troop, which was lettered ' G ' and the command given to Captain G. B. Fisher.

To return to 'C' Troop. In October, 1798, the Head Quarters and six guns in England marched from Brightelmstone to Canterbury, and in June went into Camp at Swinley, in Windsor Forest, till August, when it returned to Canterbury. In September, 1801, the division of two guns in Ireland being struck off as just stated, the Troop was made up to its full original strength. In March, 1802, it moved to Woolwich, and to Sevenoaks in April, 1803, and in June to Radipole (a small town in Dorsetshire), where it remained till December, when it marched to Christchurch. In 1804 the number of guns was reduced from eight to six, and the establishment became fourteen non-commissioned officers, seventy-five gunners, forty-six drivers, and one hundred and forty-two horses, a strength which remained unaltered in any material degree for all troops until the reductions after the Battle of Waterloo. At the time this change was made, 'H' Troop was formed at Woolwich.

In July, 1805, 'C' Troop moved into Camp at Weymouth. A plan of the form of encampment used by the Horse Artillery at this date will be found in Appendix VI. The Troop was then, as it always has been since, noted for its discipline and efficiency; and King George III. took occasion to commend Captain Griffith, the Commanding Officer, for its satisfactory condition. From the Camp at Weymouth it marched in October to Wareham, and in February received there an increase of five gunners, fourteen drivers, and twenty-two horses. In May, 1806, it moved to Woolwich, and, after eighteen months spent at Head Quarters, it marched in November, 1807, to Warley, under Captain H. Evelegh, who had succeeded to the command in 1806. A year later the Troop was ordered on active service.

In May, 1808, the Spanish National Representatives appealed to England for assistance against the Emperor

Napoleon, who had invaded and occupied Spain, forced the abdication of Charles VI. and Ferdinand VII., and nominated his eldest brother Joseph to the vacant throne. The English ministry, always ready to oppose the schemes of Bonaparte, determined to afford the aid sought for, and accordingly decided to supply money and arms, to organize and equip the Spanish forces, and to send military agents to Asturias and Gallicia. An English force was despatched in July, 1808, under Sir Arthur Wellesley to act against the French, who had made themselves masters of the kingdom of Portugal; military operations followed, which resulted in the battle of Vimiera on 21st August, 1808, and the withdrawal of the French from Portugal. After the termination of this successful diversion in favour of the Spanish cause, it was decided in October to form an army in the north of Spain of 35,000 men, to be composed of 25,000 drafted from the force already in Portugal under Lieut.-General Sir John Moore, to whom the command of the whole was given: and a division of 10,000 men to be despatched from England under Lieut.-General Sir David Baird. 'C' Troop was detailed as part of the Artillery force to accompany the latter contingent, and accordingly marched from Warley to Northfleet, where they were mustered on 1st October, 1808, and embarked on the 5th. For the official return of strength see Appendix VII. The officers with the Troop were Captain H. Evelegh, 2nd Captain J. Chester, Lieutenants W. Webber, E. Y. Walcott, and E. Barlow, with Assistant-Surgeon Peter Venables. The passage was a favourable one, only two horses being lost. The greater portion of Sir David Baird's force, which had sailed from Falmouth, disembarked at Coruña on the 29th of October. The division was then ordered to march *viâ* Lugo, Villa Franca, and Astorga to Salamanca; where it was intended they should unite with the troops marching from Portugal. Sir John Moore's instructions were to take the field immediately, and to fix some place, either in Gallicia or Leon, for concentrating the whole Army : the specific plan of operations was to be concerted afterwards with the Spanish generals. These instructions promised no good result, for the Valley of the Ebro was to be the theatre of war. No General-in-Chief was appointed to command the Spanish armies, nor was Sir John Moore referred by the English Ministry to any person with whom he could communicate, much less concert a plan of operations for the allied forces. He was unacquainted with the views of the Spanish Government, and he was uninformed of the numbers, composition, and situation of the troops with which he was to act, as well as those with whom he had to contend. Of the former, the Spanish army was divided into three principal masses, denominated the Right, Centre, and Left, consisting of 76,000 ill-disciplined and ill-provided troops, commanded by Palafox, Castaños, and Blake. They threatened the French positions on the Ebro, and were supported by a second line of about 57,000 men. Of the latter, the French army, after the disaster of General Dupont at Baylen on 10th July, 1808, had on the 1st August abandoned Madrid, and retired behind the Ebro, evacuating the whole of the Peninsula, except the portion between that river and the Pyrenees, which they held with an army of 92,000 men under King Joseph. Napoleon, disgusted with the reverses his arms had experienced in Spain, and dissatisfied with the management of affairs by his brother, determined to reinforce the French troops in Spain by 100,000 men from the Grand Army in Germany, and to undertake the direction of affairs himself.

During the operations in 1808-9 in Spain Captain

Evelegh kept a rough diary of the marches and services of his Troop, and, though it is to be regretted some of the entries are so brief, yet as a whole the diary is of considerable interest. To explain clearly the marches and counter-marches of the Troop, as well as the object of the campaign, some notes have been introduced at suitable places. A map to trace the movements of the Troop is appended, the main roads marked in sepia, the minor ones in ink. Examination of this shows that for the most part the line of march was perpendicular to the water-sheds and water-courses of a country in some places mountainous, which would imply numerous ascents and descents, as well as streams and rivers to cross. The Troop must in many instances, especially between Benavente and Valderas, have marched by country lanes, no road being marked on the map, which is taken from the best of the day, that by W. Faden, 1810. Some places, such as Portars, Tamorama, Monasteria Aveza, and Bazelle, it has not been found possible to trace or identify, but they are not of great importance. In reading the diary it must be borne in mind that a "Field Battery," the term having been adopted in 1826, was then called a "Brigade," and a Battery of Horse Artillery a "Troop." Where possible, the present designation of Batteries mentioned during the campaign is given.

CHAPTER III.

DIARY OF CORUÑA CAMPAIGN.—REMARKS ON CAMPAIGN.
—RETURN HOME.—FROM 1809 TO 1815.

31st October, 1808. Sail'd from the Downs at 8 o'clock A.M.
1st November. A fine steady breeze all day. Going right before the wind. The "Marina" made a signal and left the fleet.
7th November. Saw the land (Cape Ortegal).
8th November. At 12 o'clock anchored in Coruña Bay.
10th November. Disembarked horses. .
11th November. Disembarked guns and stores.
15th November, 1808. Downman's (B) Troop (now 'B' Battery 'A' Brigade) marched from Coruña with 1st Division of 7th Hussars.

The scarcity of transport and supplies, country carts only being available, obliged the Army to march in small successive divisions; the advance was therefore slow and difficult. On the 29th October, 1808, Sir David Baird reported as follows: "The want of provisions for the men and forage for the horses has been one of the most serious obstacles we have had to contend with. Nor do I at present feel at all easy on that subject. The horses are suffering very severely, both for want of proper accommodation and food." Again, on the 19th November, he writes from Astorga: "The local authorities have not only failed in affording us the least benefit in the respect of supplies, but have neglected to give us any kind of information of the armies or movements of the enemy."

Friday, 18th November. Colonel Cookson and 'C' Troop marched from Coruña at 11 A.M. for Betanzos, where we arrived at half-past four. Road good. It lies in a bottom completely surrounded by hills. An arm of the sea runs up to it. It is a city, but very dirty; and I was badly lodged with Barlow.

On this day Sir John Moore, who had arrived at Salamanca on the 13th November, received intelligence of the defeat of the Spanish armies of the Right and Left on the 10th and 11th November. These victories placed some 70,000 French troops free to act in any quarter, uncovered the march of the British Army, and compromised its safety. Nevertheless, Sir John Moore, though preparing for a retreat, believed in the enthusiasm of the Spanish nation. He was therefore loath to desert their cause so long as there was any prospect of success; and as the army of the Centre, under Castaños, was still in the field, he decided to unite the columns of the English Army with all haste, to abandon all communication with Portugal, and, throwing himself into the heart of Spain, to rally Castaños's army, and defend the southern provinces.

Saturday, 19th November. Marched to Guitiriz, twenty miles, a small village on the high road. Very bad road from Betanzos to this place, and one very long and steep hill. Webber and self till 11 o'clock at night from 6 getting a waggon three miles. Eight of us slept in one room of an inn—a horrid place. Poor old Schemer quite done up, and was shot.

Sunday, 20th November. Marched to Cavall, a small village on the road, twelve miles from Guitiriz. Road in general level and good, with beautiful prospects. All in one room. Bought two hares on the road, and four fowls at the door. Fowls quite yellow.

21st November. Arrived at Lugo; got quarters in house with Colonel Cookson.

22nd November. Saw the Cathedral, and had an invitation for the evening from a young lady to the house of Don Joseph de Prado.

24th November. Marched to Constantino, and halted.

25th November. Constantino.

26th November. To Doncos; terrible hills to go up.

27th November. To Portars. Chocolate.

Monday, 28th November. To Villa Franca; found Colonels Cookson and Greatly here.

29th November. Marched from Villa Franca, and arrived at Bembibre about 4 P.M.

Wednesday, 30th November, 1808. Received orders to halt. The army began to fall back upon us.

On the 27th November all the arrangements for the execution of the project decided upon by Sir John Moore were complete, when, in the night of the 28th, a despatch from Mr. Stuart, one of the British Commissioners, made known the disaster at Tudela, in which battle the Spanish armies of the Centre and Right, under Castaños and Palafox, were defeated and dispersed. This changed the aspect of affairs; the projected movement had been founded upon *the chance of rallying the Spanish armies behind the Tagus*—a hazardous and daring experiment when first conceived; but, now Castaños had no longer an army, to have persisted would have been insanity. The French could be over the Tagus before the British, and there were no Spanish armies to rally. Sir John Moore therefore resolved to fall back into Portugal. He ordered Sir David Baird to regain Coruña or Vigo, and to carry his troops by sea to Lisbon; but wishing, if possible, to unite the columns of his own army before the retrograde movement commenced, he directed Baird to show a bold front for a few days in order to attract the enemies' attention.

Thursday, 1st December, 1808. Sent Chester back with four guns to Villa Franca.

Friday, 2nd December. Marched myself with right division to Villa Franca; joined Chester again.

Saturday, 3rd December. Marched from Villa Franca to (*blank in original*).

Sunday, 4th December. From Trabadelos to Herreria.

Monday, 5th December. From Herreria to Lugo;

started at 3 A.M., arrived at 4 P.M.—about thirty miles. I walked all the day.

Tuesday, 6th December. Halted at Lugo; quartered with Chester and Walcott.

Wednesday, 7th December. Marched from Lugo to Bermonde.

Thursday, 8th December. To Guitiriz, and breakfasted at the posada.

Friday, 9th December. At 2 A.M. received orders to halt, and at 6 A.M. Dr. Macleod arrived express with an order to march again for Astorga.

Napoleon had arrived at Vittoria, the headquarters of the French Army, on the 8th November, and had undertaken the direction of the campaign. After his successes against the Spaniards on both flanks, his attention was fixed on the capital. On the 30th November he forced the Somosierra, and on the 2nd December summoned Madrid to surrender, whereupon the Junta addressed a paper to Sir John Moore, in which it was stated that "thirty-five thousand men were marching to the capital, where forty thousand others were in arms, but that, fearing an increase of force on the enemy's side, the Junta hoped that the English Army would either march to the assistance of Madrid or fall upon the rear of the French; and not doubting that the English general had already formed a junction with Blake's army (which they know to be dispersed), they hoped he would be quick in his operations." This paper was sent by a Government messenger to Salamanca, but ere he could reach that place Madrid had capitulated to Napoleon. This communication alone would not have been sufficient to arrest Sir John Moore's movement. He was too well acquainted with what facility Spanish armies were created on paper; but Mr. Stuart also expressed a belief that Madrid would make a vigorous resistance. Sir John Moore accordingly decided to suspend his retreat, and sent orders to Sir David Baird, who had fallen back to Villa Franca, to concentrate his troops at Astorga, and he himself prepared for an advance. He supposed Napoleon to be more anxious to strike a heavy blow against the English, and to shut them out of Spain, than to overrun any particular province in the Peninsula. He resolved, therefore, to throw himself upon the communications of the French Army, hoping to inflict a severe loss upon the troops guarding them before aid could arrive.

Saturday, 10th December. Marched for Lugo and

arrived at 1 P.M. Went to my old quarters with Chester and Walcott. Colonel Cookson dined with us. Five and a half leagues (four miles ninety-two yards = one Spanish league).

Sunday, 11th December. Left Lugo. Arrived at Constantino at half-past four. Four and a half leagues. Had some tea with Colonel Cookson and Doctor.

Monday, 12th December. Arrived at Castro de Piedra Feta, the Posada del Rey.

Tuesday, 13th December. Arrived at Villa Franca for third time, and went to my old quarters with Colonel Cookson.

Wednesday, 14th December. Halted at Villa Franca: General Coote Manningham and staff dined with us. In consequence of a fire at the citadel, which burnt two of the General's horses, we did not sit down to dine till nine.

Thursday, 15th December. Marched to Bembibre and recovered my new boots, left behind last time.

Friday, 16th December. To Cambarros, exactly forty leagues from Coruña and one and a half from Astorga. Plenty of honey.

Saturday, 17th December. To Astorga. Colonel Cookson and self billeted together. Greatly joined us from Coruña.

Sunday, 18th December. Marched for La Baneza; but, finding bad accommodation, Col. Hay's Brigade being there with Brandreth's, we went on to Cebrones, about five leagues from Astorga. The Alcalde had his nose broke: Chester took up a fowling-piece and fired it into the bedroom, not knowing it was loaded.

Monday, 19th December. Marched into Benavente, expecting to join the army there, but found that Sir David Baird and 10,000 men marched out two hours before we arrived, so the place was quite deserted.

Plenty of turkeys along this road from Astorga, two for a dollar. Sir John Moore and Sir David Baird met yesterday at or near Toro for the first time.

20th December. Valderas. Very slippery going down the hill in Benavente. Obliged to take out all the horses and lower down, which hindered very much. Got in here at four o'clock. Very bad road. A party of French were here last week for information. Left a horse at Benavente, but no man; and two horses at this place in care of Junta.

On the 11th December the forward movement of the army had commenced. Sir John Moore's first intention was to march to Valladolid to cover the advance of his stores, and to protect the junction of Sir David Baird's Troops, the rear of which was still behind Astorga; but on the 13th inst. an intercepted despatch informed him that the French were moving a strong force to Burgos, with the object of forcing the English to retire to Portugal. It was now certain Burgos was, or would be, strongly protected, and that Baird's line of march was unsafe if Soult followed these instructions. On the other hand, as the French appeared to be ignorant of the British movements, there was some chance of surprising and beating the 2nd Corps before Napoleon could come to its succour. Headquarters were therefore removed to Toro, and Valderas was given as the point of junction to Baird's Division, the head of which was at Benavente. On the 20th the force was united, the total strength being 19,050 Infantry, 2200 Cavalry, and 60 guns, the whole being organized in three Divisions and a Reserve—two light Brigades of Infantry and one Division of Cavalry. Four Batteries of Artillery were attached to the Infantry, and two to the Cavalry, and one was kept in reserve.

21st. Marched to Mayorga, four leagues; got in about 4 o'clock, and found General Manningham's Brigade there, with which we marched the same night to Tamorama (Bridge), where we arrived at 2 A.M. Left Sergeant Briant sick.

Thursday, 22nd December. Arrived at the village of Monasteria Aveza at 2 A.M., and slept in the convent in clothes: left a driver's horse there down a cellar.

Marched at half-past 8 A.M. to Villada, through Sahagun and Grajal, and arrived at 6 P.M. Forge lead horse fell dead on road. Dined with Sandham. Joined General Hope and his Brigade, Arbuthnot, his Assistant Adjutant General, Colonel Harding, and Downman's Troop at Sahagun, as we marched through. Found the 18th Hussars here; called on General Hope.

Friday, 23rd December. Breakfasted with General Hope. Hard at work all day shoeing and repairing. Colonel Wyatt, 23rd Regiment, called on me and stayed ten minutes. Saw Colonel Jones, Allan, and most of the 18th Hussars. At 8 P.M. marched with General Hope's Brigade to make a joint attack with the army from Sahagun on Marshal Soult at Carrion (about 10,000 men). Drummond's Brigade and my Troop taken about a mile beyond the town before dark; Raynsford's ' 9 ' Pr.Brigade (' 9 ' Co., 8th Battalion, now ' No. 9' Battery, 1st Brigade South Irish Division) R.A., arrived before we marched, and came on in rear. On the march, however, an order arrived to advance the Rifle Corps and half my Troop to Pozurama, a village about a league from Villada, and for the remainder to go back. I therefore went on with Walcott, Barlow, the Doctor, and three guns; Chester and Webber, who had a bad fall with his mare, in consequence of the frost, and was a good deal bruised in the face, etc., returned to Villada. We had very bad quarters at Pozurama; got in at 12 o'clock, Brigadier-General Allen in command. I visited the park at 2 o'clock, and laid down on the bricks. We turned out at 5 in the morning, and remained under arms till daylight.

Sir John Moore's plan was to move during the night of the 23rd December, so as to arrive at Carrion by daylight on the 24th, and to fall upon the main body of the enemy, which his information led him to believe was still at Saldaña. This attack, however, was but a secondary object, for the eighth and third French Corps were too near to admit of further success; the whole operation was one to draw Napoleon from the South, whose march from Madrid must be the signal for a retreat of the English. On the 23rd Romana gave notice the French were in motion on the side of Madrid, and in the night, whilst the troops were in march towards Carrion, the intelligence was confirmed by the General's spies, whose reports agreed that the whole French army was in movement to crush the English. The projected attack was therefore counter-ordered, and orders issued for the Army to retreat.

Saturday, 24th December. Put up our horses and returned to our quarters. Had some chocolate. At twelve marched back to Villada, leaving the German Regiment of Cavalry behind; got back about 2 o'clock. General Hope's Brigade gone. Reported to Brigadier-General Stewart, who asked me to dinner (accepted), and told me he had sent Chester with one gun and Colonel Otway to cut off a party about three leagues off. They returned at night, the birds having flown.

Christmas, 1808. Remained at Villada. Walcott went off at 4 in the morning with one gun, and a party of the 18th Light Dragoons; brought in twenty-one prisoners.

Monday, 26th December. I began to retreat with the Cavalry. Main body commenced retreat on 24th. Arrived at Valderas, three leagues; went to old quarter. Found Lord Paget and 'B' Troop there. Barlow went off early with baggage and ammunition waggons, and was nearly taken. He left one body of an ammunition waggon behind, sticking in the mud. The 18th Light Dragoons fell in with a party of the enemy, which occasioned our forming up for action over very heavy ground, which cut my horses up very much. Roads dreadfully bad.

It is difficult to reconcile Captain Evelegh's estimate of the length of the march from Villada to Valderas with the map. Both modern maps, and those of the years 1810 and 1812, make the distance, as the crow flies, twenty-eight to thirty-two miles. Captain Evelegh puts it down as between twelve and thirteen miles, or three leagues. It must therefore be concluded that the Villada shown in the map is not the place the troops marched from, but some spot with a similar name much nearer Valderas. Other accounts of the retreat of the Cavalry do not speak of this march as one of exceptional length.

While at Madrid, Napoleon heard that Sir John Moore, having relinquished his communications with Lisbon, was menacing the French line of operations on the side of Burgos. This intelligence obliged him to suspend all his designs against the South of Spain and Portugal, and to fix his whole attention upon the operations of the English Army. On the 21st December he heard of Sir John Moore's advance, and on the evening of the 22nd, 50,000 men were in full march under his personal command to intercept the English line of retreat. On the 26th he was at Tordesillas with the Imperial Guard and two other Divisions. From here he communicated with Marshal Soult, and concluded his despatch thus: "Our Cavalry scouts are already at Benavente. If the English pass to-day in their position, they are lost; if, on the contrary, they attack you with all their force, retire one day's march; the further they proceed the better for us. If they retreat, pursue them closely."

The Emperor then proceeded to Valderas, but had the vexation to learn that, in spite of his rapid march, he was twelve hours too late. The English Army had retired over the Esla.

Tuesday, 27th December. Marched early for Benavente; dreadful road. 'B' Troop marched in the column between the 7th and 18th Hussars. We followed the 10th, covered by the 15th. Arrived at Benavente at 6 P.M. Horses almost done. Poor Webber came in late with the waggons, very ill for several days. The bridge of Ezela blown up.

The Cavalry Brigade was composed of 'B' and 'C' Troops Royal Horse Artillery, the 7th, 10th, and 18th Hussars, 15th Light Dragoons and 3rd Light Dragoons (King's German Legion), and was commanded by Lieut.-General Lord Paget (afterwards Marquis of Anglesea).

28th December. At Benavente. At 11 A.M. an alarm from the Spaniards that the French were coming into the town. The whole army turned out, and my Troop was particularly alert on this occasion. It came on to rain exceedingly during the time the troops were under arms, and they all got very wet. The alarm proved to be nothing but a little skirmish with out-pickets, and we all turned in again. Sir John Moore present. The outlying pickets came in, and we destroyed the bridge of Benavente (Castro Gonzalo). Lord C. Manners dined with me.

29th December. At Benavente. An alarm at 9 A.M. The French Cavalry forded the river and attacked our pickets there, which consisted of about ninety-four men of the 7th, 10th, and Germans under Colonel Quintin, of the 10th, who charged the French very nobly three times, though so superior to him in numbers, and kept fighting till a reinforcement arrived. The enemy repassed the river, with the loss of General Lefebvre, Colonel of the Imperial Guard, who commanded, and about sixty killed and wounded. 'B' Troop and mine went down from Benavente, but mine was ordered back to take up a position on the hill. D (Downman) fired two or three shots as they went off. About 2 P.M. we marched for Puente de Vizana, three leagues off, to protect the bridge. D.'s Troop remained, and came to us at night. I made preparations for destroying the bridge, and we marched off at 2 A.M.

This attack was made by 600 Chasseurs of the Imperial Guard, who, led by their Colonel, General of Division, Lefebvre-Desnouettes, commanding Napoleon's Light Cavalry, crossed the Esla. They were held in check by the English picquets, numbering about 220 men, under Lieut.-Colonel Otway, 18th Hussars. A party of the 10th Hussars, under Major Quinton, displayed great gallantry. The enemy retreated on the arrival of Lord Paget with the 10th Hussars. The losses on both sides were about equal. The French left fifty-five killed and wounded on the field, besides the General and other officers. The English casualties amounted to fifty men.

Lieut.-General Lord Paget, in his despatch dated Benavente, 29th December, 1808, thus refers to the part taken by the Horse Artillery at the close of the engagement. "On the other side the river the enemy formed again, and at this instant three guns of Captain Downman's Troop arrived, which did considerable execution." Napoleon is said to have viewed this action from a lofty hill about a league from Benavente. General Lefebvre-Desnouettes, who had distinguished himself greatly in Spain, was much depressed at his captivity, and remarked, " Bonaparte never forgave the unfortunate." He was, however, treated with every consideration by Sir John Moore, who presented him with a handsome Indian sword in the place of his own, which had been taken. He eventually returned to France, and in 1815, as Lieut.-General commanded the 2nd Cavalry Division of the Imperial Guard (Chasseurs à Cheval and Lancers) at Waterloo, where he was also taken prisoner.

Friday, 30th December. Arrived at La Baneza about half-past 8, four leagues. Pipon breakfasted with Chester and self. Walcott on picket.

Saturday, 31st December, 1808. Marched into Astorga about 10 A.M.; constantly expecting an attack, as the enemy followed us very close. We were in orders to be in readiness to march for Bembibre at 12 at night, but were turned out at 8, and remained on the ground till 12, when we marched, but did not arrive at Bembibre till

Sunday, 1st January, 1809, at 1 P.M., the road being very slippery, and having been exceedingly impeded on the march by the baggage on the deep snow roads. Sent two guns with Barlow on picket to the church. Orders to march at 7 in the morning. All slept in a miserable place among the men.

Monday, 2nd January. At 7 A.M. marched for Villa Franca, two guns covering the rear of the Army with the 20th, under Colonel Ross. The French pressed us very close during the march; guns came into action several times. On our arrival at Cacabellos found orders to halt with the reserve under Major-General Paget. Pickets engaged continually during the night. The French cut to pieces sixty stragglers and drunken men. Our picket brought in a few prisoners. Orders to be under arms at 4 in the morning. No forage or rations.

On this day, as the army was now entering a mountainous country, almost the whole of the Cavalry were sent forward to Villa Franca, and the arduous task of covering the retreat devolved upon the Reserve. This Brigade was composed as follows:—91st, 28th, 1st Battalion 95th, 52nd, 20th Regiments; Carthew's Brigade (4 Co. 5th Battalion, now No. 2 Battery, 1st Brigade Northern Division) Royal Artillery, with 'C' Troop Royal Horse Artillery, from this date, and was commanded by Major-General the Honourable E. Paget.

On the 1st January, 70,000 French infantry, 10,000 cavalry, and 200 guns were united at Astorga; on the 2nd, Napoleon entered that town from Benavente. On his march he was overtaken by a courier from France with despatches informing him of the certainty of war with Austria in the spring. This information caused him to change all his plans. He decided to at once return to France, and fixed upon Marshal Soult to continue the pursuit of the English, placing under his orders a force of 25,000 men, of which 4,200 were cavalry, and 54 guns; this was supported by the 6th Corps, under Marshal Ney, numbering 16,000 men and 37 guns.

Tuesday, 3rd January. Under arms at 4 A.M. Moved to the top of the hill, and took a position. Found the horses just done up, and sent Walcott forward to Villa Franca for assistance. He found Webber there exceedingly ill. Walcott soon returned with an answer from Captain Downman, who commanded the Artillery there, saying he could not assist me with one horse; I must do the best I could. About 2 P.M. received accounts that the French were advancing with large columns of cavalry. Sir John Moore came back to us from Villa Franca in consequence, and the reserve took a strong position on the hill, throwing out many detached bodies of riflemen. About three o'clock the French mounted riflemen and cavalry drove in our picket of cavalry, and followed them briskly through the town, and killed a great many men who had not time to get out of it. The French then formed on the side of the town next us, the riflemen on each side keeping up a fire. The guns then opened on them, three in the road with Chester and two up the hill on the right with Walcott and self, and in a short time they retired towards the town. We also retired, the riflemen still engaged. The rest of the reserve and five of my guns continued the retreat unmolested by the enemy, the other gun (probably the howitzer) with Chester, Walcott, and self, and 95th Regiment (Rifle Brigade) playing on them during the time about a mile from Villa Franca. It then got dark, and the whole retired briskly through Villa Franca, where our rear gun broke through the bridge and delayed the column some time. It being pitch dark in the town, I rode forward and got a light, and Walcott extricated the gun. An immense lot of officers' baggage burnt in the town, with rations of all sorts. The French, supposing we should halt in the town, remained on the ground, by which we gained a day's march. Whole of the reserve arrived at Trabadelos, Herrerias, and other villages three leagues and a half from Villa Franca at 2 A.M. on

The entry in the Regimental Record of the 52nd Light Infantry for the 3rd January, 1809, thus describes the effective fire of the guns of 'C' Troop on that day:—"Two British guns which were posted on the high road leading to Villa Franca, on the slope of the hill, played upon the French column as it advanced. Among others, the French General, Colbert, fell by the well-directed fire of those guns. He was an officer of great promise, and the French bulletin emphatically announced his loss in the following words:—'His hour was come; he died nobly.'"

Wednesday, 4th January, 1809. Nothing for the horses to eat, and miserable accommodation for the men and officers. At 7 marched for Nogales. The Troop and three regiments went a mile further to the bridge. This was a dreadful march over an immense snow mountain, with ruts cut into the snow ice two feet deep and large holes, so that the horses could scarce move. The road strewed and blocked up with ordnance-carriages and others of every description; numbers of dead horses; men, women, and children frozen to death. Got into Arerias (Herreira) about 4 o'clock, with Chester and Barlow and four guns. Walcott, in the rear with two guns, did not arrive till 7. An immense quantity of dollars left on the road, and thrown over the hill on this day's march. Out-picket at Doncos this night two miles up the hill above Nogales.

> The 52nd Regimental Record gives the following curious anecdote in describing the abandonment of this treasure:—" A few miles in rear of Nogales, the road to Lugo leads over a steep mountain. Here the weary oxen were unable to drag along the heavy-laden carts, and as the enemy were pressing upon the rear-guard, it was found impossible to save the military chest. Casks containing dollars to the amount of £25,000 were thrown over the precipice on the right-hand side of the road, and rolled from one declivity to another, till they at last settled in the bottom of a rugged, narrow ravine, quite out of reach of the column. The rear regiments of the Reserve only were present when the money was cast away, and certainly not a man of those left their ranks in the hope of obtaining a portion. This discipline, however, did not extend to the 'followers,' who, as soon as they arrived at the spot where the dollars were rolling over the mountain-side, at once began a scramble, in which the wife of the regimental master-tailor, Malony (who was a merry one, and often beguiled a weary march to the men with her tales), was so successful that her fortune was apparently made. The poor woman went through all the subsequent perils and hardships of the retreat, but on stepping from the boat to the ship's side on embarking at Coruña, her foot slipped and down she went like a shot, and, owing to the weight of dollars secured about her person, she never rose again."

Thursday, 5th January. Pickets drove in about seven in the morning. We retired over the bridge, which Pasley attempted to blow up, but did not succeed. Chester and Barlow remained with two guns to defend the blowing up of the bridge. Proceeded on our march for Lugo, closely pressed the whole way. Guns prepared for action several times. Riflemen constantly engaged. About 4 P.M. reached Constantino and took a position between that and Bazelle. One gun came into action in the road half way up the hill. Large bodies of French cavalry appeared and made dispositions for charging us. The gun then opened and dispersed them after the third round. Ramie and Craig wounded at the gun on this occasion. The French riflemen got quite round our right flank. Remained in that position till dark, when we retired to the top of the hill, about two miles, and lay upon our arms about three hours in the village. Captain Squire with us. We then proceeded on our march, and arrived at Lugo about 9 in the morning, with four guns. Two guns with Walcott, forming the rear-guard, arrived about 11 on the same morning.

The 52nd Regimental Record thus describes the engagement at Constantino, which was one of the most critical during the retreat. "The skirmishing continued almost the whole day (5th), and Sir John Moore never quitted the rear-guard for a moment. Whenever the country presented a favourable situation for checking the enemy, a stand was made to give time to the weakly men to get forward. The reserve arrived close to the village of Constantino at about 4 o'clock in the evening. The village is situated on a small elevation, forming a gentle slope down to a stream within musket range. Beyond this rivulet the road crosses a small valley and ascends the opposite hill in a straight line. On the summit of this hill the rear-guard, with two pieces of artillery, kept the enemy in check, while Major-General the Hon. E. Paget, with the other regiments of the Division, descended into the valley, crossed the bridge, and took up a position with his left resting on Constantino. The enemy followed the rear-guard quickly down the hill, and commenced an attack upon the position; but after a few discharges of artillery, the firing died away, and the men began to cook. It rained excessively at the time."

Friday, 6th January. Without having been followed by the enemy. About 10,000 pounds' worth of dollars thrown over the hill this day. Chester got (*sic*). We all got to my old quarters with the priest. Found all our field officers here; called on Colonel Harding. About 2 P.M. an alarm in the town (Lugo) that the

French were near. Our picquets were some time engaged. The whole Army turned out. The French retreated in about an hour, two guns under Lempriere and two under Beane having been engaged. (Captain Beane commanded 5th Company 3rd Battalion, now 'B' Battery, 4th Brigade. He was killed at Waterloo in command of 'D' Troop, Royal Horse Artillery.) We returned to dinner. Met my friend Humphrey here, who came and sat with me in the evening. Got six bottles of Madeira from Colonel Wood. Colonels Cookson and Greatly dined with us.

Saturday, 7th January. At Lugo. Rained hard all night and this day. Sir John Moore rode out to the picquets, wishing to ascertain the strength of the enemy. Dinner at 2, but as soon as we had commenced, the "turn-out" was sounded and broke up the party. Colonel Cookson with us. Chester very unwell, so I sent him off for Coruña. We returned to quarters about dusk. The Guards had a little brush to-day.

Sunday, 8th January. Turned out very early. Sir John made a disposition of the Army, and offered the enemy battle, which was declined. Returned into Lugo about 12. I had scarcely got the horses out of the carriages, when an order came for four of my guns to go and protect the right flank of the Army; and, shortly after, the other two were ordered to go and protect a bridge (Puente de Rhabade), while arrangements were making for blowing it up. The Army joined us about 2. I marched with the Troop to Guitiriz. The blowing up of the bridge was not effectual.

At daybreak on the 8th the two armies were still in order of battle. On the French side, 17,000 infantry, 4,000 cavalry, and fifty guns were in line, but Marshal Soult deferred the attack until the 9th. On the English part, 16,000 infantry, 1,800 cavalry, and forty guns were in position. Sir John Moore, finding the French were not inclined to attack till a larger portion of their force had come up, decided, after having halted during the 6th, 7th, and 8th, to continue his retreat. Accordingly at 10 P.M., amid a terrible storm of wind, rain, and sleet, the army broke up from the position and continued its march.

Monday, 9th January. Arrived at Guitiriz about 11 P.M.; halted till 2, when we proceeded on our march to Betanzos (about twenty-two miles), blowing and raining hard the whole way. Did not get in till midnight. Many people perished on the road from fatigue and the inclemency of the weather.

Tuesday, 10th January. Got some fresh horses. Ordered to take post on the top of the hill at 9 o'clock. Remained there till 2 P.M., and marched for Coruña. The Betanzos bridge failed in the blowing up also. Lieutenant Davy, of the Engineers, blown up at this bridge. I rode forward to Coruña with Colonel Cookson, and arrived about five o'clock. Walcott arrived with the Troop about 7 P.M.

Wednesday, 11th January. Had a holiday at Coruña, and received letters. My guns were embarked.

Thursday, 12th January. Took the outlying picquet, with Downman's escort at the Bridge of El Burgo. The French close to us, and wounded an officer and several men of different regiments. Stood to our guns the whole night, which was very foggy and damp.

13th January. Relieved by Downman. I was very ill, having caught a bad cold on picquet.

14th January. Rather better. Fletcher and Colonel Mainwaring called on me, desiring me to want for nothing they had. The fleet appeared off the harbour, to our great joy.

15th January. In bed all day. Chester taken unwell on picquet. Fletcher called again, and was very kind.

Monday, 16th January. Began to embark our horses and men at 10 A.M. at St. Lucia. Thirty-two Troop horses and *(blank in original)* men on board the "William," and "Ann," and "Sally" transports; finished by 2 P.M., and had orders to warp out. Began late and did not get far out before dark. About 3 P.M., the enemy being reinforced, made an attack upon our outposts, which soon became general with all the troops upon shore. The fire from the Artillery on both sides and musketry was very heavy and incessant until dark, when the enemy retired to his original position. The 4th, 5th, 14th, 32nd, 43rd, 50th, 51st, and 95th Regiments were engaged with Truscott's (6th Company, 3rd Battalion: No. 9 Battery, 1st Brigade, Northern Division now) and Wall's (4th Company, 7th Battalion, now 'A' Battery, 1st Brigade) Brigades, R.A. The picket was commanded by Colonel Napier, who was killed. Sir David Baird wounded. Sir John Moore shot in the shoulder, and died on the road to Coruña.

Tuesday, 17th January. A strong picket was left out during the night, and all the remainder of the troops retired into the town after dark, and about 12 o'clock began embarking, which continued going on through the night, with some confusion, as it was very dark, and the boats were running foul; and very few found the intended ships. Several boats tried to get on board us, but we could only take one with fifteen men of the 36th Regiment, as we were quite full. This morning at daybreak the picket came in, and were soon followed very near to the town by the French, who were popping at them great part of the way. We now saw from our ship (which lay close to the town) large bodies of French coming in as near as they dare in different directions, and also covering the hills all round the harbour. It began to blow very hard about 10 A.M., and the master was very anxious to get the ship out of the harbour round the Castle, having told him I was sure the next thing the enemy would attempt was to get some guns upon the hills to annoy the Fleet. He made several attempts to get the kedge anchor ahead and warp out, by which we unfortunately got further in, for it blew so hard that, when we got our anchor atrip to haul, the other would not hold, and we drove further in. We were now in a dreadful situation, for we saw them getting guns down to bear upon us, and we could not possibly change our situation until the wind moderated. About half-past 12 they opened several guns upon us, and kept up a smart fire of shot and shell, to the great annoyance of the inner part of the Fleet, about eighty or ninety sail crowded together as thick as possible, and full of troops. Every ship now went to work getting up anchor or cutting cable, and setting sail, to make an attempt at least to get away. Numbers of boats were away from their ships, fetching more of the Army off, and rowing about between the ships. The shot and shell now fell very thick among them, the ships all in motion, and the confusion great. Many ran foul, and many upon the rocks. The wind, however, became more moderate, and Providence made it change two points in our favour (from S. and by W. to S.W. and by S.), which enabled us and many others to weather the Castle Point, which we barely could do, and scraped the rock without damage; and we were happy in getting soon out of their reach, with only our rigging damaged (though we lay almost directly in their line of fire) and the loss of two anchors. At 3 o'clock got quite out of the outer harbour and lay to for the Commodore with the body of the Fleet. The firing continued at the ships aground and those in the further part of the harbour till dark and after, also from the town and citadel at the enemy. A small brig ran foul of us, with five soldiers on board and not a sailor. She had a foresail and mainsail set, and one of the soldiers steering.

Arrival in England.

The captain called to them, directing them which way to put the helm. We soon got clear, without any damage.

Wednesday, 18th January. Off and on all the morning, waiting to collect the Fleet. Most of the men-of-war still in the outer harbour. Many of the transports got out during the night, and the men-of-war got hold of the rest of the Army. About 1 P.M. our convoy (the "Endymion") made signal for all masters, to whom he gave instructions, by which we found Portsmouth was the rendezvous, at which we greatly rejoiced, as it had been said we were to go to Lisbon or Cadiz. At 3 the men-of-war joined us with all the transports they could get out. Six only, I believe, were lost, which, being run foul and aground, were destroyed. About 4 o'clock the whole fleet made sail for Old England, going right before the wind. The men-of-war with us were the "Victory," "Ville de Paris," and "Barfleur" (Sir S. Hood), "Tonnant," and five seventy-four's, with three or four frigates or sloops and about 300 sail of transports. We this day changed the men of the 36th Regiment for six Artillery drivers, and Mr. Brewer from the "Lord Nelson" transport. Chester went on board the "McKay," and got my hair trunk for me.

Sunday, 22nd January. Discovered land at 7 A.M. in the morning. At noon wind quite foul, and lost sight of land. Wind very scant all night.

Monday, 23rd January. Off the Land's End; very little wind and foul. At 8 A.M. the wind fair; a nice breeze. Made all sail for Portsmouth. At 12 a frigate signalled us into Plymouth. Anchored about 5 o'clock P.M.

A note on the fly-leaf of the Journal records, "From the 18th November, 1808, to the 10th January, 1809, marched 800 miles, which is 15 miles a day for 54 days.

Thus having successfully achieved the diversion of the French from the South of Spain, the English Army arrived unbroken at Coruña. A French army of 70,000 men, with great superiority in artillery and cavalry, led by Napoleon, failed to defeat or surround 26,000 English troops. In the depth of winter 250 miles of country were traversed; mountains, ravines, and rivers were crossed, and though often engaged, the Reserve Brigade, forming the rear-guard, was never beaten or thrown into confusion. During the twelve days it covered the retreat, it was in conflict with the enemy seven times, made on two occasions marches of forty miles, and bivouacked in the snow several nights in the mountains. Nevertheless, on arrival at Coruña, this Brigade had fewer men absent from its ranks than any other in the Army. It may here be noted, to the credit of the Royal Artillery, that of the 2,636 absentees and stragglers officially reported, none are shown as belonging to that branch of the service. A great quantity of baggage was lost owing to the death of the transport mules and bullocks; and six 3-pounders, which were not horsed, and which never went beyond Villa Franca, were abandoned and thrown over the cliffs when the Army left that town during the retreat. The guns used in the battle of Coruña, seven six-pounders and one howitzer, were spiked and buried in the sand; but it is believed the French found them after the departure of the English. The hardships of the campaign were great. Lord Londonderry speaks of them thus: "I am well aware that the horrors of the retreat have been again and again described in terms to freeze the blood of such as read them, but I have no hesitation in saying that the most harrowing accounts which have been laid before the public fall short of the reality."

The same officers returned to England as had embarked with the Troop, the returns showing a loss of fifteen men and 115 horses. Many of the latter were so broken down and foundered on arrival of the Army at Coruña, that, as it was found impossible to embark them all, the worst cases were reluctantly shot. About 5,000 horses were lost altogether during the campaign.

Captain Evelegh, in speaking of the events of these days, used often to talk of Lieutenant Barlow, who was a man of great size and weight, riding about twenty-two stone. Shortly after the beginning of the campaign he knocked up both his chargers, and was afterwards usually carried on a limber. On his return to England and promotion, Captain Barlow became Adjutant to a Battalion, and forms one of the group in the sketch now in the Royal Artillery Institution of the "Garrison Staff, Woolwich, 1820."

On its return from Spain the Troop was quartered at Woolwich. On the 17th June, 1811, it was reviewed on Hounslow Heath, with 'B' Troop Royal Horse Artillery, and the 10th, 13th, and 15th Hussars. The following order was issued afterwards:

"Lieutenant-General Lord Paget has the honour to announce to the Troops of Horse Artillery, and the 10th, 13th, and 15th Hussars, which he had the honour to command this morning, that he has received the commands of the Prince Regent to convey to them His Royal Highness's entire approbation of their appearance and performance. His Royal Highness was pleased to express himself on this occasion in terms that were singularly flattering to every individual concerned, and to order that these His Royal Highness's sentiments might be known."

In August of this year the establishment of the Troop was increased by one bombardier and six gunners. In July, 1814, it moved to Christchurch, but, probably owing to the number of Troops of Horse Artillery despatched from Woolwich for the Waterloo campaign, it returned there in June, 1815. As no roster was kept for the Horse Artillery during the Peninsular War (see

Appendix VIII.), Troops were sent on active service as circumstances rendered most convenient; so that when the Army was ordered to Belgium, and the Duke of Wellington "earnestly urged to have everything that had been in the Peninsula sent out, of every description of troops, as he was sure he could depend upon them," the five Troops ('A,' 'D,' 'E,' 'F,' and 'I'), which had but returned from Spain towards the end of 1814, were included among the seven placed under orders, 'G' and 'H' being the other two. The second Rocket Troop, which, later, joined the Army, was already in Holland with the English force under Sir Thomas Graham. Doubtless the five Peninsular Troops lately returned from service were more complete than those which had been at home. The latter were not on a war footing, for Captain Mercer in his memoir relates how 'G' Troop, which had not been abroad since 1807, was completed by breaking up 'K' Troop, then quartered in the same barracks with it at Colchester. This will explain the absence from Waterloo of five of the Troops next for service. 'C' Troop also ran a risk then of being broken up, as appears in the following extract from a letter written by Lieut.-Colonel Sir Augustus Frazer at Brussels in May, 1815, to Lieut.-Colonel Hew Ross, who had just arrived from England with 'A' Troop: "Do they talk of Wilmot's ('C' Troop) coming? If not, I wish they would break his Troop up and send it and Beane's ('D' Troop) to complete us." It must be explained that Sir Augustus was then sore pressed, and constantly applying to the home authorities to obtain the additional men and horses necessary for the change of equipment, from six-pounders to nine-pounders, of three of the eight Troops of Horse Artillery in Belgium under his orders, which was effected shortly before the Battle of Waterloo.

CHAPTER IV.

PENINSULAR SERVICE OF 'D' TROOP, ROYAL HORSE
ARTILLERY.—REDUCTIONS IN HORSE ARTILLERY.—
CHANGES OF QUARTERS.—AUGMENTATIONS PREVIOUS
TO CRIMEAN WAR.

WHILE touching on the ill-fortune of the Troops of Royal Horse Artillery excluded from being at Waterloo, we may refer to the subsequent greater evil that befell one of those that was present, because it affected nearly all the Brigade of Horse Artillery, and because the Troop in question was one distinguished in the first campaign of importance in which this branch of field Artillery acted after its introduction into the English Army. The writer has special means of knowing facts connected with the history of 'D' Troop, as he possesses a number of letters written between the beginning of 1810 and the middle of 1813 by the late Sir Edward Whinyates, then second captain of it. Though these letters deal more with the general events of the Peninsular campaign than with Artillery details, yet it is believed some extracts concerning the earlier scenes in which our Horse Artillery was employed, the records of which are unfortunately so meagre, will be acceptable to those who are, or who have been connected with that branch of the regiment. As already stated, 'D' Troop was formed the same day as 'C'

Troop, and in 1809 was quartered at Canterbury. Constant rumours were prevalent at the close of that year either that large reinforcements would be sent to the English Army in Portugal, or that the Army would be brought home, should the much-hoped-for general peace be made. From these causes 'D' Troop at Canterbury was kept in a state of uncertainty for many months, till at length, after several orders and counter-orders, it was detailed on the 4th February, 1810, to march the next day en route to Portsmouth, there to embark for Lisbon to relieve 'A' Troop then with the Army in Portugal, and which, during the operation of 1809, had been so reduced through sickness, both in men and horses, as to be unfit to take the field for the approaching campaign. 'D' Troop left Canterbury with the following officers: Captain G. Lefebure, 2nd Captain E. C. Whinyates; Lieuts. W. Dunn, T. Carter, H. Mallet, and Assistant-Surgeon J. Ambrose. The strength and equipment are given in Appendix IX. On the morning of the 12th February, after a very wet march, the Troop reached the Gunwharf, Portsmouth, and was much inconvenienced by not having information of the number of vessels and what proportion of horses and ordnance each was to contain, until ordered the same day to the Dockyard for embarkation. This was eventually effected in six small craft of about 200 tons each, which were so crowded with water and forage that the men could scarce find room to sling their hammocks, or any place in which to put their kits and harness. On the 16th the fleet of some sixty ships weighed anchor and sailed for Lisbon. When, as far south as Mondego Bay, and distant some three leagues from it, a violent storm scattered the vessels, disabling one of the Troop transports, the "Camilla," her masts went by the board, her boats were stove in, and the wreck of the main topmast struck the fire from the caboose into the hold among the hay, and set it alight. Most fortunately this occurred during day-time, and after some trouble the fire was extinguished, but the ship drifted for fourteen days an ungovernable wreck in the Bay of Biscay, and, though strongly built for the whale fishery, was in imminent danger of foundering. During this trying time the courage, zeal, and activity of the men of the Troop were even beyond all praise, and it was chiefly owing to their exertions that jury-masts were rigged, and that the " Camilla," on the 18th March, reached Dansey Island in Bantry Bay, having lost but four out of the thirty-six horses on board. In a few days the vessel was able to make her way to Cork, where, after some delay, the detachment was transhipped, and on the 1st May sailed again for Lisbon. On the northern frontier of Portugal they were assailed again by their old enemy, the south-west wind, and detained twelve days, not reaching their destination till the 20th. This unfortunate portion of 'D' Troop was thus ninety-four days proceeding from Portsmouth to Lisbon, nearly as long as in later years troops took to go from England round the Cape to India, and three times as long as they now take to return.

In the meanwhile the Headquarters and remainder of the Troop, with the loss of nine horses, had arrived at Lisbon. The non-arrival of the " Camilla," which was given up for lost, prevented the relief of 'A' Troop, and Brigadier-General Howorth, R.A., about the middle of May, 1810, decided to complete it and 'I' Troop from what had arrived of 'D' Troop. Accordingly, on the 22nd May, two days after the arrival of the missing vessel, the arrangements having been previously made, detachments consisting of sixty-eight men and fifty-six horses for 'A' Troop, and thirty-nine men and twenty-five horses for 'I' Troop, were drafted from 'D,' and set out to join those Troops. The remnant of 'D' Troop—thirty-seven men and forty-nine horses—remained and acted as a depôt in Lisbon, until the recommendation of Lord Wellington should decide the authorities either to remount or recall it to England.

The disappointment caused to all members of the Troop by these arrangements can be better imagined than described; but, however, some of its officers were enabled to join 'A' (Captain Ross's) and 'I' (Captain Bull's) Troops, and with them saw the first shots fired by the Horse Artillery in the Peninsula. At length, in December, 1810, notification arrived from England that 'D' Troop would remain with the Army and receive from home a complete remount in men and horses. On the 17th March, 1811, a draft of men with fifty horses joined, others being reported *en route*, and in about a month two divisions were mounted and equipped. On the 22nd April the Headquarters and four guns marched from Lisbon to join the corps of Sir Rowland Hill, then under temporary command of Marshal Beresford, which it reached, and joined the cavalry portion of, at Villa Franca on the 10th May, 1811. The following month the division (a gun and a howitzer) left behind in Lisbon joined the Troop. Before attempting to give a sketch of its war services, it will be as well to remark that the Horse Artillery record is in error in some particulars regarding them. The first two engagements on the list of the record are "Battle of Busaco," and "Affair of Almeida." The Troop could not have been present at either. The battle of Busaco was fought 27th September, 1810, and, as has already been shown, the Troop was dismounted, and acting as a depôt in Lisbon between May, 1810, and April, 1811. The fact that some of its officers were at Busaco with the Horse Artillery that was present has probably led to the mistake. With regard to "Almeida," examination of dates, and the route by which the Troop marched to join the Army near Badajos, shows that when that action was fought, on 3rd May, 1811, it was at Montijo—a place 135 miles as the crow flies from Almeida. The record-book does not show the Troop as present at Fuentes Guinaldo 25th September, 1811, Salamanca 26th May, 1813, or Aire 2nd March, 1814, although, as will be seen hereafter, it was engaged on all these occasions. 'D' Troop was first engaged at Albuera. An account of the battle written a few days afterwards is as follows :—

"In Bivouac, near Solano, 22nd May, 1811.

"The battle near Albuera on the 16th instant was the most sanguinary and awful combat that has been fought in the Peninsula. The actors in the field of Talavera give the pre-eminence in horror to the battle of Albuera. On the 13th May the cavalry, with our Troop of Horse Artillery which occupied Villa Franca, fell back by Almendralejo to Santa Marta. On the 15th we retired to Albuera, where we were joined by more Portuguese cavalry and Baron Alten's Brigade of sharpshooters. Here we learnt that the army was marching to occupy a position near the village of Albuera, which stands within 300 yards of a stream flowing from the direction of Almendral and Torre, and falling into the Guadiana close to Talavera Real. This rivulet flows through a valley from 1200 to 1600 yards broad, bounded on either side by rising ground of inconsiderable altitude and of easy acclivity. There is a stone bridge at Albuera, and close by, one of the many fords which everywhere traverse the streamlet. Our riflemen were posted in the village and on the banks of the stream, while the cavalry with our four Horse Artillery guns (the two guns left in Lisbon had not yet joined) appuyed their left on Albuera and extended in an almost parallel direction to the stream. The first line of infantry were more than half a mile in rear of us upon the rising ground, and near the Valverde road. In their rear was an extensive plain, and to their right some high ground sloping gradually to the river, and intersected by two transverse valleys or ravines. On these last-mentioned heights the battle was fought. About 7 A.M. on the morning of the 16th instant, massive columns of French infantry and artillery, which had been concealed in a wood on the opposite side of the river, advanced by the Santa Marta road, and made a very sharp attack on the bridge. This attack was a feint, and when it appeared that the attention of the cavalry and our four guns was engaged in the defence of this point, the enemy moved heavy columns to our right with the intention of turning that flank. The heights, which became the chief scene of action, were, however, occupied by some small corps of Spaniards, and when the design of the enemy was fully ascertained, our infantry made a counter-defensive movement in that direction. The French soon brought up some heavy guns and formed their troops under cover of some rising ground, which was at right angles to our first position and to the rivulet upon which Albuera stands. To meet this movement the Spanish infantry was formed on the first of the transverse heights, and the cavalry and Horse Artillery moved into the small plain on their right, and prolonged the alignment. The French attack now formed on the rising ground in front of these troops. At this instant Colonel Colborne's Brigade, at the head of the second Division, moved up at a double from the rear, and, though having but time to form three of the four regiments, yet it instantly passed on to charge the French advance, which was in line, supported by heavy columns. The French line instantly gave way, and the brave but mad handful of men, away from support and running to certain destruction, pushed on, and got on the flank of the columns. At this moment more French troops arrived, and a fire of infantry and artillery, the heaviest and most murderous perhaps that was ever witnessed, commenced. The bugle sounded for Colborne's Brigade to retire; they obeyed. Instantly they were charged by the lancemen (lancers), who galloped in on their left flank from the plain, and issued from the body of the columns. This was a most awful moment; the fortune of the day seemed lost. The Fusilier Brigade (7th and 23rd), who supported, were almost destroyed; but at last the regular advance of Cole's Division, the steadiness of the Portuguese, and the good countenance of the Walloon Guards turned the victory; the enemy gave way, and were successfully driven from the heights with immense loss. - The advance and charge of the second Division against such masses of infantry and in such superiority of numbers was glorious, but it has been almost the annihilation of some regiments. Soult, however, though beaten, and most decisively so, carried off trophies. Three regiments lost their colours, or, more truly, the regiments being extinct, the colours remained in the hands of the enemy. We lost also one of the German Artillery howitzers (see Appendix X.), the Brigade (Battery) having suffered in killed, wounded, and prisoners, forty-five men. I am quite well and jolly, and did not get a scratch, although one of my guns was for a moment in the hands of the enemy, and I lost some men and horses. The field of battle was the most shocking spectacle that can be imagined.

The dead, actually amounting to thousands, were in heaps, and the scene was rendered more horrible by the Spaniards plundering and stripping the bodies, which consequently exposed the wounds in all their horror. Hundreds of wounded remained two days on the ground, unfed and undressed, and exposed to the burning sun—a situation infinitely *more shocking than death itself*; but the duties of humanity could not be extended to all. The next day, the 17th, both armies remained quiet, and at night the French retreated by the Solano road, having sent their baggage and many sick by the Santa Marta. Two French generals are dead, and Soult, with two others, are said to be wounded. The enemy abandoned three hundred sick in Almendralejo. It appears the strength of the enemy was about 30,000 men; 22,000 were in the principal attack on the right flank, and 4000 at the bridge. The French had about 3500 cavalry; the English were not a third of that number. The Spanish and Portuguese cavalry are nothing in a charge. They are useful in appearance, but cannot meet the French. The accounts of our prisoners, who hourly escape, and that of the French deserters, all state the enemy's loss as enormous, and go so far as to say it amounts to 10,000 men. I feel convinced it must be 7000 or 8000, if not more. The French yielded the field to us in great confusion; and, had we not suffered in the vital part of our force—had the Spaniards been a manœuvring army—the French would have been annihilated. I just learn our infantry are coming up. We shall march in five minutes. I write in great confusion."

The position of the Horse Artillery and cavalry on the right flank of the allied Army during the main attack was a very trying one. Here some of the severest fighting took place, owing to the persistent efforts of Marshal Soult to turn that flank, efforts at one time nearly crowned with success. The Troop was in the very thick of the *mêlée*; and, though the guns were repeatedly charged and ridden through by the French cavalry, General Lumley was able to check their attack at a most critical part of the battle by the effective fire of the guns of 'D' Troop. Marshal Beresford, in his despatch to Lord Wellington, thus refers to it: "I have every reason to speak favourably of the manner in which our Artillery was served and fought. The four guns of the Horse Artillery commanded by

Captain Lefebure did great execution on the enemy's cavalry."

A few days after the battle the Troop was present at the brilliant cavalry action at Usagre on 25th May, 1811, which is mentioned in a letter as follows :

"On the 18th, we followed the French with cavalry and this Troop of Horse Artillery, and continued to do so as far as Usagre, where we found 400 French cavalry, who retired. On the 25th, however, Latour Maubourg, with all the French Cavalry Division and some guns, marched from Villa Garcia to attack us. In consequence of this temerity, he suffered a loss of at least 200 men. The French dragoons did not attempt to stand us, but the instant our jolly fellows came near them, they turned and were sabred in good style. Our guns were not innocent of mischief on this day. We marched back here to cantonments yesterday (29 May), and hope to have some rest. Since the 15th we have been day and night in the fields, in a state of constant alertness."

General Lumley, commanding the Allied Cavalry, made most favourable mention in his despatch of the services of the Troop in this engagement, and the French General Lallemand acknowledged the losses caused in his cavalry division by its fire. A French military writer lays great stress on the effect produced by the English Horse Artillery on this day. He says : " Cette position est rendue encore plus critique par l'artillerie Anglaise, tirant a mitraile sur nos regiments agglomérés en avant de ce defile."

During the next three months 'D' Troop was continually on the move with the Second Cavalry Division. Nothing of importance occurred until September, when it was engaged on the 25th at Fuentes de Guinaldo (the same day as El Bodon, but some distance from where that engagement took place), and again on the 27th at Aldea de Ponte ; a letter written shortly afterwards says :

"The Troop was at Guinaldo and at Aldea de Ponte, in which latter affair, I am sorry to say my friend Dunn was wounded in the thigh. He, however, is doing quite well, and will be with us again in two or three months. He had, however, the satisfaction of putting his first shot into a column, and expediting the movements of the enemy. I really expected at Guinaldo to have had a general battle, as the French collected an immense force, and we were two days staring each other in the face. It appears that this Troop is to be continually marching, and perhaps it is really better for us to have arrived too late to accompany General Hill, as the horses cannot stand such continued work with little forage."

The following year, a few days after the battle of Salamanca, 'D' Troop (which was then on the Tagus with Hill's force) distinguished itself at Ribera on the 24th July, 1812, upon which occasion the French cavalry under General Lallemand were defeated by the force under General Long. The particulars are as follows:

On the morning of the 24th, two regiments of French dragoons and one regiment of Chasseurs, under General Lallemand, drove in the Portuguese picquet from Hinojosa to Ribera, where four squadrons of Portuguese cavalry were stationed under Colonel Campbell. His force being so inferior to the enemy, Campbell retired upon Villa Franca, from whence General Long's Brigade advanced, accompanied by 'D' Troop. The enemy withdrew beyond the defile of Ribera, through which Long advanced, and, pushing his squadrons round the town, attacked the enemy with spirit, while the Artillery fired with effect from some high ground, and near the river on the Villa Franca side of the defile. The French gave way, and retired rapidly on Hinojosa.

General Long in his despatch dwells on the rapidity of movement and precision of fire of the Horse Artillery, by which the enemy suffered considerably, adding, " I should be wanting in justice, if I omitted to express my admiration of the conduct of the Artillery under the immediate orders of Captains Lefebure and Whinyates." Subsequently a still higher eulogium was passed on the conduct of the Troop, for during a communication after the action under a flag of truce, General Lallemand made particular inquiries for the name of the officer who had commanded the guns near the river, and, on learning it, sent the following message to Captain Whinyates: "Tell that brave man that if it had not been for him I should have beaten your cavalry; but that, meeting me in every movement with his fire, he never would allow me to form for attack. Say that I shall mention his name in my orders as having been the cause of our defeat, and not your cavalry. Be sure you tell him this. Promise to give him my message."

A chivalrous feeling, displayed on many occasions, existed between the French and English armies in the Peninsula. As a further example of this, the following incident is related: During the retreat of the French Army at the close of 1812, General Junot, Duke of Abrantes, was wounded by a musket-ball in the face. Lord Wellington, on learning this, wrote to Junot to express his regret at his misfortune, and, knowing the French Army to be deficient not only of luxuries but even of the necessaries of life, offered to send anything requisite for dressing his wound or accelerating its cure. At the same time Lord Wellington informed Junot of the welfare and movements of his wife, who was in Spain. The generous offer of assistance was however graciously declined by the gallant General.

In October, 1812, 'D' Troop had the misfortune to lose its commanding officer. Captain Lefebure, who had been in delicate health, died unexpectedly at Madrid on the 22nd, from the exposure and hardships of the campaign.

At the close of the year, when the Army was forced to retreat from Salamanca and Madrid on Ciudad Rodrigo, before the much greater numbers Soult had been able to concentrate against them, the French followed the Army with a large force, comprising all their cavalry. A sharp engagement took place on 17th November at San Muños, where, so hot was the fire 'D' Troop was exposed to, that five out of its six guns were injured by it. On the next day's march (the 18th) the Troop was again engaged when the force forded the Yeltes river. During the retreat the weather was very severe, and consequently the sufferings of the troops from hunger and cold were great. On the 20th November, 1812, the Army went into cantonments.

Early in 1813 'D' Troop was inspected by Lord Wellington, who expressed his satisfaction at its fine condition and complete equipment. In March Captain George Bean joined in succession to Captain Lefebure, and in April the writer of the letters from which most of the details concerning it are taken, left on promotion. Some years later Major-General Long wrote in the following terms to Captain Whinyates, concerning his Peninsular service with 'D' Troop:

"I know of no officer who served under my command in the Peninsular War, or even in the corps commanded by the present Lord Hill, who has stronger claims upon my sense of justice, gallantry, and merit, than yourself.

"I do, therefore, most unequivocally and conscientiously declare that, during the whole and very considerable period of time that the Troop of Horse Artillery commanded by the late Captain Lefebure and yourself acted under my orders and personal observation, I never witnessed more exemplary conduct in quarters, nor more distinguished zeal and gallantry in the field, than were uniformly shown, and in several very trying instances, by every officer serving in that Troop, and most conspicuously so by yourself; and, limiting even this, my opinion to two occasions (though it would be a gross injustice to you to do so where so many others occurred), I should not hesitate one moment to assert, that your brilliant conduct at Albuera and San Muños, alone, entitled you to a full participation in every honour and consideration due to exemplary and distinguished services, which may have been bestowed upon your contemporaries.

"I have a right to make these assertions, not only because I witnessed your behaviour with admiration, but because it is the only species of remuneration in my power to render to those who, whilst serving under my command, so ably and gallantly supported the military operations for which I was often and personally responsible."

It may be remarked here that rewards at this period were much more sparingly granted than in later years. Commanding Officers then alone were eligible for medals, and it is related that when the English Army in 1815 landed in Belgium, the people would not believe any of the troops had served in Spain, because they wore no decorations. That the system then obtaining was as much too niggardly as it is now over-profuse, few will dispute.

In May, 1813, the Army broke up from cantonments and advanced. 'D' Troop with the second Division, under Lord Hill, arrived at Salamanca on the morning of the 26th May. The French rear-guard, under General Villatte, lingered too long in the place, and, after crossing the Tormes, were overtaken by the Cavalry and Horse Artillery, under General Fane. Owing to the ravines and intricacies of the ground, the guns had to make a detour, and were not able to be brought into action till the French had gained a league and a half from the city. Then, however, they opened with effect, every shot going through the ranks of the unfortunate enemy, who retired with extreme rapidity, but in great order. This affair cost the French about 200 men; few, if any, were killed or wounded except by the fire of the Horse Artillery. Seven ammunition tumbrils, some baggage, and about 200 prisoners were taken.

'D' Troop was present at the memorable battle of Vittoria, 21st June, 1813, and it took part in the actions in the Pyrenees between 26th and 30th June, 1813.

The following year it was present at the battle of

Orthes, 27th February, 1814. Major (afterwards Sir Joseph) Cairncross, in his despatch to Colonel (afterwards Sir Alexander) Dickson, "speaks with pride of the steady and destructive fire kept up by 'D' Troop, although exposed to a very heavy fire of musketry."

The Troop was specially mentioned in orders for its services on 2nd March, 1814, in the engagement near Aire. Four guns were brought into action with great effect; and one of them, under Lieutenant (afterwards Lieutenant-General Sir) W. Brereton, after a few rounds silenced two of the enemy's, and forced them to retire. The same day the second captain, Macdonald, distinguished himself in leading on the Portuguese troops, who had been forced back. He was thanked in public orders, Sir Rowland Hill taking the opportunity to state that upon the several occasions on which the Troop had been recently engaged, he had been much satisfied with all ranks composing it.

On the 10th April 'D' Troop took part in the battle of Toulouse, which closed its Peninsular services, during which it had been constantly with the Second Division of the Army, under the command of Sir Rowland Hill. A few months later it returned home.

In concluding the account of the Peninsular services of 'D' Troop, as a further evidence of the high character it held during the war, the writer may add that he recollects when at Shorncliffe, in 1862, the late Marquis of Tweeddale, who had served on the staff of Lord Hill in Spain, in talking of Artillery matters, used to speak in the highest terms of the services of 'D' Troop, on all occasions, during the war, and always dwelt in eulogistic terms on the ease and rapidity of its movements in the field. His favourite expression was, "They used to make their guns jump."

In the beginning of 1815, when Napoleon returned to

France from his exile at Elba, 'D' Troop formed part of the artillery force of the English Army then ordered to the Netherlands. It was the last Troop to leave England, and, after a very forced march, only reached the Army at Waterloo during the night of the 17th June, 1815. In the battle of the 18th it was posted with 'A' Troop in the reserve, which was brought into action early in the day. 'D' Troop suffered severely. Major Beane, seven men, and thirty-six horses were killed; and among the wounded were second Captain W. Webber and Lieutenant M. Cromie, the latter mortally.

The Troop was afterwards at the capture of Paris, and served with the army of occupation in France. Nevertheless, though having seen more war service than any other Troop—'A' and 'I' Troops excepted—it was selected by the Duke of Wellington for reduction in 1816, because it was then commanded by Captain Mercer, who, when in command of 'G' Troop at Waterloo, had incurred the Duke's displeasure by not carrying out the instructions to retire his gunners from their guns into the adjacent infantry squares during the attacks of the French cavalry on the allied position. The reason for the course he pursued—the fear of disheartening the Brunswick troops—has already been stated. This was a hard punishment to Captain Mercer, who had already been denied his brevet majority; but it was still harder upon a Troop whose services had been both constant and distinguished since 1811.

When 'D' Troop was reduced, all troops below it on the list, in spite of the remonstrances of many officers, were moved up a letter to fill the vacancy. Thus 'E,' 'F,' 'G,' 'H,' and 'I' Troops became 'D,' 'E,' 'F,' 'G,' and 'H' respectively; and in 1847 the letter 'I' was given to the First Rocket Troop. The inconvenience and confusion caused by this alteration has been very great, and it is difficult to understand how such an arrangement could have been devised. It is, however, satisfactory to state that on the reorganization of the regiment on 1st July, 1877, when the Batteries of the original 'A' and 'B' Brigades were re-united into one Brigade under the former letter, the Deputy-Adjutant-General, Major-General R. Radcliffe, wisely decided to restore to all those Batteries the letters they were formed under, and assigned that of the unfortunate but distinguished 'D' Troop to 'E' Battery, 'B' Brigade (previously 'I' Troop, raised in 1814, as the First Rocket Troop), the only existing Battery without an original letter, the Second Rocket Troop, of Leipsic and Waterloo renown, having been reduced in 1816, the year in which began those reductions which in a short time reduced the Artillery to such a state of helplessness. The six Troops with the Army of Occupation in France were then placed on a reduced six-gun establishment. Those at home were reduced to four guns, with eleven non-commissioned officers, fifty-six gunners, twenty-four drivers, and 102 horses. At the same time, besides the two Troops already mentioned, 'K,' 'L,' and 'M' were broken up. In 1819, 'B' and 'G' Troops shared a similar fate, and the future establishment of the remaining seven Troops was fixed to provide a personnel for four guns, but only horses for two and for a forge. (Appendix XI.)

To return to 'C' Troop. In October, 1815, it marched to Chatham, and to Canterbury in December. In September, 1816, it moved to Ireland, where it remained till its return to Woolwich on the 24th April, 1821. After five years at Headquarters, the Troop moved to Manchester on the 30th April, 1826.

The impoverished establishment to which the Horse Artillery had been reduced in 1819 remained unaltered for nine years, till 1828, when the two Troops in Ireland were each raised to a strength of four guns. Their periodical relief, however, by the two gun Troops from England seems to have led to confusion; for, in 1838, Sir Alexander Dickson, to whom the officer commanding the Royal Horse Artillery at Woolwich had represented the matter, writes as follows:—

"I fully agree with you as to the disorganizing consequences of the practice to bring Troops of Horse Artillery from Ireland dismounted, or nearly so. It has arisen from there being a greater expenditure of horses in Ireland than here, but I shall do my best to prevent a recurrence of it. Indeed I think no Troop should come from Ireland with less than thirty horses."

The arrangement was probably due to that destructive economy which, as will be seen later on, had reduced the Field Artillery nearly to extinction.

'C' Troop came on the four-gun establishment (Appendix XII.) on proceeding to Ireland on the 15th August, 1829. After various changes of quarters in that country, it moved to Woolwich on 26th August, 1833. It was present on the 18th June, 1836, in Hyde Park, at a review of about 5,000 men before the King and Queen and Duke of Wellington, to commemorate the twenty-first anniversary of the Battle of Waterloo. The regiments which had served there wore on parade sprigs of laurel in their head-dresses and round their colours.

On the 18th August the Troop moved into the Northern District, and, after some changes of quarters there, marched for Ireland on 13th August, 1841, when Sir Charles Napier, then in command of that District, issued the following order:—

Increase of Establishment.

"District Orders.
"Calverley, 11th August, 1841.

"Major Blachley's Troop of Horse Artillery will march for Ireland on the 13th instant, and the Major-General cannot permit it to do so without expressing his approbation of the good conduct of the Troop since he had the honour to hold the command of the District. The good order in which the Major-General has always found Major Blachley's Troop is creditable to that officer, and worthy of the distinguished corps to which it belongs.

"By Command,
"GODFREY MUNDAY, Major of Brigade."

Great pains were taken in these days to obtain men of good character for the Horse Artillery, and the certificate to character of a man who joined 'C' Troop about this date is given in Appendix XIII. as a specimen. On arrival in Dublin, the Troop was for the first time quartered in Portobello. In July, 1843, it marched to Limerick, returning to Dublin in August, 1844. The following August it moved to Woolwich.

In 1848 there was considerable stir and apprehension in England owing to the meetings and opinions expressed by the Chartists. In consequence, due military preparations were made by the authorities to frustrate the anticipated disturbances when the monster demonstration took place on the 10th April on Kennington Common. It is believed these events drew attention to the reduced state of the Field Artillery. The Horse Artillery in England then consisted of but ten guns, without any ammunition waggons, and the Field Batteries were almost non-existent (for particulars see Appendix XIV.). But be that as it may, very shortly afterwards two guns with a proportion of ammunition waggons were added to each Troop. For the detail of this four-gun equipment with which 'C' Troop marched to Leeds in August, 1851, see Appendix XV. In 1853, through the wisdom of the Commander-in-Chief, Lord Hardinge, a further increase of two guns per Troop was made; and the Troop which left Leeds on the 18th March, on its return to Woolwich was made up to a strength of six guns (Appendix XVI.) after its arrival there on 3rd May. Thus in a few years the strength of each Troop was tripled. Subsequent events fully proved how fortunate it was that these additions to the strength of the Artillery were made; for early in 1854, England, France, and Turkey entered into an alliance to resist the encroachments of the Emperor of Russia, and to assist the Sultan in preserving the integrity of the Ottoman Empire. It was accordingly agreed to despatch to the East a combined French and English force to co-operate with the Turks; the former to consist of about 70,000 men under Marshal St. Arnaud, the latter about 30,000 men, under General Lord Raglan. 'C' Troop, on 20th February, 1854, was placed under orders to join the expedition, and shortly afterwards 'I' Troop (originally First Rocket Troop, now 'D' Battery, 'A' Brigade) was added to the Artillery contingent.

The following detailed and graphic account of the services of 'C' Troop during the Crimean campaign is from the pen of an eye-witness who served with it uninterruptedly from its embarkation at Woolwich in March, 1854, until its return to Scutari in December, 1855, and who unfortunately desires to maintain his incognito. Some facts and dates obtained from other members of the Troop have been embodied in the narrative.

CHAPTER V.

EMBARKATION FOR TURKEY.—BULGARIA.—INVASION OF CRIMEA.—BULGANAK.

In February, 1854, 'C' Troop was quartered at Woolwich. Captain (now General Sir) E. C. Warde commanded. It was under orders for Turkey. Numerous changes were taking place at the time, and many of the old hands were removed—some on account of age, some by promotion, or rejection at the several medical inspections, and various other causes. Their places were filled up, and the Troop largely augmented by drafts from other Troops. Many of these were volunteers, notably from 'H' Troop (now 'I' Battery, 'A' Brigade), whose commanding officer, Captain Grant (although he told them he did not like to lose their services), highly commended them, and even, in some instances, generously allowed them to take their horses with them. In the case of the drivers many of their horses were the very best from his gun teams. Some of them lasted throughout the whole Eastern campaign, and were effective at the Curragh Camp in 1861. Other Troops supplied horses, but these were drawn in the usual way. The equipment of the Troop in February, 1854, was six-pounders. Captain Warde's promotion took place at this time, and Captain Levinge succeeded him. At a foot parade in the East Square, Captain Warde took his leave of the Troop. He addressed them to this effect, "That he had called them together to say good-bye, and to wish them God-speed. He welcomed all those who had just joined, whether as volunteers who had cast in their lot with the Troop or otherwise, all of whom bore exemplary characters; that he was sorry to have to part with his Troop, which had been his pride for so many years; that he had hoped to have taken them into action, but that his promotion left no alternative. He exhorted them to be steady under every trying circumstance, and to combine steadiness with speed, and then there was no fear but they would do well. He said, for the information of all those who had joined lately, that he had given his Troop a motto, 'It is lawful to be happy.' He thanked them for their past good conduct." He formally handed the Troop over to Captain Levinge, who was then on the parade.

The time previous to embarkation was chiefly occupied in route marching on the roads. Colonels Strangways and Bloomfield (afterwards Sir John) commanded the Horse Artillery at Woolwich at this time, and Captain (now Lieut.-General) C. S. Henry was Adjutant. There were some reviews and inspections by officers of distinction. Brigadier-General Cator was to command the whole Artillery of the expedition, and on two or three occasions he paraded so much of it as was ready, viz., 'C' Troop, the Black Field Battery, R.A. (No. 1 Company, 3rd Battalion, now 'A' Battery, 2nd Brigade), under Captain (now Colonel) H. J. Thomas, and the Ball Cartridge Brigade, under Captain (now Major-General) J. R. Anderson. The non-commissioned officers and gunners also attended at the Arsenal to have new-pattern fuses explained to them. The old fuse had to be sawn off to suit the range at the rings marked on it, and these had to be counted, which was a slow proceeding under fire; but the new fuse had merely to be punctured where the figures in tenths were clearly marked, and they could be fixed very quickly.

A little before midnight on the 17th March, Brigade Major (afterwards Colonel) Bingham came to the Horse Artillery Guard, and said the order had just arrived from London to embark the Troop; the men being called up, gave three cheers, emptied their beds in great glee, and got ready.

They embarked in the early morning of the 18th at the Dockyard, in Nos. 1, 2, 3, and 4 transports, and were the first portion of the Artillery force. Captain Levinge and Lieutenant (now Colonel) Grylls were in No. 1 "Pyrenees," Lieut. (afterwards Major-General) Michell and Assistant-Surgeon (now Deputy-Surgeon-General) Rudge in No. 2 "Murcia," 2nd Captain Willett in No. 3 "Her Majesty," and Lieutenant Earle in No. 4 "City of Carlisle." Total embarked as per Embarkation Return, see Appendix XVII.

They were the usual ship-rigged sailing transports, and carried from sixty to sixty-six horses each, the platform on which the stalls stood lay on the ballast, from the main to the fore hatch, they were fitted up at Deptford Dockyard; a few of the largest horses having been previously sent over there, to be tried into old frames used at the time of the Peninsular War, and which were found to give quite sufficient room. The instructions were to sail direct for Malta, and await orders. The four transports had a fair wind to the Straits of Gibraltar, but suddenly, on the morning of the 29th March, a gale sprung up, and Nos. 3 and 4 had to make for Gibraltar harbour, where they were detained four days, Nos. 1 and 2 going into Cadiz, and under Cape Spartel for shelter; the wind for the next fortnight was dead ahead, and the sea heavy, so the ships had to keep tacking; it increased to a gale on April 20th and 21st, then a calm succeeded, and the ships were picked up and towed by steamers. Her Majesty's ship "Cyclops" towed No. 3, and the Captain intimated that war had been proclaimed. All four vessels arrived at Malta on the 25th April. The stay there was short, just to receive orders and take a few feeds of green forage on board for the horses; the ships then sailed for Constantinople. Having arrived at the mouth of the Dardanelles, the wind was again dead ahead, and they had to anchor till picked up by steamers and towed to Constantinople, where they arrived on the 6th May. Colonel (now General Sir) R. J. Dacres and his Adjutant, Captain (now Lieutenant-General Sir) E. Hamley, had come on board No. 3 transport at Malta, and while the ship was at anchor at the mouth of the Dardanelles, they, together with Captain Willett and some non-commissioned officers, went ashore to visit a fort at the Castles of Asia; they found an old Turkish officer and some men in charge. The former insisted on considering one of the Troop non-commissioned officers as the commander of the party, and was taking him off on his arm to his room for coffee; but a Barbary Jew, that Captain Hamley had known at Gibraltar, happened to turn up at this moment, and, officiating as interpreter, soon set matters right. The fort was in a dilapidated condition. It was armed with a few very old-pattern long brass guns, seemingly without any tangent scales, or means of elevation; the carriages were of the rudest description, and could not be traversed. Stone shot only was used, and the guns could only be fired with effect when the object to be aimed at came between them and a mark on the opposite side of the Dardanelles.

The Troop disembarked on the 7th May, at Kulali, on

the Asiatic side, and were quartered in the large red barracks there. They were the first arrivals; a regiment of Turkish Lancers had to move out to make room for them. The Troop was fifty-one days on board ship, and horses were lost in all the vessels except No. 3—altogether 10 were lost. The barracks were very dirty, and plentifully populated with fleas, etc. The Commissariat bread was very poor and gritty, and the mutton (there was no beef) wretchedly thin and bad flavoured; the smell was so disagreeable when it was being cooked, that the men quite turned against it, and ate hard-boiled eggs and onions instead : these were cheap and plentiful. The pay was issued from the Commissariat chest in sovereigns, and the sergeants had to go across in caiques to Constantinople to exchange it for Turkish dollars and piastres. On one of these occasions it turned out to be a very perilous journey for two of the sergeants. In all the smaller caiques there was just room for two passengers to sit flat on the bottom, and not move, the feet of the oarsman being placed against the same board on which the passengers rest their feet, and all must then sit very quiet. On this trip the party had got well into the middle of the Bosphorus, where the current runs very swiftly, when suddenly a piece of the bottom of the caique sprung up underneath them, and let the water in. When the Turk saw this, he ceased all efforts at rowing, and considered he was on the road to Paradise. The water kept coming in, but the sergeants dare not move, as that would have only hastened the end, and the caique went with the current; hope seemed gone, when fortunately they drifted with a bang across the cable and bows of a vessel at anchor, the crew of which had been attracted by the shouting, and some sailors got down the side of the ship and caught the caique with boat-hooks and ropes as it was gliding past; otherwise it must have quickly sunk, as it was nearly full of water, and Her Majesty would have been minus two of her non-commissioned officers. After a few days, as other ships arrived, the Troop was glad to move into camp six miles away, at the "Sweet Waters of Asia," where they remained about a fortnight. At this time it had been decided that one Troop of Horse Artillery was to be with the Cavalry, and the other to be attached to the Light Division of the Army under Sir George Brown. Captain Levinge, being senior Captain, was given his choice, and he elected to go on at once with the latter. The Troop was therefore re-embarked in the same ships on the 25th of May; they remained for a day or two at anchor in the Bosphorus, and were then taken in tow by steam transports, arriving at Varna on the 30th May, and disembarking on the 31st without any mishap, after which they moved into camp a short distance outside the town, where the Light Division were assembling. The Light Division comprised 'C' Troop R.H.A., the Black Battery R.A., the 7th Fusiliers, 19th Regiment, 23rd Royal Welsh, 33rd, 77th, 88th Regiments, and the 2nd Battalion Rifle Brigade. The Commissariat rations consisted of mutton, which was of better quality than at Constantinople, salt beef or pork, brown bread, rather gritty, green coffee berries, and an allowance of sugar. The coffee berries were issued for many months, and were a source of perpetual annoyance to the troops, as they had to be roasted or burnt, and pounded on stones, there being no coffee mills procurable, or anything else to do it with. There was no rum ration at this time.

On the 5th June the Division marched to Aladyn, eight or nine miles off, and encamped there. This was a pleasant situation for a camp; everything went smoothly in the Division, and the men were in good health; the latter had sports and games, and the officers had some horse-racing. The French General Canrobert, accompanied by a cavalry escort, visited the camp, and inspected the whole Division, which was paraded for that purpose. Barley only was issued for the horses, and many of them were now suffering from fever in the feet in consequence. There was no hay, and the Troop had sometimes to go miles to get half an hour's poor grazing, but still they kept in fair condition.

Driver Thrupp, of 'C' Troop, was unfortunately drowned while bathing in the lake about three-quarters of a mile from camp.

On the 30th June the Light Division marched to Devna, about eight miles further on. The camping-ground was in a very wide sort of valley, with a rather deep and sluggish river running in the middle, having reeds in great abundance growing on its banks. Portions of the Heavy and Light Cavalry and 'I' Troop R.H.A., had now arrived, and were encamped about a mile off on the opposite side of the valley. Colonel Strangways, R.H.A., had also arrived. While at Devna, Lord Cardigan made a long reconnaissance to the Danube with a portion of the Light Brigade, during the siege of Silistria, and Lieutenant Earle accompanied him as one of his staff. On the 6th July both 'C' and 'I' Troops, and so much of the Heavy Cavalry as were in camp, were inspected and reviewed by Omar Pasha, the Turkish Generalissimo. The Horse Artillery drilled first as one Brigade, and the Pasha expressed himself as delighted with the manœuvres, particularly the movement of advancing at close intervals with guns masked, and, after coming into action, dismounting gun and carriage, etc., which was done at the particular request of Lord Raglan. As soon as the Horse Artillery cleared off the ground, the Heavy Cavalry were manœuvred by

Lord Lucan, beginning with a charge right up to the Staff. The Pasha was much pleased with their drilling also, and spoke in high terms of the appearance of men and horses, and they really were in splendid condition.

On the 22nd July Lieutenant Michell left the Troop to join his new Company (also with the Army of the East) as Second Captain. He was succeeded by Lieutenant (now Colonel) Strangways.

The English Troops had up till this time been in excellent health, when suddenly the cholera made its appearance, and on the morning of the 23rd July six men were reported dead in the Light Division, and seventeen more on the morning of the 24th, so the Division was immediately removed to Pravadi, a short day's march on the Monastir Road. About this time many men were suffering from diarrhœa and dysentery, much of which was supposed to be caused by country wine sold in the neighbourhood of the camp; so an order was obtained to hold a Board of Survey on it. The Board tried eight casks, holding about 400 gallons, and finding it very bad and sour, the Provost Sergeant was ordered to break in the head of each cask, and spill the wine on the ground, which formed a fine red pond. The owner was warned that if he brought any more such wine to camp, he would be more severely dealt with. This summary proceeding had a good effect.

August 2nd was a melancholy day in 'C' Troop camp. Major Levinge, who had not been well, was in the habit of taking sleeping draughts, and by mistake took an overdose of opium, which killed him in a few hours. There was a quiet military funeral next evening, and he was buried at the foot of a large tree in the plain near the encampment. In digging the grave, which was a very deep one, one of the men (Gunner Shaw) came upon a remarkably old coin, far down in the earth.

On August 6th, Captain H. J. Thomas, of the Black Field Battery, attached to the Light Division, was appointed to the Troop and took over the command, vice Levinge. On the same date Second Captain Willett was ordered to proceed to Varna to take command of a company of Royal Artillery there, on promotion; and, also on the same date, orders were received for the Troop to march, on August 8th, to the neighbourhood of Varna to take over a nine-pounder equipment.

The cholera, which had been raging in the Infantry, now attacked the Troop, and the first victim (Gunner Stratton) died on August 7th. Others were stricken down, and the hospital marquee quickly filled.

On the morning of the 8th August the Troop proceeded by itself on the return journey to Varna, but by a different route. They at first went nearly due south, and having crossed the river, bore towards the east, an officer of the staff (*his name is not remembered*) was sent to show the way, but he appeared to get ill, and after a time had to leave. Bombardier Fraser was left behind to attend to the men who were prostrate in the Hospital Marquee. Colonel Strangways also remained. After crossing the river on the march towards Varna, the scenery became very beautiful, the country being hilly, well wooded, and with delightful glens, but perfectly lonely. On the 9th the Troop reached its new camping ground, which was about six or seven miles south of Varna, and on the right-hand side of the Adrianople Road, as it leads to the Balkans. The Troop Arabajee was missed from the march, and when sought for by the interpreter, was found some miles back, dead on the road-side from cholera, and the bullocks still standing yoked in the araba. The site of this new camp was a very good one; it was well elevated, the road from Varna harbour being an ascent all the way, and there was abundance of grass and water; but the cholera again attacked the men, and some died, Driver Blayney amongst the number. The Troop soon became about fifty men short for work, eleven were dead or invalided, ten were left sick at Pravadi, thirty-three were in the Troop Hospital Tents at Adrianople Road—altogether nine had died of cholera. Assistant-Surgeon Rudge became ill and had to leave, and a Dr. Llewellyn of the Cavalry took medical charge. The stores of barley were destroyed in the great fire at Varna on the 10th August, and for some days after the Troop had to send to villages six or seven miles distant, and get barley just cut and unthrashed. Almost all the men who were left in the Hospital Marquee at Pravadi died at once, some of them before the Troop was well out of sight, and Bombardier Fraser rejoined a few days afterwards, having performed his melancholy duty. Colonel Strangways' tent was close by the Marquee, and he remained until all was over, and gave instructions for the burial of the men as they died. There was now no more chance of marching away from the cholera, as the expedition intended for the invasion of the Crimea was ordered to embark. The six-pounder equipment was taken down to Varna, and handed over to Commissary Rogan, who issued a nine-pounder equipment instead; these were taken up to camp, but there was only a few days now before embarkation, and no time for any drill with them; in fact, the Troop only turned out once and hooked in, to salute a regiment of French Cuirassiers, who were marching by on the road to the Balkans. With the nine-pounder equipment the gun teams were increased to eight horses, and the detachments to ten mounted men in each subdivision.

The nine-pounder equipment of a Troop of R.H.A., as laid down in Adjutant-General's Circular, Woolwich, 29th Nov., 1855, is given in Appendix XVIII.

The six last-named carriages were not issued, nor were the non-commissioned officers, men, or horses made up to anything like these numbers—in the autumn of 1855 the Troop had one forage waggon in possession.

The men who had died so far were buried in coffins made of green boughs, interlaced; afterwards there was no time or means of paying even this respect, so they were generally laid in the earth rolled in a blanket.

Brigadier-General Strangways succeeded General Cator, who had been invalided, and Colonel Lake took command of the Artillery of the Light Division. Between the 24th and 28th of August a force of Artillery, consisting of seven Field Batteries and 'C' Troop, were embarked to accompany the expedition to the Crimea.

About the 24th (a Saturday), Lieutenant Earle, with the right division, marched down to Varna and encamped near the beach. On the following Monday the remainder of the Troop marched down, and then the embarkation was at once proceeded with. The transports were lying at a great distance from the beach, and the horse boats, carrying nine or ten horses each, were towed out to them by row-boats. The process of slinging and hoisting from the boats was tedious and difficult, and two or three horses actually jumped into the sea rather than submit; these had to be towed back to the beach, some one or other holding their heads as well as they could from the stern of a boat, and re-embarked when they were in an exhausted state. The transports were not the same that took the Troop from England. The left division under Lieutenant Grylls embarked on board the "Monarchy," on which there was a number of the Rifle Brigade under Elrington. The names of two other 'C' troopships were "Talavera" and "Lord Raglan," and Riflemen were embarked on board these also. An accident occurred at the end of the slinging and hoisting, but fortunately without any loss of life. As the last horse was hoisted into the air, a party of four or five drivers fully booted and spurred, with their busbies and jackets on, who were weary with their exertions, rested against the rope which went round the horse boat; suddenly the staunchions through which the rope passed gave way, and the drivers were thrown heels overhead into the sea, going well under water; although they could not swim, none were lost. The few other men on the boat threw themselves flat on the platform-deck, and reaching down with their sword-scabbards and other things for the drivers to catch hold of, managed in this way to save their comrades, and lifted them on to the horse-boat again. The cholera now broke out on board the "Monarchy" amongst the Riflemen, so she was ordered to put to sea and cruise about, which she did for a fortnight. Unfortunately this did not do much good, as deaths still occurred, but none of 'C' Troop men were attacked. The vessel had been used as a transport for Turks, and the ship's blankets and hammocks were alive with vermin, which of course fastened on to the troops and their clothing, and could not be got rid of for many months. While on board, the non-commissioned officers and gunners received instruction daily from the Lieutenant in the nine-pounder range and equipment generally. The orders were to rendezvous at Baltschik. By the time the "Monarchy" had arrived there, the steam was up throughout the mighty fleet to sail for the invasion of the Crimea. The paddle steamer "Emperor," with the sailing master of the Fleet on board, at once took the "Monarchy" and another transport in tow, and fell into the place assigned for her, and all moved off. The largest steamers had each about two transports in tow, and the "Agamemnon" line of battle ship had at one time as many as five in tow. The sea was beautifully smooth, and the fleet and convoy extended backwards for miles and miles—farther than the eye could reach. When the fleet arrived off Eupatoria, Lord Raglan and some of the staff went on shore for a short time. Although the steamers occasionally slacked speed, and even anchored, there was no collision or confusion, as the sea was so calm.

While at anchor off Eupatoria, the ship with the centre division of the Troop on board, got aground, and before it could be got off all the equipment and a great deal of stores had to be shifted into another vessel, and afterwards put back again; this delayed that division five or six hours, and they landed after the rest of the Troop. The men worked splendidly.

On the 14th September the signal to disembark was given. Some boat-loads of the French got away first from their transports, owing to some bungling of the signals; but when the English Army once got the order, they disembarked with a good will, the sailors helping in every way. The sea was calm for a time, but after a little a moderate surf got up on the beach and became troublesome; so that men and horses were ducked in getting out of the horse-boats. However, before many hours, the whole Troop was disembarked, and guns and carriages mounted. As they were ready they moved off into bivouac with the Light Division, a few miles in advance of the place of disembarkation. It was nearly night when the Troop reached the ground with Sir George Brown. Late in the afternoon a staff officer came and requested Captain Thomas to furnish a mounted escort of twelve (including two non-commissioned officers) for Lord Raglan and his staff. They were to be experienced men, and able to handle their swords well. They accompanied Lord Raglan and some Doctors. About one hour and a half before daylight there was an alarm, and the whole

Army stood to arms. 'C' Troop hooked in ready to move off. The alarm proceeded from a sharp musketry fire at a farm-house in advance, where some riflemen were posted. When it ceased, the troops lay down again.

The infantry lay down to rest on the exact ground on which they stood in the ranks; no tents of any sort were pitched. Sir George Brown and Brigadier-General Buller lay on the ground close by; there was a good downpour of rain in the night. On the 16th or 17th Captain Thomas was taken dangerously ill, and had to be removed on board ship; and Captain John Brandling was disembarked from the siege artillery to take temporary command of the Troop. He was Adjutant of the Horse Artillery at Woolwich in 1853, and the beginning of 1854. Assistant-Surgeon Fasson (now dead) served with the Troop for a time. The exact period is not remembered, but it is possible he may have taken charge here; for at the Battle of the Alma, on the 20th, Dr. Llewellyn, who rode a pony, and wore a red girdle with a large knife in it, had some other charge than 'C' Troop, and seemed to look forward to amputations *ad libitum*. There were some cases of cholera in the Light Division while in this bivouac, and there were also night surprises, caused by firing in front, but all were in such readiness that the Infantry had merely to stand up and number off their files. About forty men were disembarked from the Foot Artillery companies and attached to the Troop, the establishment of which was now considerably augmented. Twenty-four of them were sent from Colonel Romer's company. Except the two additional mounted gunners for each detachment, nearly the whole augmentation lay with the draught horses, and these men were chiefly used as drivers. In one subdivision alone six of them were drivers of the third and fourth teams. Many of these men died, some left for the first bombardment, and others remained with the Troop until the drafts arrived from Woolwich, and it is only right to say they did all that could be reasonably expected of them. A few asked to be transferred permanently to the Troop, which was conceded by the authorities. On the night of the 18th some letters from England were delivered to the Troop; three days' rations had been served out in advance from the ship, and three days' more were served out on this date from the Commissariat. The men were in good spirits, and up till a late hour of the night were cheerfully endeavouring to burn or scorch the mutton which had been issued, by exposing it to burning heaps of coarse grass, no wood being available. About two in the morning of the 19th the Troop was startled by the screams and groans of Gunner Harold, who was taken ill with cholera. He was quite well and cheerful at 10 P.M. As it became daylight the Light Division moved out of bivouac and began the advance. As they marched on some villages and hamlets at a distance in front were set fire to by the Cossacks. Harold had been put into an araba and brought on, but he died soon after the advance began; and a party of mounted gunners fell out with spades to bury him. The body was taken out of the araba and laid on the ground, and they commenced to shovel earth on to his feet and legs first and then on to his body. He had been a very good-looking man, and, to use the words of a young soldier, Gunner Lawrence, who was engaged in the mournful task, they felt an unwillingness to cover his face; however, they were quickly compelled to shovel earth on that also, for the rear-guard of the Army was now within a few yards of them, and there was only time left to mount their horses and gallop on. Probably the araba was required for another man, as there were few of them, or it may have been thought unadvisable to carry a corpse under the circumstances; at any rate, the order from the Quartermaster-General for the immediate interment was imperative.

When the Light Division arrived near the Bulganak, which is a small stream, 'C' Troop proceeded to pass over by the low bridge or culvert which crosses it. There is a small post-house at the bridge; there are no trees, and the country about there is quite open. As the Troop approached the bridge, they met 'I' Troop R.H.A., which had been over and was then re-crossing. 'C' Troop went over, wheeled to the right out of the way, and sent two men from each detachment to fill some water-canteens at the stream, as the thirst was very great. To give an idea of the scarcity of water and the thirst that prevailed, Captain Baddeley while on the march paid a French soldier 1s. 6d. for as much water as filled his regulation water bottle. This he (Baddeley) shared amongst two or three of 'C' Troop, only asking them to leave him a little; but what was the thirst of those riding compared to that of those marching on foot. The Troop then dismounted. 'C' and 'I' Troops were thus nearly covering each other, about 100 yards apart, and the stream midway between. At this time no Cavalry or any body of troops whatever could be seen in front, nor did any one in 'C' Troop know that the Cavalry were ahead, the Light Division having been marching with the Rifles extended in front all the morning. Immediately after this Brigade-Major (now Lieutenant-General Sir John) Adye came galloping in from the front, and called out, "Where is Captain Maude?" and then added in a general way, "You'll lose the charge with the Cavalry." The Brigade-Major did not speak angrily, but only as if a sudden emergency had arisen, and that he sought help wherever he could. He galloped in towards the left of the Troop, and Brandling, who was at the centre, and many yards off, merely heard him calling out while still moving on his horse. 'C' Troop mounted, and moved off at a gallop in line, not waiting for the men with the water canteens, who, however, overtook them before they halted. The ground ascended from the stream, and it was a very heavy pull of about three-quarters of a mile on the gun horses to gain the high ground, particularly after being so long on board ship. When 'C' Troop had reached the high ground, 'I' Troop also had reached it, and Brigadier-General Strangways was there, but the troops were independent as to dressing; there was about twice the usual interval between them, and 'C' Troop was on the right. The ground in front was a sort of wide and shallow valley, about a mile across, the rising ground on the Russian side being slightly higher than that on the English side. A portion of the Light Cavalry, under Lord Cardigan, was drawn up in line near the bottom of the valley, with skirmishers out and traversing. A party of the Russian regular cavalry, rather outnumbering the English, were opposed to them, and in an exactly corresponding position, with their skirmishers out and traversing also. The distance between the opposing skirmishers was not great. The English Cavalry had previously cast off their hay nets, so as to be free for fighting, and these were lying on the ground just in front of where 'C' Troop was now halted. About a mile to the Russian right, and with their right shoulders well forward, but not quite at right angles, was a considerable body of Cossacks in loose order—that is, seven or eight deep, and with about ten yards interval between each man, covering a mile or more of country. It was a very calm afternoon, and the cavalry bugles on both sides could be heard to sound "Commence firing" to their skirmishers, and they accordingly opened fire. While the skirmishers were firing at each other Brigadier-General Strangways, for some reason, ordered Brandling to close the mounted gunners to the centre, and take them forward about one hundred yards, leaving the guns where they were at full intervals. The detachments then had the appearance of a squadron of sixty rank and file, there being ten in each detachment. Whether it was to support our outnumbered Cavalry, or to lead the enemy to believe it was another squadron, is not known; but it could not be to mask the guns, as they were well down hill, and distinctly in view from the enemy's side. While this was going on, something glittering was observed just behind the high ground opposite: it was the sun shining on the fixed bayonets of a close column of about three or four battalions of Infantry. This body came gradually in view, and marched quietly down the slope, with some guns on its right, which were at the walking pace also. "Retire by alternate squadrons" was now sounded for the English Cavalry; the Russian Cavalry also retired, but in doing so bore to their own right at once, and this cleared the front of their guns sufficiently to allow them to open fire on the English Cavalry, which they very quickly did, killing a few horses and wounding some men, the shots coming up through the Horse Artillery. General Strangways now ordered the detachments to join their guns, and the English Cavalry went to their own left, so the front was clear; the Russian guns, however, still fired up at the Horse Artillery. It appears Lord Raglan gave instructions that there was to be no general engagement brought on, but he now sent orders to both troops to come into action, which they did, quickly silencing the Russian guns, and causing both guns and Infantry to retire with loss. Both Troops then limbered up to the front, threw the right shoulder forward, but of course independently, and galloped into action against the Russian regular Cavalry, and also the Cossacks, causing them losses. The Black Battery of the Light Division was now in action as well. The Russian Cavalry quickly retired out of range, and 'C' Troop moved back to ground about three hundred yards in advance of where they first came into action, and fronted the Russian Infantry and guns, both of which had now been reinforced. Sir George Brown had by this time got the Light Division up, extended in line, but just out of view behind the ridge, and he, or Lord Raglan, desired that some men of the 2nd Battalion Rifle Brigade might be taken on to 'C' Troop guns, to act as sharpshooters, in the event of another advance into action. This Battalion had practised with the Minié rifle at Canterbury in 1853. The Light Division regiments had all, or nearly all, been at Chobham Camp in 1853.

The Riflemen were accordingly placed one on each axle-tree box, one on each trail, and three on the limber boxes; the limber gunners themselves stood on the trail handles and held on by the limber boxes; this was done with the concurrence of General Strangways, and Sir George Brown was pleased afterwards to call the Troop his Rifle Troop; however, there was no farther attempt on the part of the Russians to renew the fighting, and this ended the "Affair of Bulganak." The Troop moved back to the stream where they bivouacked for the night with the Light Division. It was generally known throughout the Army, that the Russians were strongly posted some miles in advance, and that a general engagement would be fought next day.

CHAPTER VI.

BATTLE OF ALMA.—FLANK MARCH.—CAPTURE OF BALA-
CLAVA.—PLATEAU OF SEVASTOPOL.

ON the morning of the 20th the Troop got ready quite early, and moved to where the English Infantry were massing ; there they remained dismounted for some hours. At this time Colonel (now General Sir James) Fitzmayer, R.A., who had been riding a long way out reconnoitring, returned, carrying a small Russian Cavalry carbine; he said a group of dead horsemen that were killed by shells the day before were lying at some distance in front, and that he had taken the carbine out of the arms of one of them—this was probably the first trophy. After a long wait, Marshal St. Arnaud, accompanied by Lord Raglan, came from the left, and close across the front of the English troops, who loudly cheered, which the Marshal acknowledged by taking off his cocked hat, and waving it gracefully towards the men at every cheer ; he was in the dress of a French Marshal, with the white feather over the top of the hat; he appeared to be the only French officer who wore the cocked hat that day. He was well set up, seemed in good health, and not at all the sort of man likely to die in the course of nine days, as he did. A non-commissioned officer of cavalry followed him with the tricolor, and there was a body-guard of Arab horsemen (spahis) looking very picturesque in their red and white cloaks, long guns and high saddles. The Marshal did not replace his hat till he had passed the English troops. Some time after this the whole French Army began to move off, with their colours uncased, their gilt eagles glittering on the tops of their standards. Their troops carried all they wanted; every fourth or fifth man carried a sort of large flattened water can on his knapsack, another a cooking utensil, and so on; they carried the complete *tente d'abri* also on their knapsacks. One of these little tents gave cover to three soldiers when lying close together on the ground. The English troops were without tents. The Artillery carried theirs on the waggons—in 'C' Troop about three per Division were pitched, but this depended on the situation they were in—whether advanced or otherwise.

Soon after this the English Army got into the order of march. The Light Division was in front of the left column, and in the interval between it and the Infantry Division on its right was 'C' Troop in close column of half troops right in front, and with reduced intervals to suit the space they had to move in: the right half troop marched in line with the leading companies of the Infantry. Some Field Batteries R.A. were in rear of 'C' Troop; the waggons in rear of these again. Captain Strange, R.A., had charge of 'C' Troop waggons. The other Infantry Divisions were in rear of the Light Division, and the Division which was on the right of 'C' Troop. 'I' Troop R.H.A., and the Light Cavalry (except the 4th Light Dragoons), were on the left of the English Army; the 2nd Battalion Rifle Brigade (Colonel Lawrence with the right wing, and Major Norcott with the left) were about half a mile in front, and extended in skirmishing order; the 4th Light Dragoons formed the rear-guard. The 23rd Royal Welsh was on the left of 'C' Troop, their company officers being next the Troop. The whole of the Infantry were in column more or less closed up, and all marched regularly and kept silence. In front of the Light Division one set of fifes and drums played occasionally, and one small band played occasionally in front of the Division on the right. This was the only music. All other bandsmen carried stretchers behind their regiments, having left their instruments on board ship. Brandling's dress, which he wore throughout (indeed, he had no other), made him very remarkable; the large soft, peaked forage cap of that day, the undress double-breasted frock-coat of the Foot Artillery (without the shoulder scales), brown fur gauntlets, pantaloons and hessians, a sword, with revolver on his waistbelt, completed his get-up; he was a handsome man, had a powerful word of command, and, as no one else wore a forage cap on parade at that time, his appearance was soon well known throughout the Army. He rode a small beautiful entire charger, which remained with the Troop during the entire war. Colonel Lake wore the uniform of a Colonel on the Staff, and he and his Adjutant, Captain Badderly, rode close to the Troop. General Strangways always wore the bearskin busby and uniform of the Horse Artillery. Sir George Brown rode in front of his fifes and drums, and Lord Raglan and his Staff generally rode at some distance in front of 'C' Troop. Amongst the Staff was an old Horse Artillery officer, General Brereton (in plain clothes and tall hat), who went out for amusement we may suppose; he was also on board the "Britannia" Flag-ship at the bombardment of Sevastopol, 17th October, 1854.

Having proceeded about two miles, the Army passed some groups of dead Russian Cavalry and Infantry soldiers that were killed the day before. The Infantry suffered much from thirst, and many were in a weak condition from dysentery and diarrhœa. The officers of the 23rd were anxiously exhorting any lagging men to try and keep in their places, as if they fell out, there would be no succour whatever for them, when once the rear-guard had passed. The two nearest subdivisions of the Troop did all they could to carry blankets and rifles for the weakly men. The English Infantry had left their knapsacks and great-coats on board ship. After ascending a rising ground a good distance beyond the situation where the engagement of the previous afternoon had taken place, the outlines of the Alma heights could be seen, as also some of the allied war steamers lying off the coast. A little more marching, and smoke was observed ascending from the nearest side of the heights, caused by thatch and other things which had been set on fire in a village. A little further marching, and long lines of cavalry were dimly visible on the loftiest of the heights farthest from the sea. Soon after the bright fixed bayonets of the masses of Infantry were discernible. As the Army continued its march, these things became more distinct; and, after half an hour's more marching, newly-thrown-up seams of earth could be seen. Lord Raglan now began to take frequent observations with his field-glasses; as he had but one arm, he was necessitated to pull up his horse for this purpose, and his bugler used to sound "Halt" for the Army, and after a time "Advance," and so on. During one of these halts, the colours of the English Army were uncased, and the men ordered to load: there was then a mighty ringing of ramrods. The French had been considerably in advance, on the right front, but the English Army was now drawing nearer to them; one division of the French bore still farther away to the right front nearer the sea. The war steamers were now nearer the land, and from one of them a shell was fired, which burst over the height near the sea; then another shell was fired; and then a gun was fired from the height, apparently at the steamers: this continued at regular intervals. The ground, which had been nearly level for some miles, now became a gentle descent, and those in front could see the boundary of the village of Bourliouk about three-quarters of a mile ahead, where the plain terminated. A few more yards of marching, and the men of the Rifle Brigade could be seen unmistakably springing to the alert, and peering at the village boundary; for from behind that boundary they were being shot at by Russian riflemen, and the spent bullets were finding their way right up to the army, noiselessly, and only to be observed by their throwing up a pinch of dust here and there. Lord Raglan's bugler now sounded "Halt" for the second last time, and Sir George Brown said, "What the devil are they halting for now?" Lord Raglan appeared to have finally made up his mind as to the way in which he would attack, for his bugler quickly sounded the "Advance!" Those in front now observed some sticks, three or four feet long, with bits of dark rag fastened to them like little flags. They had been put up here and there by the Russians to mark out the range. The first gun was now fired at the British Army; then the second, the shot coming right over the Troop, and Baddeley remarked that "their guns were long-ranged." The "Halt!" was again sounded, and then the whole Russian cannonade began. Some Infantry divisions in rear lay down by sound of bugle. 'C' Troop was ordered into action, and Sir George Brown was ordered to attack the position in his front. The Troop at once moved out rapidly to the front, and then to the left, to get out of the way of the Light Division. When well to the left, they broke into column of subdivisions left in front, by the right half Troop checking pace, and then covering and following (see Alma map). The object of the movement was doubtless to help to extend the line of battle of the Light Division in the quickest way, and afterwards to get as much of a cross fire as possible on the Russians. With this last object in view the head of the Troop then threw forward the left shoulder a little, and, when covered in the new direction, " Subdivisions, right wheel," and " Gallop ! " were sounded. The Troop then made for the village boundary, within about fifty yards of which they came into action. The directions were to fire up at the infantry masses near the great central earthwork. These masses appeared to be on the proper left of the work, and Brandling called out, " Try 900 yards range."

This battle was unlike the others which followed, inasmuch as it was begun as if at a review, there being perfect silence until the final instructions to attack were issued. As 'C' Troop hurried out of the interval in which they had been marching, the necessary orders were being given as to markers, deployments, etc., in the Light Division regiments. The village of Bourliouk lay rather in front of the English Army, but it was slightly to the right front of the Light Division before they began their deployments; and the boundary wall near which ' C ' Troop was now in action was merely the continuation of a well-defined boundary coming up from the village.

The line of ' C ' Troop guns was rather oblique (No. 6 being nearest) to the boundary, which just there consisted of a loose stone wall. The Rifles had not quite got to the wall ; in fact, No. 6 gun was in amongst them, but Major Norcott, in charge of their left wing, and then close by, called out to them to " Rush at it and get over," which they did by helping each other up. As the Troop stood in action the inclosures on its left were fairly studded with trees, but the actual front was more clear: that is, the flight of the shot would be only two or three yards above the top of the wall, and there did not seem to be any other obstacle to aim-taking than the smoke from the burning village. The first gun at the Alma on our side was soon fired by 'C' Troop. They afterwards fired a great many rounds from this position, and, though they were fired at in return, their quick and well-executed movements seemed to perplex the Russian gunners. The Troop had by this partly flank and partly oblique manœuvre into action managed to approach to nearly the same ground they would have occupied had they deployed and galloped straight down from the Light Division, but in this case they would have prematurely commenced (because the Light Division had not begun their deployments) a combat with about ten times their own number of Russian guns. The soundness of the course adopted was obvious: time was spent by the Russians trying to traverse their guns and follow the course of the Troop, which in reality stole into action at a rapid pace, and as a result no casualty occurred while so doing; had they gone down over the marked-out ground, they could hardly have escaped so easily.

This central position, however, could not be maintained, for it was necessary to move from the direct front of the Light Division, which was now deployed and moving down; so the Troop limbered up and retired in line, throwing their then left shoulder forward. Having gone some distance towards the rear, they wheeled subdivisions about, and, throwing the right shoulder forward, moved again into action, on ground rather to the left rear of their first position, but still close to the boundary. The path of the Troop had thus far been a kind of a zig-zag; the bend of the village boundary towards the

English left helps to explain this: that is, this slight shift of ground to the left necessitated, as it were, a push back of the Troop uphill, and as a consequence greatly increased the range.

A number of rounds were also fired from the second position. As the Light Division had not quite got down, and the Troop having now been some time under observation, it appeared as if half the enemy's guns were turned on them, but fortunately it was all graze and bound owing to the elevated position of the Russian Artillery; the burning village seemed also to be favourable, as the smoke went rather towards the enemy. The vigorous course of action pursued caused a great deal of the fire to be taken off the Light Division, their losses so far being almost nil; and, though the Troop could not see much of the results of their fire, their persistency in maintaining the position so long, tended to nullify for the time the effects of the Russian cannonade. When coming into action wheel-driver Perkins, of No. 5 gun, was hit by a shot which had grazed in front. His head was smashed to pieces, and scattered over his horses. It is now forgotten whether it was at the first or second position in action that he was killed. It is believed that it occurred at the unlimbering, when the side of the team was rather towards the enemy, and that the shot, which was flying upwards, caught him below the ear. Those at the next gun (No. 6) knew nothing of it, owing to the din of battle. It is only remembered that after the front limbering up and moving subdivisions right about, his body was then lying on the ground; he was probably one of the first killed in the battle. About the same time Colonel Lake's horse was shot, and he mounted his Adjutant's. Some part of Lieutenant Earle's accoutrements (it is believed the clasp or buckle of his sword-belt) was hit by a rifle bullet. The gun-carriages were well marked by bullets, and there was plenty of earth ploughed up and thrown about by the enemy's shot and shell.

When the leading regiments had got to the boundary, and some of them had actually got over it, the Troop limbered up and retired. It was necessary to cease firing so as to let the nearest regiments scale the boundary wall without incurring any risk from 'C' Troop guns, which had now been continuously in action from the commencement of the battle, except the two or three moments spent in shifting ground. It should be here stated that the Russian Rifle Skirmishers, who were at first behind the boundary wall, had by this time been pushed well back towards their own people by our 2nd Battalion Rifle Brigade; and as the gardens and inclosures were tolerably well filled with trees, which afforded some cover, the losses to our Infantry, in passing from the boundary onwards towards the bank of the river on their own side, were not very great. Of course, there were many open spaces which the troops had to pass over, and on these the enemy could direct their guns with exactitude. The ground would also be under fire of any troops in the vicinity of the earthworks who might be armed with the rifle; but the range at the beginning was too great for accurate firing from the old Russian smooth-bore musket. On this second retirement the Troop only went a very short distance, and, without any halting, wheeled about and advanced again towards the boundary. They did not, however, come into action. The leading regiments were now well on through the inclosures, some of them being partially hidden by the foliage; and, as the Troop could not for the present offer much further succour to the Infantry, and as a great deal of ammunition had been expended, it was deemed advisable to seize this opportunity for replenishing the limbers. In retiring for this purpose the Troop led towards the right of the Cavalry, where they dismounted close by the 17th Lancers. The first line of waggons was then brought down, and the empty boxes and cartouches were quickly filled, but even here the enemy's rifle bullets were flying about pretty freely. During the retirement a deployed regiment of the Highland Brigade passed by the then right of 'C' Troop, *i.e.* on the right of No. 6 Gun. They were marching for the boundary at a point farther up than where the Light Division were attacking. One of their men was hit just here; he was probably their first casualty. Brandling, who had galloped off to reconnoitre the village boundary, found far up to the left the entrance to a green lane, leading down to the river. He returned and mounted the Troop, which then trotted in column of subdivisions, left in front, down to the lane. It was a simple cart-track, with a low stone wall on each side, and rude gateways here and there admitting to the inclosures. The trees met overhead, and the Troop was not seen by the enemy until it emerged close to the river, where all was open; and then a light Field Battery on the very edge of the loftiest height to the left front directed their fire upon the Troop, which, however, forded the river quickly. The bank on the Russian side at that part came close down to the river, and was very steep—far too much so for any one on horseback to be able to ride straight up it. The action of the water when the river was high had caused a sort of scooping out of the sandbank for about twenty-five yards, at a point just to the right, and into this Brandling drew the Troop, *i.e.* each lead driver in succession drove close in against the bank at the right incline, and halted, the gunners placing themselves as best they could in the narrow intervals. The limber gunners alone dismounted, and then there was fair cover for all except the wheel drivers; but Brandling and Colonel Lake remained out in the open under fire of the aforesaid Battery the whole time the Troop was in this position. This Russian Battery was on the extreme right of their position, and they were the last of their guns to cease firing that day. They were some hundreds of feet above the level of the river, and they had either previously fired away their shell, or did not think proper to expend any more, for it was all solid shot they used against the Troop. It buried itself, or else only bounded a few yards in the soft sand.

It is thought the Troop may fairly claim to have been the first Artillery over the river, though not first in action over the river. Nothing passed, or could have passed further up. During this time the musketry fight was raging to the right front, in what was afterwards called the " Half-moon Battery or Central Earthwork." In a short time a wounded infantry soldier came down the hill for water, and he called out, "Lads, we're beating them; they're giving way in the Battery above." This was the first intimation to the Troop that the English were gaining ground at the Battery. Brandling had previously gone up by the bed of the river to reconnoitre, and he now returned and ordered the nearest subdivision to follow him, and the others to come on as best they could. He kept to the bed of the river for some way; then the drivers of the leading gun made a race at the hill obliquely, and, after very hard tugging, got up. The others followed in like manner. At last the whole Troop reached the top of a ridge, which overlooked a very wide and deep ravine. Along this ravine many close columns of Russian Infantry were retreating, that is, they were marching on the opposite slope, partly across the front of the Troop, from right to left, and distant about 700 yards, each man being above his left-hand comrade, and all could be distinctly seen (by the brass spread eagles on their patent-leather helmets) looking up to their left as the Troop unlimbered and fired into them. It was an exciting and impressive scene: the men looking alternately one instant at what they were stepping over on the ground, and the next up at the English, but still keeping their dressing. 'I' Troop and a Field Battery were also in action near this spot. The Guards, Highlanders, and other infantry at some distance to the right, held their head-dresses aloft on the tops of their fixed bayonets, and cheered and shouted with all their might.

It is due to these brave Russian soldiers to say that there was no running on their part, or pace other than the quick step, while they were being ploughed into by eighteen guns and numbers of riflemen as well. Having once begun the retreat these ravines were decidedly against the Russians, as they isolated the different brigades or regiments, and prevented them keeping up rapid lateral communication.

When the Russian columns had gone out of range, 'C' Troop hurried down by way of the great central earthwork, in passing which they saw the havoc that had been made in the regiment (the 23rd) they had been marching alongside a short time before. Colonel Chester, Captains Wynn, Evans, and many other officers, with the Sergeant-Major and great numbers of the men, lay dead, closely packed in front of the work which the regiment had stormed. They had nearly all been shot in the head, and were lying, some with their feet close to the ditch, and their heads down hill, and so on all the way down the slope. Captain Evans was well known. He had charge of the companies of the 23rd, which were encamped by themselves, and formed the "enemy" at Chobham Camp in 1853, in which he was assisted by Lieutenant Dyneley, 23rd Regiment, son of General Dyneley, R.A., formerly captain of 'C' Troop. Lieutenant Dyneley was mortally wounded at the assault on the Redan. The Troop went quite close to the wooden bridge before they got on to the main road leading from the river to Sevastopol. A company of sappers and miners were in the water, with their boots off, and trousers turned up as far as they could push them, either making or repairing a ford, for the Russians had almost cut the sloping props of the bridge through. Having gained the road, the Troop began to hurry up after the retreating enemy. The place was very much blocked up with ammunition waggons, etc., and just about here some foot artillerymen were carrying an elderly wounded Russian officer, it is believed a General. They had an arm under each thigh, and he held on by their necks, and seemed to call out as if in pain. An officer of Royal Artillery, however, put a stop to that mode of carrying, and the old gentleman was placed on the rear box of an ammunition waggon, for which he seemed very grateful. Just before the Troop reached the plateau above, Lord Cardigan dashed by with the Light Cavalry, and formed line to the front on the level ground; 'C' and 'I' Troops formed line behind them at "full intervals." The Russian cavalry had however been drawn across the position in long lines to cover the retreat of their army, and orders were given that there was to be no further attack made by the English. A party of Hussars were previously started in pursuit to the left, and they brought in some prisoners who had been on the extreme Russian right, and were unable to get away; amongst them a very young officer or cadet, who was little more than a boy. The Black Battery also was hotly engaged before the heights were stormed, but their position in action was considerably to the right

The Night after the Alma.   105

of 'C' Troop. Colonel Lake supervised the doings of both Troop and Battery throughout the entire battle, dividing his time equally between them.

While ascending the heights, at a point where the ground was dangerously steep for Artillery, a portion of the Infantry, it is believed the 19th Regiment, assisted in pushing up some of 'C' Troop guns; the details of this circumstance, however, are not now remembered with exactness.

The Russian cavalry was hardly out of gun range, as their drawn sabres could be distinctly seen; they were very numerous, and had not retired when darkness was setting in. After dark the Troop moved into bivouac with the Light Division, and went down, a subdivision at a time, to water; it was a long distance, and the night was far advanced when all were watered. There was great confusion near the river, and the moanings of the wounded and dying were painful to hear. Of the wounded, some were trying to drag themselves along the ground, and enquiring where their regiments and doctors were, others calling out in the dark to tell so and so, of such a company and regiment, to come to so and so; but except small water parties, no one was allowed to come down from the plateau that night. Many of the doctors were amputating and dressing by the light of bits of naked candle, and even pieces of burning port-fire.

For the next two days the Army was occupied in burying the dead and getting the wounded to the shipping. It was a great distance from the English position to the sea.

The Russian riflemen used the Liége rifle sighted up to 900 or 1,000 yards, and carrying a heavy, fine-pointed bullet. It was shorter than their musket, the barrel was browned, and the stock of the ordinary brown wood; whereas their common musket stocks were varnished black, and the barrels polished. Their gun carriages, ammunition waggons, and carriages of every sort were painted green, the guns themselves were polished, the shot found in piles on the ground inside the earthworks at the Alma was painted or varnished, but had no wooden bottoms. The Russians were strong-looking, well-developed men, they were cleanly shaved in line with the bottom of the ear, and were dressed in a sort of drab or light brown long coat, the body of the coat being let in in pleats under a shoulder piece, and a band round the waist; the trousers were of the same colour, and let into the boots, which were a kind of coarse and very roomy Wellington boot. They wore the helmet at Alma, but afterwards generally the flat cloth forage cap without a peak. The officers wore the same as the men, and could only be known by some small marks on the shoulder straps or collars, and by a peak to the forage cap, when that was worn. The knapsacks were of brown cowhide, and the men's kits were all well washed and white, but nevertheless had vermin amongst them. Each man had a small portion of oil in a bottle, which formed part of his turnscrew, etc., for the purpose of cleaning his firearms, and a large, thick, hard cake of black bread, strapped to the knapsack through a hole in the middle. They all appeared to be well cared and provided for, and the most was made of everything they had; even the muskets, which were of very old date (1832), and had been altered from flint locks to percussion, were supplied with a leather snap-cap, to keep out the wet and dirt, etc. A snap-cap was a thing unknown to the British Army at that time. The few artillery horses which were captured were black, in thoroughly good condition, and well groomed; the harness was of black coarse leather, well preserved and pliable, the girths being slit in rows lengthwise to prevent galling. We may here state that the Russian horses were considered next in quality for military service to the English, that is, they were superior to the French, Sardinian, or Turkish animals.

There can be no question as to who carried the central redoubt, for the dead bodies in and about the earthworks were, with few exceptions, those of men of the Light Division. The position of the 23rd was a very trying one, for they had to attack the work fair in front, and the ascent to it was perfectly open. A corporal of the 7th Fusiliers had the credit of bayoneting a Russian driver who was taking away one of the captured guns, and it was said he was made sergeant by Lord Raglan's orders; at any rate that was the talk over the watch fires that night.

Very few Russians were found dead on the river side of the Earthwork, but their dead and wounded were in great numbers, beginning inside the work, and so on through the ravines and hollows, and the ground was covered with knapsacks and muskets.

The English dead for the most part had quiet countenances, and generally lay at full length, often with colour in their faces. The Russians had stiffened in every variety of posture; some sitting, others half sitting, with the hands held out as if warding off something, or as if they had dropped their musket from the position of the "Present." Their faces had a glazy appearance, and some were much distorted. Near the bivouac of the Light Division lay a great many who, while retreating, had been killed by the French Artillery, after they had gained the heights on our right. An ammunition-waggon had been blown up, and there was one remarkable group of fourteen or fifteen men who had been killed by the one cannon shot going right through their bodies near the waist, as if a rank of men had just turned, and, when in perfect covering, had been caught in the back in that position by the shot, for they all lay partly one over the other, with faces downwards.

It is not correct to say that the Artillery battle first began against the French troops. There was a lull after the fire from the steamers. The first gun fired by the Russians after this was from their own left of the great recess in the hills, nearly opposite the English right, and the next fired appeared to be the companion gun of the first. The cannonade then broke out from all the commanding positions, and seemed to run round in a sort of semicircle of fire in front of the English. It is not thought the Russian cavalry could have acted with a certainty of success against the left of the Light Division during the storming of the great Redoubt. The direct descent from the heights on which they were formed up, to the hill on which the Redoubt stood, seemed to be far too steep to admit of their getting down with any degree of order, or at any other than the slowest pace.

The report current in bivouac that night and the following days was that the Russians had forty battalions (or bodies of troops, each about the size of one of our regiments) and 100 guns. This rough computation was arrived at by the interpreters questioning the prisoners, as well as by the observations of our people themselves. Each Troop of Horse Artillery, Battery, and regiment had an interpreter told off to it at that time, but some of these had deserted before the expedition sailed. As to the enemy's Cavalry, there certainly did not appear to be fully three thousand of them in view of the Allies at any time that day. They were so close to the edge of the heights on the Russian right that the light could be seen coming through between the horses' legs.

There is no doubt that certain regiments of the Light Division, and the 95th Regiment, which got mixed up with them, were fearfully outnumbered when they assaulted the great Redoubt, and the ground right and left of it. So much of them as were bivouacked within hearing distance of 'C' Troop that night, as they sat on the ground in groups, complained bitterly that when they had carried the Redoubt they were not vigorously supported at the right moment.

In addition to the English losses given in the official returns, the Quarterly Army List of that time shows that there were other officers mortally wounded who died on the second and succeeding days after the battle; and therefore great numbers in proportion of the non-commissioned officers and men must also have been mortally wounded. The returns were made up as soon as possible, but afterwards the Head Quarter Staff would be too busy to notice deaths from wounds, and the men were only shown in due course of time as "dead" in the Regimental Returns, as the news happened to reach their respective regiments from the shipping or otherwise.

As to our Infantry, the sight they presented this day could never be forgotten by those who were privileged to witness it. They moved out of bivouac soon after it was light; there was little time for cooking, and precious little food to cook, and no wood even for that. They then hung about for many hours round their piled arms, becoming both thirsty and hungry; but there was no grumbling, and if any were seen going to a doctor, there was unmistakeable illness and exhaustion in their faces. When they afterwards "stood to arms," they appeared quite light-hearted. The old type of Infantry sergeant was there sharp to his work; and when all moved off, as they well knew, to confront the enemy, the ground was clear, and no stray articles of equipment left on it to denote slovenliness or slackness of discipline. The Divisional-General even was without a tent; the

Hospital, Commissariat, comforts, and followers were almost a myth; and but very little of that sort of thing was to be seen; not that these departments broke down, as some seem to think. It was simply that, through the penuriousness of the powers at home, they had not organized them up to anything like the required standard.

A man riding on the left of 'C' Troop, and looking down the companies of the Light Division, would see that the young soldiers were in the minority as to numbers, but there they were the long service men and ten years men together, trustworthy and uncomplaining, with plenty of stamina in them, notwithstanding all the sickness they had gone through, and cholera and other evils still amongst them. One cannot help remembering the poor quality of their clothing, so inferior to that now supplied, the cloth little better than a coarse flannel, the coatee hardly meeting the waistband of the trousers, so as to hide the under garments, the high and tight collar, made to cover the high stock, the tight sleeves, the heavy chaco and heavy belts, no leggings, and a rifle in their hands they knew little, if anything, about, because it had not long been issued to them. After ascending to the level ground beyond the Bulganak, they saw the villages far ahead were being set on fire, and when objects got clearer, beyond the burning villages through which they saw they would have to fight, were the solid shining columns of the enemy as they stood up fresh from their camps, the darker-coloured patches of ground suggestive of earth batteries, and the mighty mass of cavalry with gleaming sabres farther inland, all conveying forcibly to the mind that a stern struggle was at hand. Subsequently, when under fire, they made their deployments and advanced as if at a review — no halting or wavering, but onward, onward, persistently forcing the Russians back uphill. The rest is matter of history, but a real lover of the profession would wish the country might always have line infantry of a like quality available to march against a foe.

Amongst the theories that are now started as to the right sort of man for a soldier, it seems to be forgotton, what is nevertheless the fact, that many of these good old veterans, having gone through the battles and the siege, were amongst the first to volunteer for the leading storming party against the Redan, though in so volunteering they could have expected nothing further than the credit that their company officers and comrades would accord them. Many of them were slain in the embrasures and ditches of that work. Poor fellows, they little thought it would be said of them for their long service, by some who had not been in the Crimean battles, "that they had totally disappeared in a few months under the walls of Sevastopol." We may ask how could men have possibly done better under the circumstances? They freely gave health and life, and the question to be considered is, could or would younger men have stood up so long?

On the 23rd the Army resumed its advance, and bivouacked on the Katchka. During this day's march numerous groups of Russian dead were passed. They had evidently tried to keep up in the retreat while strength lasted, but, their wounds overpowering them, they fell out and drew together as best they could. They lay generally in small circles, and a burnt mark in the grass showed where a little fire had been kindled in the midst of the group. Some had their clothing undone, exposing bad body wounds. It gave the impression that the stronger ones had lit the fires, and then, when able, had dragged themselves on after their Army, or to the next group, and so on, for no Russian wounded were overtaken. There was no chance of being able to bury or cover the corpses in any way, and our troops marched past them in silence. On the Alma side of the Katchka there were marks where horses had recently stood at picquet-lines, and on the descent to the river there were signs of confusion and hasty retreat; cooking vessels, packing cases, and quantities of cartridges in boxes had been tumbled into the ditch right and left of the road.

The Scots Greys were disembarked at this place.

On the 24th the Belbec was reached, and during that afternoon a fierce cannonade was heard in the direction of the Sea Forts of Sevastopol. It arose in consequence of some of the allied war vessels having gone rather close in to reconnoitre. The village at the Belbec was very picturesque, being situated in a charming glen. There was the usual red-and-white sentry-box on the footway at the bridge; the ground on the Sevastopol side of the river was covered with low copse, and there was a long ascent before the level road was arrived at. The bivouac of 'C' Troop was in a very advanced position, being at the extreme left front of the Army. It was placed there by Lord Raglan in person. After it was so placed, General Airey, the Quartermaster-General, who had also been present, galloped off to the left by a narrow cart-track to reconnoitre, accompanied by a mounted Tartar guide only, in white cotton clothing and black sheepskin cap. This track would, no doubt, lead to McKenzie's Farm.

On the morning of the 25th the flank march to McKenzie's Farm began, and the route all the way was through forest ground, with a thick growth of underwood. Into this 'C' Troop entered by half-troops, and some sappers and miners were ordered to accompany, so as to assist in cutting down branches and removing impediments. The Infantry, which entered at the same time as 'C' Troop, were at some distance to the right. It

Arrival at McKenzie's Farm.

was very hard work indeed to get along, as the underwood was dense and higher than the horses' girths. There was no road or opening of any sort for miles; the camp-kettles, gun buckets, etc., were torn off by the bushes, and had to be carried by the men, and the sappers themselves had to be taken on the guns, or they must have been left behind. At one time the Troop came on a broad dusty road, and another at right angles to it. Here they saw Lord Raglan with some of his staff examining hoof-marks in the white dust. The question was, were they made by Russian or English horses? The Troop Farrier was sent for, to give his opinion, and he had no difficulty in saying they were Russian. The Troop again plunged into the copse, and, after a wearisome struggle, they came upon several small open spaces. In some of these there was a quantity of dry salt fish, about as large as mackerel, strewn over the ground. It seemed as if some commissariat conveyance had been upset or pillaged. After a little more marching, the roof of McKenzie's Farm could be seen over the stunted trees and high bushes, and some commotion and words of command were heard in front; so the Troop hurried on to the open ground at the Farm. The centres of threes of the Scots Greys were holding the horses of the other men who had just been dismounted, and sent into the wood beyond the open space to skirmish. 'I' Troop, R.H.A., had been sent down the road to the left, where they got some guns into action, and stopped the further retreat of the Russian baggage party. There was a short pursuit by some of the Light Cavalry, who got "loot" from the baggage conveyances. Amongst the things secured were some costly Hussar uniforms. A large quantity of captured ammunition was blown up by the sappers and miners. The first part of this day's march did much injury to the horses' legs, particularly those in the guns, tearing and scarring them in all directions.

The Infantry of the Light Division soon arrived on the ground, and, after a short halt, they and 'C' Troop began to descend the road which is cut in the side of the cliff (see Balaclava map), leading to the plain below, and on to the Tractir Bridge; the ammunition waggons and carriages had joined the Troop on the open ground at McKenzie's Farm. There were signs of surprise and confusion at the beginning of the descent, arabas and packages had been tumbled over the cliff by the Russian drivers previous to taking flight. When the Light Cavalry reached the plain below, a portion of them started away to the left, to reconnoitre the country beyond Tchorgaun. On this day there was a rather remarkable sight in the 13th Light Dragoons, namely, an officer in wide-awake and *bona fide* mufti, except sword, leading one of their Troops; he was a volunteer from another regiment. That night the Troop and Light Division bivouacked on the hills near the bridge. In some gardens close by there was an abundance of vegetables, which afforded a great treat to all. Sir George Brown was asked to use one of the Troop tents at this bivouac; the old General was still without his own. A driver (one of Colonel Romer's men) was attacked with cholera while on his horses, descending from McKenzie's heights; he died during the night, and was buried in the early morning on the slope of the hills facing the bridge.

On the morning of the 26th the Light Division marched on to Balaclava, 'C' Troop accompanying. When the Infantry got near Kadikoi and the inclosures to their left of it, they spread out in skirmishing order. The inhabitants of the village, however, took to flight on the approach of the troops, making for the hills in the direction of Sevastopol. The Infantry now began ascending the heights right and left of the gorge leading to Balaclava; those on the left, as soon as they gained the slopes of the conical hill, opened musketry fire in the direction of the hills farther on, and which are on the left of the harbour. It was said the Russian troops in the fort had come out to offer opposition, but 'C' Troop could see nothing of that, as the conical hill, and the hills on its left, which were afterwards called the Marine heights, effectually shut out the view on that side. Immediately after the Infantry commenced firing, the Troop proceeded at a moderate gallop down a narrow cart track through some paddocks and inclosures. This track led close by the foot of the conical hill, and close by the foot of the hills which are on the left of the harbour, and so on into the little seaport town of Balaclava. There was quite a grove of trees at the head of the harbour, and outside of this 'C' Troop formed up. Neither water nor town could be seen from there, the Infantry had ceased firing, there was a perfect calm, and the place looked like a beautiful glen; any loud talking or words of command echoed all around. During some part of the advance this day, a number of Riflemen, under Major Norcott, were carried on 'C' Troop guns.

Lord Raglan now came up with his staff and interpreter, also a villager they had taken prisoner. The 77th Regiment had ascended the heights on the left, and other Infantry those on the right. Nos. 1 and 2 guns were taken forward to the head of the harbour, but not unlimbered. Lord Raglan could see the fort, which was situated on a high rock at the mouth of the harbour. When the villager was questioned by the interpreter, he declared there were no guns there; but instantly a shot was fired from it at the staff, which went close over them, cutting away branches of trees, and disturbing some wild fowl; immediately afterwards a shell was fired, which burst amongst the staff, and a splinter tore the back of one of the officers' coats from the waist right up to the collar. He was dismounted, and, fortunately for him, he turned his back and ducked his head to avoid the shell; after the explosion he shook his fist at the villager, who did not seem to mind it very much. Lord Raglan now ordered the two guns to come into action against the fort; then the howitzer (No. 3) was brought forward, but owing to the height of the fort, they were found unequal to the range. The left half Troop was then taken to the left, up the heights, which are very steep, and it is a great distance by a winding road to the top. The four sets of breast web harness, which at that time were carried by a detachment, were hooked on in front of the gun horses, and eventually the three guns were got up. They were unlimbered and run forward by hand to the edge of the precipice overhanging the Black Sea, where there was just room for them at close intervals (see map of Balaclava Plain and Plateau). The height was very great, and from there the fort could be seen right into, the distance being 650 or 700 yards; the guns, and the men running about, were quite visible. The "Agamemnon" and a small steamer were outside, and had been firing shell at the fort, while the left half Troop was getting up the heights. Colonel Egerton, 77th Regiment, was close to the guns with some of his men, who had also been firing into the fort for some time, but the commandant still held out; however, after five or six rounds from each gun of the left half Troop, a little white flag was displayed over the battlements, and "Cease firing!" was sounded. Brigade Major Adye, R.A., and Captain Gordon, Royal Engineers, accompanied these three guns up the heights.

There were some very fine grapes in a vineyard half way up the heights, which were most refreshing to all. When the left half Troop came down, the whole Light Division were marched back to the plain near the village of Kadikoi, where they remained until the 29th or 30th. Some things were picked up in the village, left by the people who had fled, amongst them a very fine fur cloak, which the Troop asked Colonel Lake to accept. He said he would be glad to sleep in it at night, and kept it accordingly; but there were inquiries for it, and it was given up. This is no doubt the cloak which an old Greek insisted on going to Lord Raglan about: it is said his lordship gave him his own cloak until this one was found. The men got some cabbages and onions from the gardens here; they were much appreciated, but there was only sufficient for one day's consumption.

On the 29th or 30th September, the Troop marched up from the plain of Balaclava on to the plateau before Sevastopol, some Infantry accompanying. They bore rather to their left, and halted on ground afterwards occupied by the French Siege Artillery. From this they got their first glimpse of Sevastopol, and beautiful it looked in all its strength, with its white fortifications, enormous buildings, and numerous green-coloured domes, etc. There was a clear view from this to the sea near the mouth of the harbour, and the embrasures of numerous recently erected earthworks could be seen. All along the line of defence works were in rapid progress, for the shovelsful of earth were visible as they were tossed up by the working parties. A mounted Russian officer came out from Sevastopol, halting at some distance on a rising ground, and taking a quiet survey of all that was going on. After he withdrew, a few shots were fired from the town, but they did no harm. The Troop bivouacked near that ground that night, and on Sunday, 1st October, they were ordered away to the right, to what was afterwards known as the Right Attack. On the way they passed close to the house afterwards occupied by Lord Raglan, in the inclosure at the back of which 'I' Troop, R.H.A., was holding Divine Service Parade. The camping-ground of 'C' Troop at the Right Attack was near the Light Division, but in front of it, and the nearest to Sevastopol of all the camps. The exact spot of ground was on the right of an intermediate ravine, between the Careenage Ravine and the Left Attack. Just to the left of where No. 6 Gun stood, there were four or five moderately large trees, which were at once cut down for firewood, and there was a very small spring of water which came out of the bank underneath the trees. Then in front of the guns there was a slope upwards for about 350 yards to a heap of ruins, and in these ruins there was a strong picquet of Infantry. The troops used to call it "The Picquet-house Hill." Behind here, in the early days of October, the Troop frequently remained for hours, all hooked in and "standing-to-horse." This picquet had orders not to allow any one to show themselves from our side; but if, by chance, a peep was got over the heaps of stones, some of the Russian war-vessels could be seen—notably the three-decker line-of-battle ship, "Twelve Apostles"—riding at anchor in the roadstead or great harbour, with every yard set, every rope in order, and standards flying.

The sailors' encampment was on the right rear of the Troop. The most stringent orders were given out that the men were not to take off any part of their clothing, or undress themselves in any way. The cloaks and valises were taken off, so as to be out of the way of those sent out as working parties, and that the men might put the cloaks over them when lying on the ground at night. Slow matches were kept burning, the horses were all kept harnessed and saddled, merely the cruppers undone to prevent galling. They were rubbed down and groomed while in this way. Only about a dozen were sent at a time to be watered, and only a very few saddles removed at a time to have the backs cleaned and examined. The men were not allowed to move from their subdivisions, or to go near the tents of the sailors or Infantry, or make any unnecessary noise. In short, every precaution was taken so as to insure a rapid turn-out. The wallets at that time were a combination of wallet and rocket pipe, made of stout hard leather. It was found that from exposure, or the length of time they had been in use, they had contracted, and were too small to receive the rockets, so they were slit up the inside, or partition, and rockets fixed in them, each mounted gunner carrying two. Captain H. F. Strange had now rejoined his company. When the Troop first moved on to the plateau, the Sergeant-Major and a number of drivers, with upwards of sixty draught horses and some waggons and carriages, remained behind in the plain of Balaclava, for the purpose of drawing up siege guns and material from the harbour to the Siege Train Depôts. The Quarter-Master Sergeant had been taken ill at Bulganak, and was not again effective; and the soldier intended to be clerk was also sick and away from the Crimea. This was a great drawback, considering the way in which the men and horses were divided. The Troop turned out every morning one hour before daybreak, and moved a short distance to the front, towards the before-mentioned heap of ruins occupied by the Infantry picquet. Sir George Brown was always present, walking up and down close by the guns, and remaining there about an hour after daylight, till all was clear, and everything reported quiet. After the first two or three mornings the Troop, instead of remaining in front in the early morning, went away an hour before daylight to the ground at Inkerman, and watched the ravines in that direction. The Russians sometimes fired at the Troop, but did no harm, and the fire was never returned. There were continual alarms and surprises, with turnings-out night and day, owing to sudden musketry firing. On one occasion, during day-time, when the Troop had hurried towards Inkerman, and could not make out the cause, as all was again silent, Captain Lushington, Royal Navy, came up the ravine and told Captain Brandling that it arose from the capture of a small Russian water party. The nearest English Infantry picquet captured some of them, but the Russian non-commissioned officer, or, at any rate, one of the party, would not allow himself to be taken, and had to be destroyed. Such were Captain Lushington's exact words. It was a pity such a brave fellow could not be spared!

One officer, two non-commissioned officers, and twenty-four pairs of draught horses, with their drivers, attended nightly at the Siege Train Depôt, for the purpose of taking guns into the Batteries after the latter had been partially made; these were divided into two teams of twelve pairs each, and the siege guns had sheepskins or some other material tied round the tires and felloes of the wheels to deaden the sound as much as possible. Major (now General Sir) Collingwood Dickson, formerly 2nd Captain of 'C' Troop, was always to be found in or near the Batteries at night, assisting with his advice and directions as to drawing in the guns, and afterwards getting the horses away quietly. Nearly all the route down to the Batteries was exposed to the fire of the Great Redan and other Russian works, and the firing was casual, so as to annoy the working parties. The enemy had a trick of firing two or three guns together in the same direction, one only being loaded with shell, so that the noise of the burning fuse might distract attention from the shot which accompanied it.

There must have been some very good system of signalling carried on by the Russians from their outlook on the Inkerman ridge or heights, for if any considerable body of English troops were assembling for any purpose near the Light Division Camp, although they could not be seen from Sevastopol, there was certain to be a cannonade opened from the neighbourhood of the Malakoff, towards the ground on which they were signalled to be assembling. One Sunday, at a church parade, as soon as all the troops off duty of the Light Division were assembled on the Victoria ridge, but of course out of view of Sevastopol, and the chaplain, the Rev. Mr. Egan, had commenced the service, an enormous shell from a mortar was fired up; it was a considerable time in the air, and the fuse was kicking up a precious row, coming unmistakably nearer and nearer to the square, so much so that almost everybody ducked, except Sir G. Brown and the parson, who continued reading. The shell fell just beyond the rear rank of the men on that side of the square farthest from Sevastopol, burying itself a great depth in the earth. There was some silent laughter amongst those on the parade, and loud laughter amongst those left to watch the tents. The clergyman still continued, but one of the Infantry colonels, and also an Aide-de-camp, who failed to see any fun in the thing, pointed out to Sir G. Brown that the square was under fire, and Sir G. Brown coolly said, "Well, if they are, tell the Brigade Major to take them farther back." They had just removed about 100 paces, when the next shell burst beautifully close over the ground they had left.

About this time the Troop was employed (without

their guns) in escorting the Tartars who took ammunition down to the trenches; they were also employed in assisting to mount guns in the Batteries, the Lancaster guns included, and a party, consisting of Bombardier Lockwood and some gunners who had a knowledge of siege guns, were directed to join the Siege Artillery, Left Attack. These were men who for the most part had joined the Horse Artillery at home, after previously undergoing some amount of training in the Repository, they served in the bombardments, in their Horse Artillery uniform, and did not rejoin the Troop for many weeks, until the Siege Artillery was largely augmented from home.

On three occasions before the 25th October the Troop was ordered to Balaclava, as an attack was expected there; they generally returned on the evening of the day they went down. On the first of the three journeys to Balaclava in anticipation of the Russian attack, the whole of the common spikes of 'C' Troop were lent to the Cavalry, and some of their non-commissioned officers and men were instructed as to how they were to be used in case any of the enemy's guns were captured. The spikes were left in their possession till after the Battle of Inkerman; it is well remembered that on these three occasions the men had to eat some of the fat of their uncooked pork with the biscuit: unpalatable as it was, there was no help for it, for no other thing was to be had. On one of these occasions, Captain Morris, 17th Lancers, came over to the Troop after arrival in the plain, and said to Brandling, "John, I think we'll have no fighting to-day; they've been showing themselves, but have now withdrawn." It was noticed that he (Morris) seemed eager for the fray, and though on the Head Quarter Staff, and wearing Staff forage cap and frock-coat, that he evidently intended to lose no opportunity of being in action with his own regiment. About the 23rd October, the party left with the Sergeant-Major at Balaclava plain rejoined; the horses had undergone such severe straining work that they were naturally in a very low condition and suffering from galls. A great many of the drivers with them were from the batches of Foot Artillery sent to augment the Troop, after disembarkation at Old Fort. There had also been many deaths from cholera in the party. Although no one had died with the Head Quarters of the Troop before Sevastopol up to the 25th October, yet dysentery and diarrhœa had set in with severity, and from the worry, loss of rest, want of nourishment and proper medicine, some of the men got so low that they were past recovery, and many died off immediately afterwards; when cholera attacked them, they had no chance. From about the time the army arrived at Balaclava, scurvy had made its appearance, and as it was all salt meat ration before Sevastopol, it made things worse. The legs of those affected swelled very much, and after a time broke out in running sores.

The ration was simply biscuit, meat (generally pork), green coffee berries, and sugar, with the allowance of rum. No tinned meat, dried beans, or vegetables of any sort whatever; and though the coffee and sugar looked well enough on the ration returns, it was a miserable allowance when prepared. There was a great scarcity of wood, and water was both scarce and dirty.

The horses got little or no hay, and the barley was so heating to the feet that many of them were quite lame.

CHAPTER VII.

BATTLE OF BALACLAVA.

ON the morning of the 25th October, the Troop went out as usual, an hour before daylight, to the ground at Inkerman. The spot from which they watched on this particular morning was a short distance from the English picquet that was on the left of the line of picquets running across the Inkerman ridge, and it was partially concealed in the scrubby brushwood. A short time after the Troop had returned to their camp, news was brought in that Balaclava was attacked. The men had had nothing to eat or drink.

It was Brandling's custom on all alarms to take the first one or two guns that were hooked-in and be off with them. An old 'C' Troop driver named Stacey, who had served with distinction under Sir de Lacey Evans in the Spanish wars, acted as bâtman. This man bridled up the charger, and Brandling had merely to kick off a pair of shoes, which he wore about the lines, pull on his hessians, and mount; so he was invariably amongst the first out. Those who happened to be last in turning out on an alarm generally heard something further on that particular subject. It is worthy of remark here, as illustrative of the kindness of Sir de Lacey to old soldiers who had served under him, that he continually inquired after this man, and when in Bulgaria spoke in glowing terms of his soldierly qualities to Major Levinge. He even asked him to call at his tent whenever opportunities offered, and tell him how he was getting on.

Everything was in such a state of readiness that the Troop was hooked in, mounted, and trotting away in a few minutes through the tents, on towards the Woronzoff Road, intending to reach Balaclava by that route. When they arrived where this road begins to descend, masses of Russian Infantry were then crossing the bottom of the valley, and their troops had also carried by assault the farthest Turkish redoubt. No English Cavalry were then in sight (it appears they were drawn in under the bend of the Plateau at this time); so it was not considered safe for the Troop to proceed that way any farther. The guns were therefore wheeled about, and they went straight for the "Col." At this time news arrived that Captain (now Colonel) G. A. Maude had been very badly wounded. There was no regular road then, and the ground to pass over was very rough, sterile, and covered with stones. It is nearly two miles from this part of the Woronzoff road to the Col, and that portion of the journey told very severely on the draught horses.

When the Troop arrived near the Col, the French Cavalry (Chasseurs d'Afrique) were approaching it from their camp at a trot also, and the officer in command held up his sword and halted, to let 'C' Troop through the barrier first. This break or gap in the line of circumvallation was at that time called the "Barrier." It afterwards went by the name of the "Col," or "Col de Balaclava." There would be about one regiment of Chasseurs, certainly not more than four squadrons, if so many, descending at this particular moment. Having entered the descent to the plain, they kept to their left, and went in close under the line of circumvallation, but the Troop went straight away for the middle of the plain, where there was some portion of the red-coated Heavy Cavalry formed up, with the Scots Greys in the centre. The latter could be distinctly recognized by their head-dress and colour of horse, and the others by their brass helmets without plumes. When the leading subdivision of 'C' Troop had, as it were, wheeled left about three-quarters, to descend through the barrier, this body of English Cavalry had been already formed up, and did not move until it moved to attack in the charge afterwards. This serves to fix the exact time that 'C' Troop and the Chasseurs d'Afrique entered the plain, and further that so much of the Cavalry had been formed up, and were actually waiting, during the time 'C' Troop was proceeding at a fairly rapid pace from the barrier to them. Had there been no Cavalry there, the Troop would not have gone out to the middle of the plain on an objectless journey, and without any support.

For simplicity we call the plain of Balaclava next Kadikoi, the inner plain, and that on the other side of the ridge, where the Light Cavalry charge subsequently took place, the outer plain.

We call Canrobert's Redoubt, which is the farthest off and on a conical hill of great height, No. 1; then the next to it (which is on the ridge), No. 2; then, at a good distance, comes No. 3, also on the ridge; and last of all No. 4, which was tolerably close to the Sevastopol end of the ridge, and next the line of circumvallation. Some accounts say there were six redoubts, and represent Nos. 2 and 3 as being close together, but we prefer to say there were four, as that is the way they were spoken of at the time of the battle. When 'C' Troop entered the plain, there appeared to be no Infantry in it except the 93rd Highlanders, in line, at a considerable distance away to the right, and beyond the entrance to Kadikoi. Indeed, there had been no time for any English Infantry to get down; for when 'C' Troop was proceeding along the plateau towards the Col, they saw some few men on their right hurrying across towards them from the positions occupied by the 3rd or 4th Infantry Division before Sevastopol (which was called the English "Left Attack"), but these were only in parties like companies, or half companies, and had evidently been started off as they could best be spared for the emergency. They were hurrying in any sort of order, dressed in their red coatees, carrying their blankets loosely over their shoulders, and were the vanguard of the Infantry force which afterwards got down to the plain. It is believed that the Infantry disembarked on the 14th September, with a blanket and one change of linen only (rolled up inside), that they left their great coats on board ship, and had not received them on the 25th October; at any rate, they used the blanket and not a great coat in the trenches up till 17th October. The French Cavalry continued their course under the line of circumvallation in the direction of the English Light Cavalry, and 'I' Troop, R.H.A., then behind, or near No. 4 Redoubt. As 'C' Troop proceeded onwards, left in front, about seven or eight horsemen came trotting along the top of the ridge from No. 2 towards No. 3 Redoubt, so that they saw into both plains. They were the Russian Cavalry General and his staff, doubtless keeping abreast of their own Cavalry, which at this time could not be seen from the inner plain. Immediately afterwards the left front corner, as it might be, of the Russian Cavalry showed itself. They were coming over the ridge at a rapid trot, and bringing their right shoulders forward. When well over and fully in view (*i.e.*, when the rearmost ranks had just passed the crest), they were found to be a very considerable force, in either close or quarter distance column. There were no skirmishers, flankers, or scouts, but it is thought that possibly there may have been some few guns very close up in rear. However, if there, they did not attract the attention of any one in 'C' Troop, though all were looking in the direction of the column. The front had the appearance of three large squadrons, and the depth from front to rear when halted, as they were in a moment or two afterwards, was about the same as the extent of front; so that at the halt and closed up they had the appearance of a nearly equilateral figure. When moving they seemed to be a little deeper, owing to the slight tailing off always consequent on such a number of cavalry moving at a trot, when the columns are closed. There appeared to be no Lancers with this column; certainly no Lancers with flags to the lances, as they are easily distinguished, nor did there appear to be Irregular Cavalry of any sort with them. It is well known that there were Lancers in Liprandi's force, and numbers of Cossacks also. Therefore, they must have been somewhere outside the inner plain; but, be that as it may, this force confronting the Heavies was not more than 2000 at the very outside, probably less. Any one with experience in *bonâ fide* mustering of Cavalry by actually counting the men (and not trusting to the states) will know that squadrons of eighty men are not on parade every day, and that to manœuvre twenty-five of such squadrons in one close or quarter-distance column, at a rattling good pace such as these men were moved at that day, is all but impossible, as the men in the centre are crushed out of all shape and dressing. The intervals between their squadrons must have been very slight, so slight, indeed, as not to be observed from the ground where 'C' Troop saw them at their nearest, about 450 yards distant, before the collision. The column could in no way be seen through from front to rear, as would be the case in a similarly-formed body of English Cavalry at the present day, with their twelve yards intervals. It is believed our own Heavy Cavalry were not quite the strength they were afterwards given out at, for many horses had been lost at sea and from other causes, and some few horses on the sick list were left in the lines on the day of the battle. At any rate, when three English squadrons were engaged on the Russian front, as they were in a few moments after this, the Russians rather overlapped the English.

The Russians continued to bring the right shoulder forward until their centre was about opposite to the Scots Greys, who were in the centre of the English Cavalry, and they then moved on. There was a slight rising ground rather to the left front of where the Heavy Cavalry stood, and Brigadier-General Strangways (alone at this moment) was on this rising ground, looking towards the Russians, but having his right side towards 'C' Troop, so that he was well seen on his dark-coloured charger. The Troop, with the gun horses very much jaded, had now got to within about three hundred yards of the left rear of the Cavalry, and Brigade-Major Adye (who had just left General Strangways) met Brandling, and said, "You are to move on to this rising ground, —(pointing to where General Strangways was), and come into action against this mass of cavalry." But Brandling called out, "I cannot reach it in time, and all will be confusion. I'll go to the right, where I'll be of more use." The leading subdivision (No. 6) immediately afterwards threw forward the left shoulder a little to pass by the rear of the Heavy Cavalry, from the rear ranks of which, during the passage to the right, it would be about a hundred and fifty yards. At this moment the Russian Cavalry halted, and, whether from unwieldiness or bad timing of the orders, it so happened that their central officers or leaders in front pulled up before those on the flanks, but only to the extent of from ten to twelve yards. The flanks, however, did not curve round, but kept tolerably parallel with the central line. There was no such thing as prolonging the front ranks of the column, though it might have such an appearance from other parts of the field; indeed, there was no time for it. It was simply that the officer in chief command of those who were to go on in the attack seemed undecided for a moment as to how he would proceed. It was, however, but momentary, for they instantly moved on, only not so fast, and the dressing in front was not corrected. The first attacking squadron of the Greys now moved out (not very fast—it was said there were some obstacles immediately in front of the Greys). After a moment the Russians halted again, and there were some pistol or carbine shots discharged from their central squadron at the first squadron of the Greys. Then the Russians moved on, but their pace was so slow that it could hardly be called a trot. The first Squadron of the Greys had now quickened their pace, and in a moment or two had passed into the space where the central squadron of the Russians had hung back. The first squadron of the Greys got in partly between the files, dismounting some of the Russians, and partly at the angles formed by the Russian centre checking. They then spread out something like a fan, going through the distances between the Russian ranks, which at the moment were not quite closed up, owing to the before-mentioned tailing-off. The course taken by this squadron of the Greys could be easily observed by their red coats and grey horses. The Russians, as far as they could be seen in this particular body, had black horses, wore a black oilskin cover, over a very broad-topped old-fashioned shako, and a dark grey overcoat. They were altogether a black-looking mass.

Other squadrons of Heavy Cavalry had, of course, moved off in succession to the attack. At this time six riderless black Russian horses, in single file, broke in on 'C' Troop, snorting and trotting in and out through the guns. They were a portion of the results from the crash with the first squadron of the Greys. The Troop trumpeter caught one of them (a great beauty), but Brandling ordered him to let it go; and after a time they careered away again to their friends on their own side of the field. Brandling told the trumpeter immediately afterwards that he was sorry he had given the order, as the animal would have made a splendid field trumpeter's horse.

'C' Troop, which had now got well out beyond the right flank of the Heavy Cavalry, wheeled subdivisions to the left, and halted to watch the results of the charge, and wait for an opportunity to come into action. The gun-horses were very much done up, as they had been forced to their utmost consistent with keeping them on their legs, and they had come about five and a half miles without any rest, half of it at least (including the steep descent through the Col) was over very bad ground. No wonder they reeled and trembled, they had been underfed ever since they disembarked on 14th September; for days at a time they were without a mouthful of hay; the trumpeter used to go to Balaclava with a pair of horses and ammunition waggon minus the boxes, and would often return unable to get any from the shipping. Sometimes he would manage to secure a truss of 56lbs. for about 130 horses, and, poor brutes, still harder times were in store for them; but this day's work undid a few of them for ever.

By the time 'C' Troop had halted, the whole Russian

Cavalry may be said to have halted, for the tussle was going on along its whole front with the other squadrons of Heavy Cavalry that had been already formed up, when they (the Russians) came over the ridge; but a squadron of Heavy Cavalry, which had in some way been detached to the right, now passed at a good distance in front of 'C' Troop, and at a splendid pace, the men sitting well down, and in good dressing; in this form they tore in on the left flank of the Russians, and catching them, as they did obliquely, and on the bridle arm, unhorsed whole troops of them. There was now no longer any doubt what would be the result, the dismounted Russians were running back, some through the intervals between their comrades, and some came out of the left of the column altogether and tried to run back that way.

The mass of riderless horses helped to block up everything, and all was confusion, so that no matter what was the determination of those at the rear of the Russian column, they could do no more.

There were also some attacks on the Russian right, and right front, by other independent or detached squadrons of the Heavy Cavalry; but the results of these were not observed so well by 'C' Troop. From the ground upon which the Troop was halted during the time of the fight of the Heavy Cavalry, the pennons of the 17th Lancers, a portion of the head-dress of some of their men, and some of the busbies and upper parts of the dress of men of 'I' Troop, R.H.A., could be distinctly seen: they were formed up behind, or near the end redoubt; and any one in 'C' Troop had only to look in the direction of their left front to see them: the other regiments of the Light Cavalry Brigade could not be seen from this ground, they were hidden partly by the ridge, and knolls about the end Redoubt, and were farther in the direction of the outer plain, or else farther back towards the line of circumvallation.

It should be mentioned, that owing to the momentary check experienced by the Russian centre from its collision with the first squadron of the Greys, the whole force had rather a remarkable appearance, and this no doubt caused some to imagine that the Greys had penetrated into the heart of the enemy, and were quite cut off; on the other hand, if the English right and left squadrons had been started first, the check from their collision would have tended to correct the dressing of the Russian front, by giving their centre time to come on.

But now to go back before the Russian Cavalry made their appearance, or had begun to cross the ridge to attack the Heavy Cavalry, another portion of Russian Cavalry moved out from the direction of No. 2 Redoubt; they were in one line, and were about the strength of what a very strong eight troop regiment of English Cavalry on home service would be, there were certainly not more than four hundred sabres in all.

They moved on at the trot towards the 93rd Highlanders, then in line, and at a considerable distance to the right rear of the line of the Heavy Cavalry: that is, they were covering the entrance to the gorge of Balaclava. Barker's Battery (B Battery, 2nd Brigade now) was close to the 93rd, and fired some rounds. The 93rd also fired a volley. There appeared to be no saddle emptied or any confusion whatever in the Russian Cavalry, who however did not approach much nearer, but wheeled by fours or troops, and went straight away for a long distance in the direction of their own left. Then the heavy guns on the Marine Heights fired shell at them, and caused them some losses, after which they led away for Canrobert's or No. 1 Redoubt. This body could not have joined the main body of the Russian Cavalry in time for their attack, for the simple reason that they were not quite clear out of the inner plain when the main body had entered it about a mile higher up. It may be mentioned that 'C' Troop, at a reconnaissance on the 19th February following, came across a corpse of one of the Russians killed by the Marine guns on this day; and also that these heavy guns could very nearly reach the ground at the foot of Canrobert's Hill. They were occasionally fired at Russian patrols.

To return to the Heavy Cavalry fight. Soon after the attack on the Russian left flank by the before-mentioned detached squadron which passed obliquely in front of 'C' Troop, and, no doubt, owing to the numbers of riderless horses and dismounted men everywhere about, they (the Russians) began to retire. In doing so they seemed to go by fours or sections to their left, and then at once in a direction that took them left about three-quarters from that in which they stood when fronting the Heavy Cavalry. They were accompanied by all this lot of loose horses and men on foot. Many of the latter had now secured horses, and were mounting, but there was a formidable body of them (certainly one-half) that had never been reached or touched by our people; for when all the squadrons of the Heavies had executed the charge at the front, and partially on the flanks near the front, their strength may be said to have been expended. It was stated that they could make no impression on the Russians, owing to the thick overcoat they wore; but it is believed our men's swords were not sufficiently sharp, and as for those of the Russians no attempt whatever had been made to sharpen theirs. The few picked up on the ground were as blunt as they could be.

The very formation of the Russians (bad generalship though it was) helped to consolidate them, make them support each other, and keep our dragoons out.

The cutting and hacking was only carried on about as far as the fifth rank from the Russian front, and about as far inwards as the breadth of twelve horsemen on their flanks near the front. On the left flank, which was in full view of 'C' Troop, certainly two-thirds of the flank nearest the rear was quite untouched: the remaining third next the front would be rather more than the breadth of front of the detached squadron which charged in in that way, and which landed its left, on the left of the Russian front rank. Probably on the Russian right flank, the attack may have extended farther towards the rear, but the same rule holds good: only a certain number of horses standing sideways could have been ridden down or destroyed at the first crash, and the horses inside these would hardly feel it, or suffer inconvenience from it. Any of our men riding in between the Russian ranks would find it a losing game, for they must enter in single file or two abreast at the most, and then they would be cut at on both sides; from one rank by the men reaching back over their horses' croups, and from the other by the men merely leaning forward in their stirrups; but besides this, the Russians carried a large loaded pistol (which our people had not), and any number of men riding in single file between their ranks, would have been quickly disposed of. The Russian Cavalry had a white raw hide thong about three-quarters of a yard long, one end fastened to the trigger guard, and the other somewhere in the front of the saddle. If previously loaded, the soldier had merely just before the last moment to pass his sword to his bridle hand, draw his pistol, discharge it towards the enemy, let it fall by the horse's shoulder and take the sword in his right hand again, provided he timed it properly; or, he could take the rein in his sword hand for the moment, and discharge the pistol with his left hand.

Our troops had the mastery in strength of men, and power of horse, of which they gave grand proof in unhorsing the enemy right and left, and it was thought, that if it had been possible to have taken the Russians in rear, or right rear, the whole mass would have thrown down their arms, or at any rate that great numbers of their dismounted men would have been driven into our position, and made prisoners of war.

Even after our first three attacking squadrons had collided on the Russian front, the enemy seemed to carry forward the weight of battle a very few yards, but not to carry our Dragoons with it: this is easily accounted for by the slight descent from their side, by their preponderance of numbers, and by the few more dashing who broke through from the corners, where, owing to our squadrons being weaker, there were none of our men to oppose them. When our remaining squadrons closed with them, it had more the appearance of a blocking business from our side, and after the first crash our men knocked or pulled them off their horses in every conceivable way. Of course there were some of our own men knocked off also, who were staggering about with bleeding faces, etc., etc. There did not seem to be an upheaval, that is, the untouched Russians in the centre and rear neither reined back nor went about; when the untouched retired, they did so in as regular a way as could be expected considering the number of loose horses and dismounted men; had there been more Heavy Cavalry, the Russians could have been followed for about 500 yards with advantage.

The Cavalry camping-ground, part of which was not far from the place of encounter, had not been quite cleared; and amongst other things left were a few sick horses fastened to picket lines. Some of the more dashing or venturesome of the Russian Cavalry managed to slip away from their column—possibly from the right front corner, or, at any rate, from some part of the right flank, and, getting through our people, found their way into this camp-ground, where they badly injured these picketted horses with sword cuts. There were also some tents, which had been partly pulled down, lying about, with a few arabas or vehicles of sorts; and, as there were some very low trodden-down fences there also, the Russians, by a stretch of imagination, may have considered it a park, and reported it as such. Hence it might have in this way been embodied in General Todleben's work, but there was nothing else at all resembling a park of Artillery or stores in Balaclava plain. In retiring in the way described, the Russians came across the front of 'C' Troop, which had meanwhile begun to move forward. The severest fighting appeared to be at the Russian front, and they were the last to retire. Some of our people were still entangled with them, and the guns could not as yet be brought into action. The Russians, however, halted short of the ridge, and their officers could be seen holding their swords up and endeavouring to rally them, and get them into order, which they very soon would have done, but 'C' Troop now came into action, and fired forty-nine shot and shell at them, at a range between 700 and 800 yards, with admirable results, the 24-pounder howitzers making splendid practice. This effectually prevented the Russians rallying, and they quickly retired, keeping a little inside the crest of the ridge, and thence over into the outer plain. Being so far from camp, and so many waggon horses away at the siege work, Brandling was anxious about the expenditure of ammunition, so he asked for a verbal report at the instant of "cease firing." The total as above was called out in a loud tone, and thus it is remembered for this one particular occasion.

The reason it was thought there might have been guns close up behind the Russian Cavalry was that at this point, amongst a number of dead, a Russian driver and his horses were, at a later period of the day, found killed by a shell. This, however, was the only reason, and he may have been a driver of something else than a gun.

The Troop then limbered up to the front, advanced about five hundred yards, and changed front to the right, which brought them under the fire of the Russian guns near No. 2 Redoubt. It then advanced in echelon of half Troops from the left, in the direction of some squadrons of Russian Cavalry that had been pushed out towards their own left in the inner plain, and were fronting the Troop. The left half Troop came into action against them, and its fire was very successful. The Russians were on the sky-line, and some of their casualties could be seen, after which they quickly retired.

Just before coming into action this time, one of No. 6 limber wheels was hit by a large shot from No. 2 Redoubt. It came close over Brandling's shoulder, almost grazing his ear, and struck that part of the felloe next the ground at the moment (on its upper surface); but, strange to say, the wheel was not quite disabled, though partly split. It was looked upon rather as a curiosity, for it did service for many months, and was evidence of the stability of English material and workmanship.

The Troop now retired some distance towards the Heavy Cavalry, which had in the meantime also advanced and changed front, and was in fact covering the Troop, though a long way behind. Throughout the remainder of the day, although frequently manœuvred about, as their services were called for, the front was generally in this direction.

Some time after this there was a lull in the battle,

the Troop was dismounted with their left resting somewhere near the slope of the ridge, and fronting in the direction of No. 2 Redoubt; from this they could not see into the outer plain or valley. The Heavy Cavalry was not very far from the Troop at this time, some of them were a very little in advance, and more upon the crest of the ridge. All seemed pretty quiet except occasional shots from the direction of No. 2 Redoubt: suddenly, Brandling who had been away to the front, came galloping back, calling out, "Mount, Mount," and when he came close in, he remarked in a loud tone to an officer, that the Light Cavalry had begun an advance on the other side of the ridge. The Troop at once moved off at a rapid pace to their front, in the direction of No. 2 Redoubt, keeping their right in the inner plain, but their left gun was sometimes on the crest of the ridge, and sometimes off, owing to its windings. When they halted and came into action, they were so placed, that those at the left gun had a clear view into the outer plain, and could see the 4th Light Dragoons at a considerable distance down to the left front, near the foot of the hills on the other side of the plain; and straggling parties of men, chiefly of the 13th Light Dragoons and 17th Lancers, returning up the plain and making for the ridge; some of them were dismounted and leading their wounded horses, some were on foot whose horses had been destroyed, others riding back with various sorts of wounds. The 8th Hussars at this time could not be seen owing to a bend in the hills. The Heavy Cavalry were near the Troop, but not all in one line. The Troop was then under fire from guns concealed in or about No. 2 Redoubt, which were also playing on the Heavy Cavalry; these guns seemed to slacken fire for a time, as if they had limbered up to change their position, and then to come back into action again; but the ground about No. 2 Redoubt is very deceptive; it is slightly higher than that on which the Troop stood, and widens out, and there is capital cover for guns; all the Troop could see was the smoke after each discharge, and they fired shell in that direction. The Heavy Cavalry kept manœuvring and shifting about, but still they suffered numerous casualties here; they and 'C' Troop retired independently of each other, keeping to the crest of the ridge, upon which they afterwards halted: the 4th Light Dragoons and 11th Hussars came obliquely across the outer plain, and passed to the rear, where they and all the other remnants of regiments were mustered. The 8th Hussars came back by the line of the ridge, but on the outer side. All were cheered as they passed by the Heavy Cavalry and 'C' Troop. Numbers of badly wounded also came slowly up to this place, and passed on towards the rear, reeling in their saddles, some calling out, "Lads, look at my poor broken arm or leg," as the case might be, etc., etc. Captain Brandling and the other officers of the Troop held their flasks to these men's mouths as long as the contents lasted. Many of the head-dresses were smashed and torn by shell and grape shot. Captain Morris, who commanded the 17th Lancers, was terribly wounded about the head, and was carried past the front of the Troop towards Kadikoi, calling out loudly, "Lord have mercy on my soul." He had served with great distinction in India.

'C' Troop now moved well out into the middle of the inner plain, and took up a position about six hundred yards from, and facing, the opening between Nos. 1 and 2 Redoubts. They threw forward the right shoulder for this purpose. They did not, however, unlimber, or, at any rate, there was no firing from this point. While there, a Sergeant-Major of the 11th Hussars came out from the opening between the Redoubts and made for the Troop. On his arrival at the guns Brandling said to him, "Who on earth gave the order, Sergeant-Major?" and the man answered, "Oh, sir, God knows! We heard, 'Come on! come on!' called out. My horse was shot when I was down at the bottom of the plain; this is a loose horse of another regiment I am on, and this is a Russian loaded carbine I have been defending myself with against some Lancers, who attacked and knocked me about." His story was quite true as regarded the horse and carbine, and his jacket bore evidence of the struggle he had undergone, for the wadding was all sticking out through the rents made by the lances. He also said that the Russian Infantry were hidden in enormous masses at the foot of the hills on the other side of No. 2 Redoubt, and all about there. This was the last man observed by 'C' Troop returning from the Light Cavalry charge, and how he crossed the bottom of the outer plain amongst the Russians, and got out where he did, is only known to himself.

After a short time the Troop moved back to the ridge, but keeping on the inner side, the Heavy Cavalry were then in rear and right rear of the Troop. The Russians appeared to be a little on the aggressive again, for they brought some guns into action on the ridge in advance of No. 2 Redoubt, and fired into the Troop and Heavy Cavalry. 'C' Troop came into action and fired a few rounds in the direction of the Russian guns, and then some English Infantry moved off apparently to dislodge the Russian Artillery, who were in advance of No. 2 Redoubt, but the latter retreated. The Infantry, or those with them, then blew up some ammunition which the Turks or Russians had left behind. One of the Russian shot fired before the Light Brigade attack had a most curious effect, having grazed just at 'C' Troop guns, it flew onwards and struck fair on the edge of a dragoon's sword when at the "slope," about a foot from the hilt, and so passed in between him and the man on his right. Strange to say, neither of the men was injured, although the sword at the point where it was struck was bent or driven bodily inwards to the shape of the shot.

Brandling had heard that Captain Nolan, of the 15th Hussars, who was on the Quartermaster-General's Staff, had been killed, and he looked about on the outer side of the ridge for the body. Having found it, he came back and took with him Bombardier Ormes (afterwards Riding-Master O. Orme), and four limber gunners with spades to bury it. The bombardier, on his return, said that the poor fellow's chest had been quite broken away, and the gold lace and cloth of his jacket very much burnt by the shell which killed him, and which must have burst close by; also that there was only one officer present, who appeared to be a friend, and was much affected, and who took off his watch and sword. The body was then laid in the earth as it was, there was no time to dig a deep grave, as occasional shots were then being fired at the Troop. Nolan's appearance was well known to all, both in Bulgaria and the Crimea, as he wore the scarlet forage-cap and uniform of his regiment. The grave is in the outer plain, and there is a slight bend inwards in the ridge near that place. It would not be visited by the English for some months (probably until the time the Sardinian Army was encamped on the Tchernaya), as the ground was abandoned that night, and for a certain period considered neutral. When Lord Lucan was told that Nolan was buried, his Lordship said, "Ah, I wish we could get poor Charteris' body." The latter officer was his relative.

About this time a large body of Russians, supported

by Artillery, were looking as if they meant another attack. So the Troop again moved into action, and this portion of the enemy retreated in a few minutes. These were the last shots fired on this day. A Circassian, in national costume, advanced with 'C' Troop guns, and very gravely shot with bow and arrow at the Russians.

Soon after this Lord Raglan visited the plain, and complimented General Scarlett, in the hearing of 'C' Troop. His Lordship spoke in this way to Scarlett, "Now tell me all about yourself." Scarlett replied, "When the Russian column were moving down on me, Sir, I began by sending first a squadron of the Greys at them, and"——but at the word "and" his Lordship struck in, saying, "And they knocked them over like the devil." He then turned his horse away, as if he did not need to hear any more. He seemed very much annoyed and bowed down over the loss of the Light Brigade, and was pointing out with his arm the ground over which he intended the advance should have been made. He and Scarlett were only ten yards in front of 'C' Troop at the time, no divisional staff being present. It was also understood that he complimented Captain Brandling on the timely arrival of the Troop, and the part taken by it in the Battle; and further, he ordered that it must now remain on the ground with the Cavalry, and not even go back to its old camp at the Right Attack for that night.

As to the part taken by the French Cavalry (Chasseurs d'Afrique), what was observed by 'C' Troop was this: At the moment when the 4th Light Dragoons and 11th Hussars were retiring obliquely across the outer plain, after the Light Cavalry charge, they (the Chasseurs) were placed thus: three squadrons in line halted, facing and within about one hundred yards of the foot of the Fedioukine hills, with their backs to Sevastopol.

A portion of their men were about two-thirds of the way up the hill-side in front of the regiment, in the stiff brushwood, in skirmishing order, with intervals of about eight yards. They were halted and firing (mounted) towards the top and over the hill, which is steep. It was awkward work for them, and they had some killed and wounded. If this particular force stood in this position when the Light Cavalry began the charge, there was no time for them to go to their left, get up the hills that way, engage in a combat, and then get back again before they were seen by 'C' Troop. There were no field guns with them.

As night set in, the whole of the troops withdrew out of the plain. As long as there was any light the Russian Cavalry could be seen extended in long lines right across the bottom of the outer plain. When it was dark, General Scarlett came to 'C' Troop, then near the ridge, and said, "Artillery, try to light fires with this long dry grass, so as to make the Russians believe we are staying here all night."

After a time the Troop withdrew to some gardens or enclosures which are situated on the Col side of Kadikoi. Here the surgeons were attending to some wounded Cavalry, in a sort of outhouse or shed; the moanings were heard all night. Near here 'I' Troop, R.H.A., also remained. The night was far advanced before any water was found. It then had to be lifted from a great square well, and, as it proved to be very foul, the horses refused it. The men of 'C' Troop had no food of any sort that day, and they had to bivouac without cloaks, blankets, or valises, which were not brought to them from the old camp for the next three days. An hour before daylight the troops found their way out again into the plain, but everything appeared to be quiet.

During the day 'C' Troop moved to where the Cavalry were encamped, up in a sort of corner or recess, on the left-hand side of the road before it enters the Col. There were some holes and traps of various sorts dug in the ground in front of the camp by the Turks, in case the whole Russian Cavalry should be tempted to charge in. This camp was in full view of the Russians on the ridge, and they could see everything going on in it. Here the Troop and some Cavalry remained for a time. During the night of 27th October there was a stampede of Russian horses that had broken away from their picket lines; also some night and day alarms. On the second day Captain Fellowes, of the Divisional Staff, and the Trumpet-Major 17th Lancers, went with a flag of truce towards No. 2 Redoubt, to inquire after the wounded and prisoners. The Russians informed them that "their dead were buried and their wounded well cared for." Afterwards a second flag of truce was sent, asking permission to send some clothing and effects to the prisoners. On this occasion the Russians were more gracious; they gave consent, and then a third flag of truce was sent with the things.

An incident occurred during one of the lulls in the battle, which shows how cruel the Turkish soldiery can be, and how disposed they are to mutilate their enemy's dead. Nearly all the signs of confusion caused by the Heavy Cavalry charge had been cleared away; the men suffering from slight cuts and bruises about the face and head had had time to get righted, and settle themselves in the ranks again; the badly-wounded and contused had gone to the rear, and all was as quiet in the Brigade, and in 'C' Troop, as at a Review. Three Russian Hussars and a private of the 4th Dragoon Guards lay stretched on the ground at some distance in front. They had been already examined by our men, and were considered to be quite dead. At this time a Turkish soldier was observed running in from the direction of No. 3 Redoubt on the ridge. As he approached one of the Russians (who was lying face downwards with arms extended right and left), he suddenly brought up the butt of his musket in the air, and drove the fixed bayonet into the back of the Russian at the waist, and in a second he had repeated the stab. All who saw it roared out, and a Doctor of Heavy Cavalry galloped out to cut down the Turk; but the latter merely continued his run in the direction of Kadikoi, kicking up his heels and grinning as he went. Now it so happened, and this is the most painful part of it, that this particular Russian had been only badly stunned in the charge, and was not dead until killed outright by the Turk; for, when stabbed, he began writhing about on the bayonet. To sum up, the Turk (who was himself leaving his post), not knowing the English character, bayonetted what he thought was a dead Russian, in the hope that the act might please the English soldiery then looking on.

It was considered, by the Naval authorities and others who observed from the Marine Heights, that the Turks in No. 1 Redoubt stood their ground well against overwhelming numbers, but that those in the other Redoubts retreated prematurely.

Alluding to the bluntness of the Russian swords, it may be stated that the dead soldier of the 4th Dragoon Guards had red or fair hair, which was cut as close as possible, and therefore well suited to show any wounds. His helmet had come off in the fight, and he had about fifteen cuts on his head, not one of which had more than parted the skin. His death-wound was a thrust below the armpit, which had bled profusely.

It was given out that the Russians killed some of the wounded English during and after the battle; but the men who had been taken prisoners, whether wounded or otherwise, and released towards the end of the war, stated that in no single instance had they seen a comrade put to death in cold blood. The number of horses with broken legs and entrails hanging out (upon which they would be treading) would be very great, and it is always a charity to shoot them at once; so it is to be hoped that the shots observed in the bottom of the outer plain after the charge arose from this cause.

It may be remarked that no one in the inner plain had a better view of the Heavy Cavalry charge before, during, and after its execution than the men of 'C' Troop. They were not occupied with any dressing, and had merely to look to their front, and to their left while passing by the rear of the Heavies, to see all; and the ground is such that while passing by the rear they saw over the heads of their own Cavalry (except a very few yards just in front of the latter,) the clear ground right up to the enemy's horses' feet. The dress of the Russians was a red broad-topped stiff felt chaco, with brass double-headed eagle in front, and an oilskin cover over all. Underneath their great-coats they wore a dark green jacket, with coarse orange worsted lace; trowsers of sky blue, with red piping down the seams, and a narrow strapping of leather from the fork to the bottom. Their horses were in good condition; they used layers of felt, or some soft substance sewn together, under the saddle, and a blue shabracque with red edging, and their Emperor's (or some other) initials in red at the corners.

One special act of bravery on this day deserves to be mentioned. It was not what is sometimes called a doubtful case, but was the talk and admiration of the men in the Division over the watch-fires on that and many subsequent nights. Victoria Crosses had not then been thought of. It was performed by a subaltern officer of the 11th Hussars, Alexander Roberts Dunn, afterwards Lieut.-Colonel of the 33rd Regiment, and who met his death by the discharge of a sporting gun on the advance to Magdala, Abyssinia. When the 11th Hussars were retiring after their charge, and when they were far down the outer plain under a flanking fire of riflemen on the Fedioukine hills, a sergeant, who was on a slow and jaded horse, could not keep up with the remnant of the Regiment, and each stride left him farther behind. Three Russian Dragoons, one of whom it is believed was an officer, closed on the sergeant and commenced to hack at him: they had effectually cut him off, when some one in the ranks called out that "Sergeant So-and-so was cut off." Now Dunn was a rich man, having large possessions in Canada, and he had already contemplated selling out of the Army, so he could not hope to gain anything by the course he instantly determined on, and which appeared to take him to certain death; added to this his charger was a most notorious kicker. Without asking any one to follow him, and no one knew what he was going to do, he rode away from his squadron, and on to the rear to the rescue of the sergeant. The 11th were now riding fast under a galling flanking fire (their retreat at one time had been barred by Russian Lancers), so Dunn was soon left far behind, and there were none to retire after the Regiment from whom he might expect succour. He closed on one of the Russians, and quickly despatched him with his sword, set the distressed and used-up sergeant free to continue his retreat; then applied himself to work, and disposed of the other two, after which he lost his charger, and had to escape on foot. Although he at once sold out of the Army, he was afterwards (on the unanimous testimony of the men) decorated with one of the first of the Victoria Crosses, when that order was instituted.

CHAPTER VIII.

REMARKS ON, AND FURTHER RECOLLECTIONS OF, THE BATTLE OF BALACLAVA.

THE drawing up of these additional recollections and observations was brought about in this way. After the first account had been written out, an effort was made to give a trustworthy computation of the total numbers engaged, and the actual losses in each regiment or corps at the battle of Balaclava, so as to make it more generally interesting. In trying to do this numerous occurrences of interest came under consideration, and it was deemed advisable to give them either in detail or not at all. One thing led on to another, till this part of the history grew into its present proportions.

It is offered solely in a spirit of justice, and not for the sake of contradicting other published accounts of the campaign, with which it is occasionally in conflict.

An observant actor in this day's battle could not fail to see how dangerous it is to interfere unduly with cavalry when once it has been started to the attack under competent leaders, and he would be impressed with the desirability of a cavalry officer asking for the fullest instructions time admits of before proceeding to execute any attack, and, further, the absolute necessity there is of soliciting co-operation from other arms of the service, or, at any rate, of sending them the best notice possible, so as to make some provision for contingencies. Thus the Russians, having about 78 guns, did not a fire a single shot to support either advance of their cavalry, although they had every advantage of ground. They pushed forward the larger column of cavalry at a rapid pace, quite a mile in advance of any support, and notwithstanding the advantage of ground was still all on their side, their Cavalry General, or guiding spirit, whoever he was, pulled them up to the helpless position of the 'walk' or 'halt,' and then left them in a situation, of all others the most favourable, from which to be easily routed by the English, who were not half their strength. Eighteen or twenty guns trotted a few hundred yards down from the ridge, and brought into action against the 93rd, would very likely have forced that regiment and Barker's Battery out of position. We have seen that three, at least, of our Heavy Cavalry regiments were for about fifteen minutes waiting out in the middle of the plain, all ready to hand to be dealt with in the same way by the Russian Artillery. There can be no mistake about this period of time during which these regiments were alone, no matter what has been said to the contrary; however, having decided to use his cavalry against the 'Heavies,' if the Russian commander had kept on even at the "trot," the very weight and density of his column must have overborne our four ranks of dragoons, for that is the actual number they would have ridden against, and in this case 'C' Troop would have had to take themselves back towards the Col, the gunners probably behind defending the guns. It is believed that the Russian officers in front were at the last moment left without orders, that their Cavalry General, who would be still somewhere on the proper left of the column, had meddled with them unnecessarily, and, having pulled them up to the 'walk' or 'halt,' there was no time left to get messengers to the front with instructions, before they were actively engaged.

The position here given of the Greys differs from some other accounts, but nevertheless it is the fact that that regiment had helmeted Cavalry on both flanks, and there were no troops whatever between the rearmost squadron of the Greys and 'C' Troop, R.H.A., while the latter was passing by the rear of Scarlett's men.

It is not so certain that Cardigan could, as some think, have safely pursued the Russian Cavalry after their retreat from the charge of the Heavies. They (the Russians) at first retreated fairly left about three-quarters, from the way they fronted at the attack, a few of our dragoons, as easily seen by their red coats, being mixed with the rearmost. They then halted, tried to rally and re-form, at some short distance down the Balaclava side of the ridge, when 'C' Troop opened fire upon them. After this, instead of at once retiring over the ridge, they went rather parallel with it for a little way, still on the Balaclava side, and left the inner plain at a point fully three-quarters of a mile below where they entered it. Be it remembered that all this time the crest of the ridge in advance of No. 2 Redoubt was clear for the Russian Artillery to have operated upon any pursuit by our Light Brigade. The golden opportunity occurred at the instant they saw the Heavies begin the attack, for then the enemy had moved down into a real trap, and their Artillery could not have fired into our people without injuring their own. It would have been very agreeable fighting, particularly for the 17th.

From the right rear corner of the Russian column, when our Heavies began the attack, to the nearest regiment of the Light Brigade, would be, perhaps, 550 or 600 yards, and the Chasseurs d'Afrique must have been near our end of the ridge then; but supposing Cardigan construed the order that he was to defend the position he was then in, and not leave it, people will ask, was there no authority to set him in motion? After the detached squadron of Heavy Cavalry had passed to the attack obliquely across the front of 'C' Troop, there was not a man left in the exact front of the Troop, nor yet on the right of it away towards Canrobert's Hill; so the commanders must have been somewhere in the curve round between the left of 'C' Troop and the Light Brigade. The vineyards or orchards said to have been in that part of the field had been so trodden down and levelled that by the day of the battle they could hardly be designated as obstacles, and they did not interfere with the view.

It is an error to suppose that the above squadron of Heavy Cavalry became detached, and remained so by accident alone. They remained, or were allowed to remain, designedly detached, and that at a great distance, for upwards of fifteen minutes. It is quite possible that the advance of the Russian Cavalry up the outer plain may have been a surprise to Scarlett, as he was below the level of the ridge. The group of horsemen, however, as previously seen by 'C' Troop trotting along the crest, could mean nothing else, to any one who ever even saw a Review, than that it was composed of a superior officer reconnoitring the ground, followed by his staff, trotting as fast as he could, and having a clear view into both plains. Then comes the question, Who halted Scarlett before the Russians came over the crest, (for halted he was, and fronted towards the ridge when 'C' Troop came down through the Col), without informing him they were coming up the valley, and why was not this detached squadron instantly recalled by bugle sound or messenger? This subject is alluded to at page 400, Vol. IV., of "Kinglake," where it says, "The

Russians moved very slowly in the outer valley, and ought to have been seen by General Scarlett when a mile distant." It was, however, impossible for that officer to have seen them after he began to march his Heavies towards the middle of the inner plain, because the whole height of the ridge, from which he was then some distance, intervened to prevent it. It appears our Heavies had marched under specific instructions, but, at any rate, there were no men out as skirmishers or scouts towards the ridge. If the Russians had not halted as they did, the services of this detached squadron would not have been nearly so effective, because the collision would have occurred some moments before they could have got in to help at the encounter.

Although, owing to the variety of accounts that have been given, the movements at this time seem difficult to understand, still the whole thing is very simple. Both brigades and 'I' Troop, R.H.A., are at, or near, our end of the ridge. Lord Lucan, in pursuance of instructions, orders the greater portion of the Heavies to march direct across by the plain towards Kadikoi, so as to be in readiness to help in that quarter, and they accordingly move off, one squadron being in advance, Lord Lucan remaining for a time, at any rate, on the ridge. Scarlett is about 800 or 900 yards on his journey, when, from some warning or other cause, he halts and fronts towards the ridge on his left, from which he is then 700 or 800 yards. This is how he was when first seen by 'C' Troop, and the warning to him may have come from the guns of 'I' Troop, which were just in advance of Cardigan's Brigade, and about this time fired a few rounds down the outer valley, afterwards retiring and forming on that brigade. This is going on while 'C' Troop is on its journey to Scarlett, and the main body of the Russian Cavalry not yet on the crest, or in sight of those down in the inner plain. There is a lull at the instant—in fact, excepting the Chasseurs d'Afrique, the only movement seen in the inner plain is that of 'C' Troop, and the party of Russian Cavalry leaving, or about to leave, the plain far away by Canrobert's Hill.

At page 400 of "Kinglake" it is stated, Lord Lucan "saw the Russian Cavalry moving very slowly up the valley before they crowned the heights; that he found time to travel after General Scarlett, halt, form, and dress his attacking line, etc."; but at page 137 "Kinglake" says of this: "Lord Lucan's attention having been called by an A.D.C. of Lord Raglan's to the advance of the Russian Cavalry up the valley, he (Lord Lucan) gave his parting instructions to Cardigan, galloped on, and overtook Scarlett's column, etc." At page 133 of the same it is stated: "An A.D.C. of Scarlett's saw the Russian Cavalry on the crest, and was the first to inform Scarlett, who instantaneously fronted the Heavies towards them." It will be seen that all three accounts differ. Against the foregoing accounts there is the indisputable fact that Scarlett's squadrons were already halted on the ground from which they charged, when 'C' Troop, with jaded horses drawing heavy guns, came down through the Col, and that Brandling instantly made up his mind to go to their support, there being none of the larger force of Russian Cavalry then in view. The distance from the Col to Scarlett was very much greater than the distance from the crest to Scarlett. If the Heavies had continued their march uninterruptedly, they would have reached Kadikoi by the time the Russians came over the ridge, and 'C' Troop would have gone elsewhere than to the middle of the plain.

The extensive plain was so bare of our troops, that

any one of average intellect had no difficulty in taking the whole situation in at a glance; but what one wondered at was, that when the enemy's cavalry invaded the outer slope of the ridge so far up, the Light Brigade, supported by 'I' Troop, R.H.A., was not immediately ordered forward to the primary attack at that point, and messengers sent to move up the Heavies, then at the halt, to second the attack; and this view of the case is strengthened by the fact that our authorities on the ridge could see exactly what numbers they would have to contend against, whereas Scarlett, who was 700 or 800 yards down from the slope, could not tell but that the whole Russian force of all arms was coming over against him. The point at which the Russians crossed is the lowest part of the saddle; it is very regular, and would have been admirable ground for the combat.

Although there was fair cover for our Cavalry at the end of the ridge, and they may have been out of sight of the enemy, still Liprandi knew they must be thereabouts, as they had not gone up on to the plateau by the Col or the Woronzoff Road, both of which routes were plainly in his view. Between the time of the Russian Cavalry General receiving the order, when far down the valley, and his own arrival on the crest, our Heavies had gained the middle of the plain, and lay invitingly ready for his attack, and he accordingly, after some further progress, changed direction to his left for that purpose, thinking probably that he could scare away so small a force as our Heavies were, without even crossing swords. This is no doubt how it was conceived and attempted, for otherwise he could have entered the inner plain much sooner by coming at once obliquely across the ridge, without wasting time in continuing his direct advance up the valley, and so going over more ground. The Russian idea of attacking a park of artillery at Kadikoi was most likely an afterthought; no park was there: besides, their direction was not exactly towards Kadikoi.

Now let us glance at the orders said to have been given Cardigan previous to the Heavy charge. He does not say he received such instructions, for instance, as the following: "If this Cavalry continues its advance towards you, take care you attack it in good time, and Scarlett, to whom I am going, will come up and take it in flank; but should it change its direction and move down on Scarlett, take care you attack it in flank." Cardigan's version of the order given (*vide* page 210, Kinglake) runs thus: "I was ordered into a particular position by Lord Lucan, with orders on no account to leave it, and to defend it against any attack of Russians; they did not however approach the position." Lord Lucan's version of the order is in the same paragraph, and runs thus: "I am going to leave you. Well, you'll remember you are placed here by Lord Raglan himself for the defence of this position. My instructions to you are to attack anything and everything that shall come within reach of you, but you will be careful of columns or squares of infantry."

We cannot define the exact pace at which the Russian Cavalry moved up the outer valley; but we do say that if they were keeping abreast of their commander moving on the crest, they must have been going as hard as horses could trot. We say further, and this must be specially borne in mind, that there was no way of seeing into the outer valley, from Scarlett's side, except by the crest of the ridge, and that a man so observing the Russian Cavalry before they commenced the shoulder forward movement to cross over, must, unless he was fraternising with the Russian commander, have been on the crest between where they (the Russians) afterwards crossed and Cardigan's Brigade. In fact, the observer, having his back or side turned to Cardigan, would be looking towards the Russian commander, the enemy's Cavalry being as if about to cross over between the two; so that, until the Russians commenced this crossing movement, they were going straight for Cardigan.

In any case Lord Lucan seems to have decided not to be present with Cardigan's then probable initiatory attack; otherwise it was much easier and quicker for him to have brought forward the Light Brigade the very short distance necessary for the encounter, than to have ridden 700 or 800 yards to Scarlett in anticipation of events.

At the instant when the instructions are said to have been given to Cardigan, the Light Brigade, with the six guns of 'I' Troop, fresh and ready on commanding ground, was a more formidable body for repelling the Russians than our Heavies were without any guns; for 'C' Troop at this moment was too far off to be safely reckoned upon for assisting before the encounter, and one regiment of Heavies seemed very much detached from the others: that is, they appeared to be at the halt and lying back nearer the line of circumvallation.

It matters little whether the instructions to Cardigan were, as Kinglake states, given at the instant of Lord Lucan leaving the ridge, or a few minutes previously. They were, according to Lord Lucan, certainly given after Scarlett had marched off, for he said to Cardigan, "I'm going to leave you." If the orders were given to Cardigan before Lord Lucan saw the Russian Cavalry advancing, then it is certain Lord Lucan followed one of three courses until such time as he did see them advancing: that is, he either remained with Cardigan, or went forward on the crest, or went down into the inner plain after Scarlett, and then returned to the crest; for he says, "I saw them before they crowned the heights," etc., and he could not have seen them except from the crest. Now, if he remained near Cardigan on the crest till the Russians made a change of direction to their left, to convince himself that they were fully intent on crossing over, is not the whole theory about "overtaking Scarlett's people, and then halting, forming, and dressing them before they had traversed more than half the breadth of the valley," contrary to the known and unquestioned proceedings and experiences of 'C' Troop? Then, if the Russian Cavalry had not begun to move up at the time Scarlett marched off, is not the idea that "they moved very slowly from the time they began ascending the outer valley" equally opposed to facts, inasmuch as Scarlett had only marched about 800 or 900 yards, whereas the Russians went over more than double the distance up the outer valley before they made a change of direction at all? Further, if it was Lord Lucan, in person, who really halted, formed, and dressed Scarlett's people, how is it possible, having regard to the movements of 'C' Troop, to accept the idea that he remained with Cardigan till the enemy made their change of direction, and then gave him this long and formal order, together with the hint about being careful of Infantry, the change of direction, as is well known, having been made quite close to the outer side of the ridge?

The remarks and criticisms on this particular point may perhaps be pardoned, seeing that the important services of 'C' Troop at this crisis have been entirely ignored or overlooked by historians; also because three superior officers have already given to the public accounts which contradict each other; and the effort to elucidate doubtful points ought to be welcome to all ranks.

Lord Cardigan hampered by his Orders.

In consequence of the multiplicity of orders that were given during the day, it was easy for members of the Cavalry Staff to differ in their narratives; but there is only one feasible construction that can be put upon the doings at this particular moment, and that is, that Cardigan, towards whom the Russians were advancing, was left to defend the exact ground he was then on, Lord Raglan and the whole of the Allied Staff being up the heights behind him, and that the Heavies were halted in their march to Kadikoi, to wait the course of events as to whether the enemy would really attack, and, if so, the mode thereof: that is, whether he would bring forward his Artillery to shell the Light Brigade out of their position, supporting the attack by Infantry, for Lord Cardigan was told "to be careful of Infantry." This, too, seems to have been in anticipation, as apparently there was none of that arm advancing against him, and it could not be said that there was any full development of the Russian plans until they came over the crest to the inner plain. It is but just to say that Cardigan may have felt hampered with his orders, and perhaps have thought he was to be careful to defend the exact position he was then in. He could see Lord Raglan and Staff up on the heights behind him, and he may have inferred that, in the absence of Lord Lucan, future instructions would come to him from the Commander-in-Chief. Kinglake in his plan shows a passage down the face of the steep acclivity, by which the Guards are about to descend (we do not say they did descend by this route), and Lord Raglan is near this spot. If there really was such a passage, the defence of the approach to it from the plain may have been uppermost in Cardigan's mind; otherwise it is difficult to see how the ground on which he stood was a position of any great importance for defence in the general acceptance of the term; for there was a line of breastwork, near the top of the acclivity, throughout its extent, from which the French Infantry could fire on the enemy's troops below. Cardigan was reminded that he was placed there for the defence of the position by orders of Lord Raglan, but Kinglake shows that up till then Lord Raglan had given two simple orders: one, that the whole of the Cavalry were to take ground to our end of the ridge; the other, that a portion of the Heavies were to march towards Kadikoi. At any rate, a swift horseman from the ground of the Heavy charge could have reached Cardigan in ample time with instructions to take the enemy in right-rear with a part, or the whole, of the Light Brigade.

The action taken by 'C' Troop during and after the Light Brigade Charge now deserves a short notice. The fair inference is that Brandling received no warning of the attack about to be made by the Light Brigade. He was not the man to lose an opportunity of using his guns, and if he had been at the usual commander's post, instead of being, as he happily was, some distance in front, because he had come down with independent authority, the charge would have been all over without any one in 'C' Troop being aware of it. This is borne out by the fact that after the Troop had advanced rapidly into action in the direction of No. 2 Redoubt, the 4th Light Dragoons were, as already stated, at some considerable distance to the left front; therefore, that regiment, which belonged to the support, must have passed the left of 'C' Troop, but of course out of view, before Brandling galloped back, calling, "Mount! Mount!" The 4th when thus seen were in compact order, and moving rather towards the foot of the Fedioukine hills: that is, the distances from front to rear, between the different bodies composing the regiment could be clearly seen through ; if the 4th in column had been going straight away towards the Russians, those spaces could not have been seen by 'C' Troop, for then the different bodies would have been covering each other from the Troop, instead of in the lateral direction. The regiment had evidently gone out by the right of the Russian broken-up Battery, but those in 'C' Troop knew nothing of this Battery at the time. There was then no smoke from guns in that part of the plain, nor was there sufficient indication of a Battery having been broken up to force itself on the view: that is, there were no groups of horses, either standing in teams or lying disabled on the ground. The 4th were easily distinguished by their tall cylindrical-shaped chacos, by the figures of the men in their jackets, and by the white pouch belt. They were the body of troops that caught the eye at the instant. Other things beyond them seemed too distant to attract the attention of Artillerymen busy with their guns. 'C' Troop naturally considered the front of the battle as being on the ground about No. 2 Redoubt, which was much nearer to them, and from which there was then a Russian cannonade. The belief at the moment was that we were attempting to retake that part of the ridge. No one in the Troop then knew the exact nature of the attack in the outer plain, nor the full extent of the havoc wrought, till they saw the last of the contingents of disabled coming back, and the regiments of the Brigade with their sadly thinned ranks.

In some plans the left of the Heavies during the attack of the Light Brigade is shown to be farther into the middle of the outer plain than was the case.

Unquestionably if before the Light Brigade attacked, both Troops of Horse Artillery had been ordered to make a vigorous advance into action towards No. 2 Redoubt, to have distracted the enemy's fire, the losses to the Brigade even going in the direction they actually took, would have been less, but with a timely explanation to the Artillery as to when they should cease firing, the Brigade, during its advance, and as soon as it had passed the line of our left gun, might have thrown forward the left shoulder, have swept over the hills about No. 2 Redoubt, probably with little loss, and, most likely, have re-taken that work. There was the very man on the ground to have given effect to the wish, if requested, in the same way he did at Bulganak. Brigadier-General Strangways' appearance was known to every soldier in the Army, and he was much spoken about by linesmen long after the war was over. No one in the field was so easily found as he, with his snow-white hair and moustache, and black busby; he was the only Horse Artillery officer who rode apart from the Troops: he even dispensed with an orderly, lest he might weaken a gun detachment; and the Brigade-Major, in his cocked hat, only helped by contrast to make the Brigadier the more conspicuous. There were Field Batteries and Infantry then, not far off, to have backed up this movement. We know for certain that the Allies had $23\frac{1}{2}$ squadrons, but if there were, as some say, two regiments of Chasseurs d'Afrique, it made $27\frac{1}{2}$ squadrons; and the Allied Cavalry, taken as a whole, were quite a match for the 34 squadrons of Russians. There was no other safe way of attempting to re-take the position than by advancing along the crest and slopes of the ridge, and winning it back bit by bit. If this had been successfully carried out, it must have gone hard indeed with the Russians at the bottom of the outer plain, and it is doubtful if they would have got back all their troops and guns over the bridges and fords, much less have taken away our captured guns, for their people on the

Formation of Light Brigade.

Fedioukine Hills were, in great measure, a fixture, and must have thought of making good their own retreat by the Tractir Bridge, in the event of the others giving way. The Brigade was, however, sent by the most fatal path of all, being exposed to three sides of an immense parallelogram of fire, and every inch of this ground ought to have been better known to our authorities at Balaclava, who had been free to ride over it, than it was to the newly-arrived army under Liprandi.

Before the attack the Light Brigade was formed up thus: First line, the 13th on the right, 17th in the centre, 11th on the left: two squadrons each regiment. Second line, the 8th (one squadron and a half) on the right, the 4th (two squadrons) on the left, under Lord George Paget; so that of the first line, the first squadron, the right half of the second squadron, and the sixth squadron would be uncovered.

At the same time that the advance was ordered, the 11th were ordered not to move with the first line. According to Kinglake, pages 400 and 401 (it is Kinglake's 4th volume which relates to the Battle of Balaclava), the Brigade was carefully divided into three lines to expose as few men as possible, and the 11th were to form a second line with the 4th. Lord George does not state that he received any orders about the 8th being ordered from his line, to form a third line by themselves. At any rate the 11th were not sent to align themselves on the 4th, nor were they immediately sent behind the 17th to form the second of the three lines. Lord George says he received no instructions about the 11th; but, whatever the intention was, it did not save the regiment, for their losses were heavy.

In the regimental historical account of the battle, drawn up at the time by the Commanding Officer, Colonel Douglas, it is stated that " the order to attack the Russians was then given, and at the same time the 11th were ordered to fall back. The regiment thus acting independently, a deadly fire of shot and shell assailed them on both flanks and in front, and men fell on all sides from the enemy's Riflemen on the right." Colonel Douglas always strenuously disputed Lord G. Paget's claim to having authority over the 11th at any period of the charge or retreat. As a matter of fact, the regiment was more or less in echelon to the 17th, during the advance to the Battery. The first line, with Cardigan in front, led straight at the Russian Battery; the 11th led so that their right went through the right of the Battery. The support, however, did not follow in correct line, for the 8th bore to their right. Beyond all doubt, any one in authority riding near the first line at the beginning of the advance could have made a moderate change of direction without halting, and with the greatest ease, if he so desired, by bringing forward the shoulder, and instructing the Brigadier and officer of direction where they were to lead to, or up to about 400 yards, Cardigan could have been easily stopped altogether, and at this distance men and horses were being knocked over. The Russian Artillery intervals seemed to be fully as large as our own, and the extent of front of the Battery of eight guns would probably be 140 yards. It is believed that the complement of non-commissioned officers and men, excluding sergeant-majors and trumpeters, actually in the ranks of the first line did not exceed 230; halve these by placing them in two ranks, and add for three-squadron intervals (squadron intervals were less in those days), and it would give about 145 yards, so that the line, even if intact, would have nearly fitted within the flank guns. This gives an idea how much less in numbers the two regiments were than one four-squadron regiment is on parade at home. At any rate, they were so decimated that there was ample room for those left to get through the intervals between guns without any check of pace, and then some, at least, set to work to deal with the Artillerymen, while Lord Cardigan states that he continued on until he was confronted by a portion of the enemy's Cavalry beyond the Battery. The 11th, after a short halt at the Battery, bore more to their left, and made a dash at some detached Russian Cavalry; but this body of Russians gave no chance of collision, for they fell back, pursued by the 11th, till the latter found themselves in front of the main body, drawn up with their backs to the Aqueduct. The 11th, although alone, were not vigorously attacked. They commenced an orderly retreat, followed by the Russians, and there was hand-to-hand fighting all along with those more adventurous than the rest. At this time they were joined by the 4th, when both regiments fronted and checked the further advance of the enemy. Suddenly, however, two squadrons of their Lancers appeared in rear, having come out of the Tractir Bridge Road, and there was nothing left but for the two regiments to go about again and cut their way through, when some desperate hand-to-hand encounters took place. This is taken substantially from Colonel Douglas's historical account, so far as concerns his regiment.

When 'C' Troop retired from their most advanced position, after supporting the attack of the Light Brigade, to a second position more or less on the ridge, the guns were unlimbered, but there was no immediate firing from this point. A great many wounded and disabled had already passed to the rear by the left of the Troop. At this time Lord Cardigan rode up at a quiet pace, *i.e.* the same pace at which some of his men had ridden up before him, from the direction of the enemy in the outer plain, and halted within a yard or two of the left of No. 6 Gun, which was fairly on the crest of the ridge, the other guns of the Troop being more or less on the slope towards the inner plain. He had no trumpeter, orderly, or orderly officer with him, but he was attended by Cornet Yates, Adjutant of the 11th Hussars, who was in the uniform of that regiment, and who rode one or two yards behind. This officer had been acting as Brigade-Major to the Light Brigade during the illness of Lieut.-Colonel Mayow, the proper Brigade-Major, but the latter came on the ground before the advance began. It seems doubtful, however, whether he reported himself to Lord Cardigan as effective or not, but at any rate there was either no time or no inclination to properly relieve Cornet Yates, and send him back to his exclusive regimental duties. As a consequence there were two Brigade-Majors officiating with this Brigade of nine squadrons and a half, which circumstance could not well conduce to harmony. It was besides no secret that Lord Cardigan and Colonel Mayow were not the very best friends; those in 'C' Troop observed this on the few Divine Service and other parades they attended with the Cavalry at Devna.

Lord Cardigan was in the full-dress pelisse (buttoned) and uniform of the 11th, generally, and he rode a chestnut horse very distinctly marked and of grand appearance: no officer in the Cavalry Division at all resembled him in face, figure, or seat on horseback. The horse seemed to have had enough of it, and his lordship appeared to have been knocked about, but was cool and collected. He returned his sword, undid a little of the front of his dress, and pulled down his under-clothing under his waist-belt (military men who have even had a simple set-to at single-stick, mounted, with a sword-belt on, will easily understand this). He

then, in a quiet way, as if rather talking to himself,
said, "I tell you what it is—those instruments of theirs,"
alluding to the Russian weapons, "are deuced blunt;
they tickle up one's ribs!" Having re-fastened his
uniform, he pulled his revolver out of his saddle-holster
as if the thought had only just struck him, and said,
"And here's this d——d thing I have never thought
of till now." He then replaced it, drew his sword, and
said, "Well, we've done our share of the work;" and
pointing up towards the Chasseurs d'Afrique, in our
left rear, added, "It is time they gave those dappled
gentry a chance"—this had reference to the colour of
their horses. After this, he asked, "Has any one seen
my regiment?" and the men, thinking it was the regiment
dressed, like himself, in the crimson overalls,
answered, "No, sir." The men inferred from the
question that he knew nothing as to the position of
the 11th. The thing did not occupy a minute and
a half or two minutes. He then turned his horse and
went further back by the outer side of the ridge in the
direction in which some of his men, wounded and others,
had retired before he came to the gun at all. While he
was at No. 6 gun, he could not have seen his supports,
for his back was turned nearly in the direction from
which some of them came a moment or two afterwards;
indeed, no one at the gun did see those supports just
then. They did not know that Lord Cardigan had led
an attack, or how the regiments had been formed up;
in fact, they were altogether in the dark on the subject.
Brandling was three or four yards on the right of the
gun fronting towards Lord Cardigan, but not joining
in conversation, and the detachment standing at their
posts heard and saw all: no other officers or staff were
present.

A few moments after Lord Cardigan left, the 4th

Light Dragoons came obliquely across the outer plain,
either at a trot or canter, but they broke into a slower
pace as they passed within about 100 or 150 yards of
the left of 'C' Troop on their way to the rear, and at
this time the 11th Hussars were contiguous to the 4th.
While the latter regiment passed on, Lord George Paget,
its Colonel, rode over to No. 6 gun, and it so happened
that he halted on the very spot of ground Cardigan had
been on. Lord George looked like a man who had
ridden hard for a mile or two, and was heated and
excited. He said, in rather a loud tone, "It is a
d——d shame; there we had a lot of their guns and
carriages taken and received no support, and yet there
is all this Infantry about—it is a shame." It was quite
true there was a very large sprinkling of English Infantry
at this time, adjacent to that end of the ridge. Meantime, Cardigan had come back and was close behind
Lord George while he was speaking, without the latter
knowing it. Lord Cardigan stopped Lord George talking
further by calling out his name, and, on the latter turning
round, said to him in an undertone, "I am surprised,"
and tossing his head into the air, added some other
remark which was not heard. Lord George lowered
his sword to the salute, and without saying *anything*,
turned his horse and rode on after his men. Lord
Cardigan then went forward along the ridge in the
direction of the enemy, met the 8th Hussars, and returned with them. In passing the Heavies, the latter
cheered. Lord Cardigan acknowledged it with his sword,
and so passed on to the rear by the left of the Troop.
From the time that Lord Cardigan first came to No. 6
gun till he had finished speaking to Lord George Paget
and passed on in the direction of the enemy to meet the
8th, not more than four or five minutes at the outside
had elapsed.

This is a faithful account of what was seen and heard by the detachment at No. 6 gun at this momentous period of the battle, about which so much has been said and written. The detachment never thought otherwise than that both these distinguished officers had bravely done their duty. It seemed as if Lord G. Paget was only showing a reasonable or excusable amount of excitement and indignation that such an opportunity of capturing some of the Russian cannon should have been lost through want of supports; and, on the other hand, it seemed as if Lord Cardigan (who, as it was afterwards shown, had the greatest cause to grumble about his own particular supports), even in such an anxious and exciting time, and himself fresh from a personal encounter with the enemy, thought of discipline, and so suppressed any further remarks at the time from Lord George.

At this distance of time we are not absolutely positive whether Lord George or the 8th got back first. We believe it is as we have stated, but it does not in the least affect the particulars. It was on his coming the second time to the gun that Cardigan heard Lord George talking loudly, and at once interposed. If the 8th were back before Lord George, then it was on Cardigan leaving the gun the first time that he went to meet them, but whether first or second time matters little. It occurred thus: He had turned backward from the gun when the first cheer was given by some Heavies. He then halted, turned about as if to to see what it was for, saw it was in compliment to the 8th returning, trotted towards them, turned about in front of Colonel Shewell, and took up the "walk." This portion of Heavies, which cheered, had just that moment moved from the outer slope to the crest, and halted in column, their rearmost Troop or squadron being about fifty yards rather to the left front of No. 6 gun: that is, their right was barely clear of the front of the gun. And now occurred something rather painful to witness. As the 8th came in view of No. 6 Detachment (who were looking past the left-rear corner of the Heavies' column for the returning regiment), it was seen Colonel Shewell was in front, and Colonel Mayow behind on the left of the other officers. The moment Cardigan got his back turned round to the 8th, Colonel Mayow pointed towards him, shook his head, and made signs to officers on the left of the Heavies, as much as to say, "See him; he has taken care of himself." Men here and there in the ranks of the 8th also pointed, and made signs to some of the rearmost men of the Heavies, whom they were passing left hand to left hand. Colonel Shewell neither saw this nor took any part in it; there was, as well, a little undertalk from one side to the other consequent upon the excitement. Of course Cardigan did not know what was going on behind him while he was smiling and raising his sword to the cheers. He was thus, in a way, held up to ridicule, not only to some of his own Brigade before they had completed their retreat, but also to the rearmost troops or squadrons of this portion of the Heavies. Now, if this was the first seen of Cardigan during the charge by some of these private soldiers in the ranks of the 8th (which was also Major Calthorpe's regiment), will it not help, in a great measure, to account for many of the reports which were afterwards circulated?

It is a mistake to suppose the Russian skirmishers on the Fedioukines were quite silenced by the Chasseurs. Jets of Russian musket smoke were seen on the top of the hills from a fire directed at the Chasseur skirmishers themselves. This accounts for the quicker pace of our people retiring from that direction, because they were longer under fire, whereas the 8th were enabled to take up the "walk" earlier in their retreat. Cardigan's line of retreat was between that of the 8th and 4th. There was then a sort of tacit keeping away from him for a time; no congratulations on his escape were offered him in the hearing of 'C' Troop. People began to think he was to blame for what had befallen his Brigade; but when Lord Raglan came down, and it was seen to what quarter he first went and his angry gesticulations, it was evident all the blame was not with Cardigan, although he appeared much cut up when he re-passed No. 6 Gun after his interview with the Commander-in-Chief.

The question of the support given Cardigan may be summed up thus: Lord George states Cardigan rode back to him and said (*vide* page 170 of the Journal), "We are ordered to make an attack to the front; I expect your best support," and Lord George answers, "You shall have my best support." Then Cardigan galloped back to his first line, and the attack began. Lord George adds (page 209 of his "Journal") that, as far as he knew, no one else heard Lord Cardigan give him this "solemn injunction." In proof of having given his best support, Lord George, at page 178 of his "Journal," says he was 100 yards in rear at first; the first line started at a brisk trot, and he followed at a decreased pace to get his proper distance of 200 yards, giving the word "4th direct," he himself being in front of the right or directing squadron of the 4th, and Colonel Shewell in front of the left squadron of the 8th; the two officers would thus be only about forty yards apart. Before proceeding far Lord George found it necessary to increase his pace, to keep up with the increasing pace of the first line; and, after the first 300 yards, his whole energies were exerted in shouting, "Keep up; come on." Afterwards the 8th began to incline away to their right, and then Lord George, with a remarkably good cigar in his mouth, reins in one hand, sword in the other, his overalls a mass of blood from wounded horses, and Cardigan's words haunting him, did all he could, by voice and gesture, to bring the 8th to their place in his line. Colonel Shewell, he says, heard all his shouts, but was unable to rectify the interval, and he adds that, as regards Colonel Shewell, he knew he was dealing with one of the most honourable, gallant, conscientious, and single-minded men he ever associated with. The whole of the foregoing is in Lord George's own words, and the character of Colonel Shewell is the same, word for word, as that given at page 331, "Kinglake's History"; indeed, a great deal of Kinglake's account of the battle is precisely similar to Lord George's. Lord George then says the 8th not only inclined away from him, but fell behind the dressing, and after that he saw no more of them.

Meanwhile, having seen that the 11th had disengaged from the first line, Lord George endeavoured, by a still more increased pace, to form a junction with that regiment. This was his second increase, but he does not further define it, or say if it was a "gallop out," or merely a "canter." He saw terrible evidences of the slaughter of the first line, from the bleeding objects which lay in his path. About this time the first line, which had been in the centre of the valley, now inclined to their right, and the 11th inclined to their left, and by the time he got to the guns, he had so overtaken the 11th that his front rank was nearly in line with their rear rank. He believes the number of guns to be eighteen, that the ten on the proper left were attacked by the first line, and subsequently by the 8th; that the 4th attacked the next six, and the 11th the remaining two. All the foregoing is from his "Journal"; and

Kinglake, at page 274 of his History, as if speaking for Lord George, says, "Lord Cardigan's words haunted him, and it seemed to him (Lord George) that no evil was so great as the evil of lagging behind." Lord George does not profess to say he made personal inquiries for Lord Cardigan at the guns.

Now come certain statements which, to any one who has ridden in the mounted arms, are so difficult to reconcile with the idea that the best support was given by the rearmost line, or with the account of the distance it was behind. Lord George (page 208 of his "Journal") prefers to call the "Charge" an "Advance." He was aware of the weakness of the four squadrons, first line, before they started, and he saw the carnage they were undergoing.

Kinglake, at page 291, says, "It was before our supports had come down, and whilst the English were still combating in the Battery, or pushing their onset beyond it, that the enemy for a moment exercised dominion in rear of the first line." Could the enemy have swept in from the halt, without previous preparation, along a front of eighteen guns (the number Lord George supposed there were), occupying probably 840 yards' frontage, or even Kinglake's estimated twelve guns, and have then exercised dominion, while the supporting line, already at its speed, and with its object in front, was passing over a distance of 300 or 400 yards? At page 302, Kinglake, it is stated: "A party of the 17th Lancers, under a sergeant, were busy hindering the enemy withdrawing their guns." This must have occupied some short time, and then Colonel Mayow appears on the scene, pistol in hand, and tells these men if they remain in the Battery they will be cut to pieces. There is no smoke to prevent him seeing the men, but he seems not to have seen the 4th coming on in support, and he says he could not see Lord Cardigan. If this statement is strictly correct, it would be significant of the distance Lord George was behind; and Lord George himself says (page 70 of his " Journal "), " When I got to the guns and saw all their host advancing, I looked in vain for the first line, and could never account for them till I came back and said, 'I am afraid the 13th and 17th are annihilated, for I saw nothing of them.'" This seems to be an admission that the survivors of the first line had got completely away after their brush with the Artillerymen, before Lord George reached the Battery. It is also an admission that there was no smoke at the Battery, otherwise he could not have seen the advancing Russian host, which were, of course, beyond the Battery, and which, oddly enough, Kinglake says, had about this time been driven in on their second reserve by Col. Mayow and 15 men. The Colonel was a fortunate man to have been able to accomplish this.

At page 285, Kinglake, it is stated that a few horsemen on the left of the 17th outflanked the proper right of the Battery. Lord George is in conflict with this also, for he makes it appear that he led the 4th at that exact part of the Battery, into which, Captain Morris says, Lord Cardigan led, followed by the 1st Squadron of the 17th. To prove Lord George's plan correct, it would be necessary to show that the whole of the first line, except about twenty men under Morris, made a sharp right incline when at the " charge "—an almost impossible thing to do—and that the twenty under Morris made a sharp left incline, leaving such an extensive gap that the 4th, when they got up, could see nothing of the first line. The idea of Cardigan with the first line choosing to incline across the muzzles of the guns, and so remaining longer under fire, instead of passing at once into the intervals, is unlikely.

Kinglake, at page 352, mentions the case in which an officer of the first line, during the attack, and when not far from the Russian Battery, had his horse shot under him; but that he had time to catch a loose horse, mount, join the 4th when they came on, and advance with them to the guns. This must have occurred after the pace had been put on; and it is not doubted, but to any one of experience, the problem presents itself: Could the officer have accomplished all this by himself in the open plain while the supporting line was galloping a distance of 350 or 400 yards; and, if farther back than this, they were hardly giving best support.

Now as to the support given by the 8th, at page 315 (Kinglake), it is stated, "Colonel Shewell, with the 8th, maintaining a well-steadied trot, continued his advance past the proper left of the now silent Battery, pressed on 300 or 400 yards farther, and then halted from three to five minutes in a region out of harm's way, where he seems to have expected an order would reach him." It is not stated from whom he expected the order. There was no smoke from the Battery then, but, like Lord George, Colonel Shewell seems not to have made personal inquiries for Lord Cardigan at the moment: at least, at pages 328 and 329, Kinglake, it is stated that the 8th, having resumed their advance (not by the direct rear of the Battery, but keeping rather to the circuitous route), Colonel Shewell meets Colonel Mayow, and asks if he has seen Lord Cardigan, and the latter answers he has not, for he had previously come to the conclusion that he could not see him at the Battery; and about this exact time (*vide* page 339 of Kinglake) Lord George, who has also not gone on by the direct rear of the Battery, is made to say to one of his officers, "We are in a desperate scrape: what the devil shall we do? Has any one seen Lord Cardigan?"

If Colonel Shewell had only cast his eyes behind him during the time he was at the halt, he would have seen there was no support whatever coming on, and he would then have known that there could be no one senior to himself from whom to expect an order, except Lord Cardigan, whose line he had not followed straight, and Lord George, from whom he had ridden away. It seems incredible that a regiment of only one weak squadron, and a half, with a Lieut.-Colonel, Major, Adjutant, and seven other officers, if left to themselves, could not have led straight after three squadrons,—for that is how they covered at the halt,—but should have deliberately begun easing off to their right, and going away from the dressing hand, so that by the time the Battery was reached, they were altogether outside the left flank of it. This contradicts Lord George's idea that the 8th assisted in the attack of ten guns on the proper left. In saying this, however, of the 8th, it must be understood that nothing disparaging is here intended towards that regiment, nor is it imputed that those composing it moved in any other way than in conformity to orders. The statement of Kinglake, as to Morris and some men of the 17th being outside the proper right flank of the Battery, tends to confirm the Russian account that it was a Battery of eight guns only (No. 3, Don Battery); and the statement of Lord George, that he could see nothing of the 13th and 17th, leads one to the conclusion that he must have been very far behind, or else that there is some error in the account given of the doings of Colonel Mayow at the Battery.

Lord George says he was unable to quit the right squadron of the 4th, and go the short distance which separated him from Colonel Shewell, to find out what that officer meant by leaving his post in the line; but commanding officers, when the line is at the trot, have often to move across the front, at the increased pace, to point out and correct any glaring loss of interval, without in the least disturbing the moving base, which keeps on at an unvarying pace, and this is not looked upon as a difficult duty. There was also the alternative of pulling the base squadron of the 4th up to the walk for the instant, and insisting on the 8th coming to their proper place, for the keeping of the support together was the primary duty.

The squadrons of the 4th were only about twenty-six or twenty-seven file each before starting (*vide* Regimental State in Lord George's Journal), and therefore easily handled; and the greater the casualties, the greater the need for staunchly seconding the man who was leading the attack in the thick of the fire.

At the time the 8th were at the "halt," Lord George was "a passive observer at the silent guns." Now the ground across between the 4th and 8th was pretty level; the 13th, which led at the proper left of the Battery, was practically annihilated, so there was nothing to materially interfere with the view of either Lord George or Colonel Shewell, and they could not have been so far from each other as to have made the uniform of their regiments unrecognizable. The busby, with its red bag flying, worn by the 8th, was at that time a scarce and remarkable head-dress, and might have served to distinguish that regiment; for the 11th, who also wore it, Lord George knew were on his left front, and there were no other busbies with the Eastern Army except in the Horse Artillery.

At this moment Lord Cardigan says he was in personal encounter with some Cossacks, slightly wounded, and nearly dismounted (*vide* page 404, "Kinglake's History"). Assuming the number of guns to be eight, this encounter of Cardigan's would probably be going on from 180 to 200 yards or thereabouts from Colonel Shewell's left when halted.

Kinglake, in his plan, page 252, shows the position of the guns to be about 300 yards below the entrance towards the Tractir Bridge, and midway in the plain, where it is half a mile across on the level. Lord George in his plan shows their position to be about 400 or 500 yards below that of Kinglake. There would, very likely, be eight or more waggons, as well as eight limbers. Some of the drivers, when they saw the gunners being cut down, tried to make off with their teams and carriages, and in this way the Battery got spread over more ground; so it is easy to understand our people may have magnified the number of guns. The survivors stated at the time that the last round was like a salvo; had there been eighteen guns, a salvo of grape concentrated on the four reduced squadrons, must have emptied every remaining saddle. The situation of the great bed of graves, *débris*, etc., as seen by 'C' Troop the following year, was quite in accordance with Kinglake's idea of the position.

As to the supposed position of the Russian Battery, it may be stated that on the morning after the reoccupation of the position by the Allies, when 'C' Troop exercised over the ground, there was, about midway across the plain, a something which had very much the appearance of the remains of a low breast-work or narrow bank, with hollows here and there, as if for embrasures; but it had sunk and packed, and was so overgrown with coarse vegetation, that it was difficult to trace out. Whether it was thrown up by the Russians on the day of the battle, after the Light Brigade Charge, or subsequently, will probably never be known; but it had not the solid turf of the surrounding ground, and it gave one the impression that it had been constructed about the time of the battle, and was soon afterwards partially razed.

It is not generous to say (*vide* page 214 of Lord George's "Journal") that "if Cardigan during his advance had looked to his right, he would have seen our guns in the different redoubts which it was Lord Raglan's intention he should attack, and, seeing them, he would have known that those were the guns he was to capture, and the fatal charge would never have been made," or that he could have "thrown up his left shoulders" so easily after speed was put on, and under a destructive fire. Lord George says he himself was unable to keep his own line, which was fewer in numbers, together, going on the straight, and with covering and distance only to attend to. Lord Raglan, however, did not order "an attack" by Lord Cardigan, but that the "Cavalry were to advance rapidly to the front, and try to prevent the enemy carrying away the guns, etc.," the guns, as every one knew, being on the ridge and not in the valley. The front of the Light Brigade was a newly-made front, the making of which neither Lord Raglan nor Lord Cardigan had anything to do with (*vide* "Kinglake," pages 224-225, as to Lord Raglan's instructions, and how they were carried out; and page 401 of the same, for Lord Cardigan's first apprehensions as to his new position). In fact, looking at the best maps, the left of the Light Brigade could hardly have been out of gun range from the Fedioukine Hills, in the position it was moved to before Lord Raglan's order arrived. There was nothing to prevent the Russian troops at the lower end of the valley from being seen before the Light Brigade moved off, and any traveller visiting the locality could judge of this matter for himself.

The foregoing quotations from Lord George's Journal

imply that Lord Raglan's order was read, or the tenor of it given, to Lord Cardigan, and that the choice to charge or not lay, in a great measure, with that officer, though he (Lord George) knew Lord Cardigan had distinctly denied this (*vide* "Kinglake," page 248), which book Lord George says he had read and re-read with avidity, and which was printed eleven years before Lord George's "Journal." But this part of the idea is finally disposed of by Lord Lucan himself, where he says, "I galloped far down the valley, having directed that I was to be followed by the Heavy Brigade, etc." Why far down the valley, having four of our captured guns up on the ridge towards his right, and having the Light Brigade on his left front, if the direction of the attack was not strictly in consonance with the orders he had given Lord Cardigan? And Kinglake clenches this by saying, at page 236, that Lord Lucan in his despatch two days after the battle, acknowledged he knew the guns meant in Lord Raglan's order were our guns which were lost by the Turks on the ridge. Kinglake in his plan at page 252, represents Lord Lucan to be so far down the valley as to be nearly abreast of the ground about No. 2 Redoubt, and the first line not yet into the Battery. Be it remembered that at this time the 8th are said to be at the trot, and also that the Russians were soon to sweep in and exercise dominion in rear of the first line, Lord George not being far enough down to prevent them doing so.

In confirmation of Kinglake's idea of Lord Lucan's position, we know that Captain Charteris A.D.C. was killed a good distance down the valley, for Lord Lucan consulted Brandling in front of 'C' Troop as to the possibility of recovering the body, and Brandling, brave and venturesome though he was, thought it could not be attempted. As to seeing the Redoubts, why every soldier in the Army knew about them; and no doubt Cardigan would have been very glad to have thrown up his left shoulder, and attacked the position at No. 2, if he thought he dare do so, instead of going past it to the distant Russian troops in his front, and following out what he believed to be his orders; but clearly No. 2 Redoubt must have been enveloped in smoke from the enemy's guns near that part, and Canrobert's or No. 1, holding three of our captured guns, was on quite different ground.

Lord George states, "he believes no one when he started was insensible to the desperate undertaking about to be engaged in." If so, it might be reasonably expected that, as next in seniority, having seen the slaughter of the first line, and having promised his best support, he would on arrival at the Battery have sought out Cardigan for instructions as to whether he was to go on or what he was to do, for he must have supposed that the Brigadier, if alive, had charged in before him. The 4th were at the halt, or nearly so; and it would have been a good opportunity, as the guns were silent, to have brought the 8th, who could not have been far off, to their proper place in line. Colonel Mayow, if then present, in his conspicuously plain blue dress, ought to have been easily seen. It would also have been a good opportunity for Colonel Mayow, if he saw the 4th, to have consulted with Lord George about missing Cardigan at such a crisis. Lord George, however, led the 4th out of the Battery in a direction bearing to his left, and in this exact state that Regiment was seen by 'C' Troop when they first looked into the outer valley.

At page 206 of his Journal, Lord George says, "I ought to have reported Colonel Shewell for disobedience of orders, but I determined to talk the matter over with him, and most amply was I rewarded." He does not give Colonel Shewell's excuses, or any hint of the forces that were at work which prevented that officer backing up his chief in the straight line of the attack; but goes on to say, "bear in mind the difficulty of controlling a body of Cavalry that has once got out of hand." The 8th could not have been very much out of hand at the trot, nor could the 4th have been so if they were at such a pace as to admit of the Russians exercising dominion in rear of the first line.

Withholding Colonel Shewell's reasons seems unfair to that officer, and is decidedly so to Lord Cardigan, whom Lord George on the same page charges with not having brought his Brigade out of action as he ought to have done, though he excuses himself for not being able in the early stages of the advance to put on a spurt and go the short distance of about forty yards across the front to Colonel Shewell, and stop him going away, notwithstanding that he had a few minutes previously faithfully promised Cardigan the best support of the line entrusted to his command. There were twenty-one combatant officers with these three and a half weak squadrons of Lord George's, and probably not one of that number had been hit at the time the 8th inclined away.

Lord George considers he ought to have reported Colonel Shewell. Quite so, but with how much greater cause, apparently, might Cardigan have reported Lord George, who had it within his power, certainly in the early stages of the advance, to have brought Colonel Shewell back to his proper place; whereas Cardigan, being in front of all, could not well have gone back and brought the support up to the regulated distance so long as Lord George was permitting the enemy to exercise dominion between the two lines.

Then, as to Lord George's charge against Cardigan, "of not having brought his Brigade out of action as he ought to have done," it is grating to the feelings of any unbiassed survivor of the Battle, so far as it concerns the supports. How was it possible for Cardigan, when he was pursued back to the Battery, even if the supports had been in his view, to have turned about, his pursuers still after him, and their number probably increasing, to follow Lord George some hundreds of yards? and then, by making another turn, have gone across through the enemy 400 or 500 yards more after Colonel Shewell, or *vice versa*, and thus have gathered up his supports? in fact, before getting back he must have made a circuit of the lower part of the valley, to accomplish this. If it were possible to have done so, had either of these officers who had ridden so wide of the true point of their Brigadier's attack any right to expect to be thus followed? One cannot help noticing how Lord George has twisted Cardigan about (if we may use that expression) to make ends meet. He first, at page 195 of his Journal, has him in the centre of the valley for a considerable distance, then, inclining to his right as he approaches the guns, and attacking the ten on the left; then at page 204, he represents him going headlong to the guns without looking to right or left; at page 210, as leading the first line down the right of the valley, and this he says is fair reasoning that Lord Cardigan was unaware of the fate to which his personal retreat had left the second line, and while he in a qualified way acquits him of having passed the 4th in his retreat, he on page 214 says, "there certainly still remains the question, how Lord Cardigan in his retreat could have failed to meet the 8th in their advance."

Seeing, however, that after the 4th Light Dragoons were observed in the distant position already indicated, 'C' Troop had time to fire some rounds at the enemy, then limber up, retire to another position and again unlimber, before Cardigan came towards them from the direction of the enemy, it was perfectly impossible for that officer, in his retreat, to have passed his supporting regiments. Lord George says, "that he was the man who in the greatest degree had to complain of Cardigan's conduct, that he considered himself the man the most aggrieved at it, having always been of opinion that it was his bounden duty, after the solemn injunction he had given, to see him (Lord George) out of it; and that Cardigan when forced to retire should have left no stone unturned to find him out, etc." This is an interested opinion, and Cardigan was not alive to retaliate. By the way, "forced to retire" is a mild way of putting the case for the Brigadier; who alone, or nearly so, was outnumbered and overmatched in personal combat; though Lord George takes care to describe his own condition, under less trying circumstances and with his officers and men about him, as a "desperate scrape."

In a letter of Lord Lucan, dated 30th November, 1854 (page 417, "Kinglake"), it is stated Cardigan made objections to the advance, that Lord Lucan entirely agreed with those objections; but said, "The order is from Lord Raglan." At pages 401 and 249 of the same, Lord Lucan's words are, "I am aware of it, I know it, but Lord Raglan will have it, and we have no choice but to obey."

At pages 147 and 248 of the same, it is stated Lord Lucan directed Cardigan "to advance, without enjoining an attack," and that he either "read over or gave him the tenor of Lord Raglan's order." This last Lord Cardigan denies, and (*vide* page 250 of "Kinglake") had no recollection of having received the first. Colonel Douglas says nothing about any order being read to Cardigan; merely that Lord Lucan ordered Lord Cardigan to attack the Russians, and this is strengthened by what Lord George says; for Cardigan would hardly go to him and say, "We are ordered to make an attack," if he did not so believe it, nor would he be likely to ask for "best support" if he thought he was merely to make a quiet steady advance, and there is also Lord George's idea that all were impressed beforehand with the desperate character of the undertaking.

Taking all these things into consideration, how could Cardigan have thought of stopping until he had crossed swords with some portion of the enemy? What an example of wavering he would have set his men if, for instance, when at the gallop, he had suddenly dropped back through one of his squadron intervals on pretence of seeing where Lord Lucan was! Where the Heavies were, and if the attack was really meant, how was he to see through the ranks of his line without thus dropping back through an interval, and this while his men were falling thickly in view of Lord Lucan? As a matter of fact, had he so dropped back, he would have seen Lord Lucan at the "gallop" in his right rear almost, if not quite within bugle-sounding distance of him, the Heavies not on the crest, but moving down the slope into the valley after him, and no appearance of sham or feint about the matter. This exactly explains how Colonel Douglas may have been misled; if he happened to look towards his right, or towards the right of the 8th, he would possibly have seen Lord Lucan and staff at the "gallop" (they were easily distinguished in their plain blue coats; one of them wore an oilskin cover over his cocked hat, which was very noticeable, and all were without their hat feathers); the Heavies in motion, having Scarlett in their front in the remarkable helmet and blue coat, with his separate group of staff, and every appearance of a general advance. He knew the French Cavalry were near his left before he started; and in his remarks (*vide* Lord George's Journal) he says, "I thought all along I would have been supported."

It is clear Cardigan was powerless to make his own arrangements about supports. We may feel sure, if he could take the precaution of going backward to warn Lord George, he would certainly, if he had had the authority, have added to the warning; let the 4th take ground at once to their right, and cover and follow the 13th, and, when you come abreast of the 11th, bring them on with you, they covering the 17th, for the 8th are to fall behind and form a third line by themselves; or would he not most likely have placed the 4th himself, as that should have been the primary move? He could not then have imagined there would be any other change attempted, for if he had thought the 11th were to form a second line by themselves (see pages 250-251, "Kinglake," where it says, "As altered at the moment of directing the attack, the 4th and 8th formed a third line, the 11th a second"), he would without doubt, as he was returning to the first line, have warned Colonel Douglas also as to "best support," but the 11th must have been ordered out of the first line at the very moment of moving off, and Lord Lucan did not depute Cardigan to do it, or even take him with him to see it done (*vide* "Kinglake," page 401, where it says, "Cardigan strenuously opposed the 11th being removed, but Lord Lucan moved across his front, and directed them not to advance, etc."). Strong proof as to this latter point is that Cardigan, on his return from the charge, asked men of 'C' Troop for tidings of his regiment.

"Kinglake," at page 276, says, "Lord George during the advance, without knowing it, brought the supports to the exact form the Divisional General intended to order." If Kinglake is correct in this, as well as in

Lords Cardigan and George Paget. 187

what he says at pages 274-275, about the orders given the 11th never having been communicated to Lord George, about the officers of the 8th considering theirs the directing regiment, about Colonel Shewell being resolute in keeping down the pace, and the two squadron leaders of the 4th not suffering themselves to be hurried, although Lord George is crying out, "Keep up," while all the time the first line is fading away in the distance, and their riderless horses everywhere around, then the whole affair shows a lamentable want of unity, which, under such serious circumstances, is quite distressing to dwell upon.

"Kinglake," page 297, says, "It might be thought that since Lord Cardigan had left a main part of his Brigade in the fangs of the Russian Army, he, when resolved to fall back, would have sought to turn his retrograde journey to a saving purpose by flying to Lord Lucan or General Scarlett, and entreating some squadrons might be pushed forward to extricate the remains of his Brigade." This point should be looked at in a fair and liberal way. At page 400, "Kinglake," Lord Lucan states, "So soon as the Light Brigade moved off, I instructed my A.D.C. to have me followed by the Heavy Brigade. I then galloped on, and when far down the valley, I observed the Heavy Brigade in my rear suffering, etc. I would not allow them to be sacrificed, as had been the Light Brigade. I caused them to be halted, etc." Thus, so soon as the 8th Hussars have started on their well-steadied trot, Lord Lucan starts on his gallop, going by the right of the ground over which the 8th are passing; and here one wonders which reached the point far down the valley first—the Divisional General at the gallop, or the regiment that started nearly at the same instant at the well-steadied trot, and which would not pay attention to the shouts of Lord

George, but would insist on inclining towards the ground the Divisional General was going over.

Lord Lucan then (*vide* pages 322, 324, and 325), having perceived he had entered on the path of destruction, accepted the cruel alternative, let the chain break asunder, and said to the Acting-Adjutant-General, "They have sacrificed the Light Brigade; they shall not the Heavy, if I can help it." Two successive movements in retreat were then made to get the Heavies out of fire, where they accordingly remained halted, Lord Lucan judging that position sufficiently advanced to protect the Light Cavalry against pursuit. If the reader can fancy himself standing at the point where the Heavies are out of fire, the 4th, 8th, and 11th being still down the valley, but numbers of wounded from all five regiments passing by him, he can form an idea of the amount of protection the Light Brigade had against pursuit. This is exactly how the Divisional Staff saw it. There they were looking on.

The risk to be incurred and the uselessness of the object was obvious to all, before Lord Lucan could have got far down the valley. He says he waited till the Brigade had moved off, but horses were tumbled over by cannon shot in Cardigan's line soon after it was set in motion. They lay even farther back than where Nolan's body was found. Brandling's exclamation about it while the Troop was mounting before moving off to the support was this: Holding his hand in the air and letting it fall on the front of the saddle, "My God! there's a bad business over here; they've sent the Light Brigade into the heart of the enemy's position. They'll never get back; they're being shot down right and left!"

Now cases often occur at large camps of manœuvres, where an efficient officer, against his own will, is ordered by a senior, to take his regiment or command, whatever it may be, into some position in which the umpires pronounce it to be annihilated, and they are left to stand or sit at ease; people remarking, "Oh, they've made a mess of it, they're wiped out in disgrace, etc., etc," and so the officer who suffers naturally looks with dislike on the one who has been the cause of the mishap; keeps away from him, and gives him the widest berth he can for a time. In how much greater degree would this be the case in real warfare? with one, who, before he attacked, pointed out what his men would be exposed to, and received the reply, "I am aware of that;" who was further told that his front would be narrowed for him against his wishes; who knew that the line he led had been destroyed from the causes he pointed out; who had just saved his own life, solely by his sword and the good qualities of his horse; who could not see the supports of his own Brigade when in extremities; and who, if he saw Lord Lucan at all, saw him making movements in retreat away from him, with the red Cavalry, General Scarlett having no authority (*vide* "Kinglake," pages 325-326).

As to the censure for not entreating help, it has been amply shown, that, except the right of 'C' Troop, the whole mounted force, English and French, were on the crest and in the outer valley, with unimpeded view of the terrible state of affairs. General Scarlett, an elderly man, older than the Divisional General, saw it, and pointed it out (*vide* "Kinglake," page 299).

At page 254, "Kinglake," it is stated, "Colonel Mayow was busied in general with the troops, and did not ride much with the staff." But what troops, and what staff? Colonel Douglas says nothing about him, and Lord George does not speak of him, so it may be supposed he was with the first line, or with the 8th, or midway between them, or somewhere between the 8th and the Divisional Staff. Captain Morris, commanding 17th Lancers, said that "Lord Cardigan put himself in front of his right squadron and led like a gentleman, in capital style, nothing could be better" (*vide* "Kinglake," page 295). This would be No. 3 squadron in the first line. The Brigade-Major should have been in line with, close to, and supervising the three leaders, who were close in front of that particular squadron; so that his head would be turned the whole time towards Lord Cardigan, who was only four or five horses' lengths distant either on his right or left front.

If Colonel Mayow was really in this position, it may be that on the instant of arrival at the Battery, he allowed Cardigan to slip farther ahead of him, and that the unfortunate relations which existed between them prevented him from willingly and devotedly seeking out his chief at once.

There is still, however, Cornet Yates's presence with Cardigan to be accounted for; and when there are such contradictory statements, it is only natural to enquire for the probable whereabouts of Colonel Mayow in the charge down to the Battery; if he was at the proper post, he must have well known, as the officers of the 17th knew, that Lord Cardigan was in front. The ground was fairly covered with coarse dry herbage, and any dust thrown up by the Brigadier's group of two or three could not hide the view; the smoke from the bursting charges of field-shells was a mere nothing, and dispersed instantly. There was certainly the smoke at the Battery, and if Cardigan was seen to enter that, it was hard to understand how it could be impartially stated he was not at the guns, or that there could have been any great difficulty in finding him at the rear of the Battery, if he had been properly looked for. Then there is the cogent reasoning that if Cornet Yates had not been with the first line, he would be with the supports, and have gone towards the left with the 11th or 4th, or to the right with the 8th; in either of these last cases, how could he have had the opportunity of accompanying Lord Cardigan as an effective officer up to No. 6 gun?

As "Kinglake" has it, Colonel Mayow after a time took a party of the 17th on to attack the enemy in rear of the Battery; his view as to the necessity of this step being in agreement with Cardigan's, the wonder is, he did not instantly order the men on, without permitting this lengthened pause, for they probably belonged to the squadron which had been behind Cardigan; the left of the 17th had moved on under other authority.

These few practical remarks on the Light Brigade charge may perhaps not be considered out of place here, because both Lord Cardigan and Lord George Paget, on the instant of coming out of action, halted close to 'C' Troop, each relating a portion of his own doings; also, because Colonel Shewell with the 8th Hussars, accompanied by Colonel Mayow, passed out of action within three or four yards of the left of the Troop, whereas the extra Brigade-Major rode up with Lord Cardigan; and the statement of the simple facts may help to clear up disputed points. It was only at this time that Lord Cardigan, Lord George Paget, Cornet Yates, Colonel Shewell, or Colonel Mayow were with or near 'C' Troop that day, with the exception that Cardigan passed by later on, to make his report to Lord Raglan, so there can be no mistake in the matter; and the circumstance becomes more interesting when it is remembered that after Lord Cardigan and Cornet Yates were dead, quotations from Lord George's Journal were given to the public, the Journal itself being subsequently printed, in which it is made to appear that language was used at the *moment of meeting* quite dissimilar to that (and that only) which was actually spoken in the hearing of those on the left of 'C' Troop, Captain Jenyns of the 13th not being present at all. It must be clearly borne in mimd that the account here given has nothing to do with possible conversations afterwards. Captain Jenyns, who was well known, was not near 'C' Troop that day. A man writing of his day's doings may be easily mistaken as to words, time, and place; not so with others, who only see and hear him once, and that for a very limited time during that particular day or particular occasion.

The reason the Light Brigade Officers were so well known to 'C' Troop arose in this way. The 17th and 4th were quartered in the West Square, Woolwich, only two or three years before the war broke out; the 4th were subsequently quartered with Horse Artillery at Canterbury, and at Chobham Camp in 1853; the 8th, 13th, and 17th were also at Chobham. Many non-commissioned officers and men who were drafted into the Troop before leaving England had drilled with the Regiments in "Fifteen Acres" and elsewhere; the 17th were for a time at Kulali with the Troop, the 8th were near them at Varna, and there were some parades with the Brigade at Devna; so that, although the Troop belonged to the Light Division, they were continually acting with the Cavalry also, and became quite conversant with the faces and names of the officers. Cornet Yates had previously served in the 17th Lancers at Woolwich.

Colonel Mayow was indeed a fine soldier; he was well on in years, and all who witnessed his return from the charge, in command of some 17th men, minus any officer of their own, felt that he had made a name for himself, and that he could give confidence to troops in the hour of trial; this group of Lancer-men themselves seemed not a little proud of him, and they were bright and cheery.

At the same time, those who were brought in contact with him in the Crimea, and afterwards when he was Assistant-Quartermaster-General at the Curragh, knew that when once he took a thing into his head, he retained a most obstinate opinion about it, and that he was not likely to give way or compromise any differences he had with Cardigan. He was a cool, stern man of experience, and could hold his own with any one.

According to "Kinglake," page 247, Lord Cardigan, in a communication to Lord Raglan two days after the battle, when all was fresh in his memory, stated that he was ordered to attack the Russians *in the valley* with the 13th and 17th. Colonel Douglas, in his "Historical Record," drawn up when the proceedings were fresh in his memory, also states that *the attack* was ordered, and that the 11th were ordered to fall back, thus acting independently. Lord George does not say, if after the first line moved off, he was timed or instructed in any way as to distance, pace, etc., or if he was aware of Colonel Shewell having received other instructions that did not come through him (Lord George). Military men must judge for themselves as to whether Lord Cardigan's authority was narrowed or not in the Charge of the Light Brigade; but, as Mr. Kinglake truly says, "Many who could throw light on the affair maintain silence," and that "the time has not arrived for conclusive decision."

There must certainly be some in existence who could give information as to the origin of the high speed in the first line—that is, the bugle sounds for the increase of pace, and who ordered it; also, how near the Divisional Staff were to the first line when the speed was so increased, and whether the 4th and 8th had passed, or were abreast of, or were behind the Divisional Staff, at the instant the speed was increased in the first line.

These are important points for consideration. In a memorandum in the beginning of his Journal, dated 25th July, 1875, Lord George says his account of Balaclava was in Mr. Kinglake's possession for two years, and that the latter said he had learnt more from it than all other accounts put together.

Before the above date many of the Balaclava men had died. Cornet Yates died in 1862, so he was past replying. Captain (Lieut.-Colonel) Morris died in 1858. Colonel Shewell died about 1859, so it is possible Colonel Mayow supplied the statement of the conversation he and Colonel Shewell are said to have had as to where Lord Cardigan was, etc., etc., when they met beyond the Battery. Lord Cardigan died before Mr. Kinglake's account of the battle was printed, but Colonel Mayow was alive at that time. Colonel Douglas died May, 1871, but the modest protest of that brilliant soldier is given at page 249 of Lord George's Journal, where he says, "As to him (Lord George) rallying the 11th at any time, I cannot admit it. How unfair it would be that such a statement should go forth to the world." Lord George himself describes the 11th as being a compact little knot when he met them; they were therefore not out of hand, and it is difficult to understand how the word rally can apply. At any rate, when the 4th and 11th in their retreat passed by 'C' Troop, the regiments were not dressing in one line, as if in united command. The 11th were farthest off, but lying back, and seemed to be commanded by their own officers. Some other officer must have taken the 4th on to the rear while Lord George came over to have his say at the left of 'C' Troop, until interrupted and cut short by Lord Cardigan.

Lord Cardigan (*vide* "Kinglake," page 249) says he warned Lord Lucan that the enemy's Artillery was on both flanks and also in front, and the ground covered with riflemen; but Lord Lucan (*vide* the same page) believes the warning only pointed to the flanking fire from the Fedioukine Hills, and not to that on the ridge or to the forces in front, and that this was Lord Cardigan's objection. Lord Cardigan's account of this, however, must be perfectly correct, for the simple reason that the Battery in front could not but be seen. The ground is such that a solitary man would be seen; and as to the other flanking fire from the ridge, it spoke for itself, and everybody saw it. The Russians, during the interval between the Heavy and Light Charge, never missed a chance of firing a shot, when they thought they could do so with advantage, up at 'C' Troop and the Heavies, and every two or three minutes there was a quiet muttering in the ranks, "Look out! here's another," when the smoke from the discharge of a gun on the ridge was observed, and the well-understood black spot was seen in the air coming towards our people. It was one of these that smashed a limber wheel in 'C' Troop, and another that landed in a remarkable manner on a dragoon's sword blade.

According to "Kinglake," pages 250, 401, Cardigan was enjoined to advance very steadily and quietly, and keep his men well in hand; the idea being that he should use his discretion, keep his four squadrons under perfect control, and halt as soon as he found no useful object to be gained, but great risk incurred. Cardigan (*vide* Kinglake, page 269) insists that he himself was not the originator of the high speed; perhaps information as to the bugle sounds at the moment will come to light some day. If Lord Cardigan had adhered strictly to his original statement to Lord Raglan, and that only, namely, that he was ordered to attack the enemy with the 13th and 17th, and left it to others to settle amongst themselves as to who was arranging the details about his supports, their pace, distances, direction, etc., he would have been all right; information on these points would have leaked out little by little. Every unbiassed survivor of his first line would have backed him up in his statement, for numbers of men in the ranks heard the orders given him; and it was believed, that of those who made no halt at the guns, no one went farther in the direct line into the Russian position than he. The true feeling of the troops at the time is only known to those who mixed with them, on that and the following days and nights. While they conversed with sorrow over their lost comrades, they thought they had been thrown away, and that the whole affair was a heavy misfortune; but at the same time they considered that possibly their efforts had cowed the Russians sufficiently to prevent an immediate re-attempt at a general engagement on the position. No one dreamt that the charge would be looked upon as it afterwards was, or that there ever would be such a thing as a Balaclava Banquet. After a few days the great promotions consequent on the losses, and the augmentations, made the recipients content, and they began to speak of the affair as part of the fortunes of war. As time went on, certain survivors talked themselves into a prominence they were not credited with on the night after the battle, while many deserving modest men have been forgotten.

Mr. Kinglake justly alludes to cases where some who were sick returned to duty in time to participate in the charges; the period however of intense depression, and it was a long period too, arose some time before the charges took place, we mean when the Turks had left the ridge, and there were no troops between the enemy's cannon and our Cavalry. After the supports began to file into the plain, there was then a prospect of fighting on less unequal terms. Before the charges took place, the tents were down; the Quartermasters had got away with the few books and things they could remove, and a man had either to be in the plain as an effective, or out of it as a non-effective.

Once again let us refer to "Kinglake," page 297, where it is asked, "Was. Lord Cardigan warranted in leaving those Regiments (*i.e.* his supports) to fight their way in? etc." The casual reader, taking up the book, might suppose there was some obstruction of ground or other cause to prevent the Divisional Staff seeing the course taken by the Brigade in fighting their way in, or the condition they were reduced to then and afterwards. It is easy to understand Mr. Kinglake's difficulties in getting together the accounts of the battle, so many people siding one way or the other, but it would certainly be unworthy of any survivor, for interested motives, to prompt such harsh questions as to what Lord Cardigan had left undone, at any rate in fighting inwards. What are the facts on this head? First we maintain the Brigade was not across the middle of the outer valley, as has been stated, and as is shown in some plans, when they began the advance. Colonel Douglas in his record says, "No sooner had these events terminated (*i.e.* the retreat of the Russians, after the 'Heavy' charge), than the Light Brigade received orders to move and take up a position across the hills, separating the valley of Balaclava from the other, down which they subsequently advanced; and at the bottom of which, with their backs towards the Tchernaya, the Russian Cavalry had just formed. The valley led down by an easy slope towards their position, about one mile and a half off; they were posted with batteries in advance, the valley gradually widening out in their front." He then describes the formation of the Brigade; and says, "In this formation they received orders to attack." Colonel Douglas's was the outermost regiment, and he certainly ought to know the ground he stood on. How significant this is of Lord Raglan's idea of the true front of the Cavalry Division when he despatched his order; and, is it not also significant of how little Nolan contemplated what was going to be done until the first line was moved off? Now couple Colonel Douglas's account with the circumstance that when 'C' Troop had mounted, the then inward flanks of both 'C' and 'I' Troops were about equidistant from the crest, but not far from each other; and having regard to the weakness of the Squadrons to which 'I' Troop had been contiguous, occupying, as they did, so little ground, and that Nolan's body was found just outside the ridge, is it not proof that the Brigade could not have started from the middle of the valley, but rather that they were moved with premeditation gradually down from the slope, and were some distance on their advance before the directing squadron, with Cardigan in its front, was fairly in the middle of the valley? also that Nolan, who, though willing enough to accompany the attack to the true front, as the mass of Cavalry had previously stood, when he found he could not dissuade from the course taken, made up his mind to have no hand or part in it, and was trying to get out to his right when he was killed?

When Cardigan was questioned the same afternoon by Lord Raglan, his fearless answer was, "My Lord, I received the order to attack in front of the Troops." Lord Raglan believed and accepted this explanation, and five days later wrote of him (*vide* "Kinglake," page 363) "that he had behaved with steadiness, gallantry, and perseverance." Probably no Cavalry officer was ever in a greater predicament than Cardigan was as he approached that Battery; his personal Aides had thinned off from various causes; he saw the chances were entirely against him, and as often as he thought it, to use his own words, "a mad-brained trick," so often would he remember it was forced upon him by his Divisional General; that Lord Raglan, then looking on, "would have it." To have halted anywhere within 300 yards of the Battery could have done no good, for he would have received the salvo of grape all the same, and the Artillerymen would not then have desisted for a moment, whereas, by charging home, he at least shut up that number of guns from firing on his supports.

It was unfortunate for Lord Cardigan that he kept his yacht, with friends on board, in Balaclava harbour, and that he asked Lord Raglan's permission to sleep there, as it gave people opportunity to talk, and they made the most of it; still times were hard, and others were not behindhand in availing themselves of the very few habitations that were about. Lord George alludes to it, but he himself, a year afterwards, lived altogether in a house in the town of Eupatoria, while his Brigade was under canvas on the desolate beach, a distance quite as great from him as the head of the harbour was from the plain at Balaclava, when, as he says, "horses were dying, and great numbers of officers and men were down with sickness."

As 'C' Troop found the body of Captain Nolan and buried it, it may not be out of place in these remarks to say that that officer was never looked upon by the troops as the madman he is described to be by Lord George Paget. The Troop had excellent opportunities of noticing him in Bulgaria and elsewhere. His remarkable dress, the only one of the sort with the Army, made him conspicuous. He rode a great deal round the Artillery camps, observing all he could, and getting information, but in such a quiet, gentlemanly way that his voice was seldom heard. He was known to be an enthusiast in the greater individual training and better equipment of the Cavalry soldier, things which have since had to be attended to. Doubtless, Lord Raglan selected him to convey the written order because he was a swift and sure horseman, and the moments were precious. Lord Airey died before the issue of Lord George's Journal, so he was past saying a word in defence of his former A.D.C.

The losses in the Light Brigade during the twenty or twenty-five minutes occupied in the attack and retreat were great. They are given on the opposite page.

Note.—The 128 of all ranks for the 13th Light Dragoons is from their Historical Record, which adds that, "in re-forming after the charge they could only number nine (mounted), exclusive of officers." Other accounts say the regiment was but 112, all ranks, before the charge. Beyond doubt horses turned up in all the regiments long after the first roll call. They had been ridden back by whoever wanted, and were lucky enough to catch them. To those in 'C' Troop there seemed to be more than nine Troop horses left in the 13th, when encamped for the next few days inside and outside the Col. The historical information of the 13th is not so complete as that of the other regiments. The casualties in officers' horses of the 8th are included in the numbers in the Return, but there is no information on this head for the other regiments.

The nine non-commissioned officers and men wounded of the 4th Light Dragoons is from their records. Other accounts say they had a greater number of wounded. It is believed that many of the prisoners of the 17th succumbed, but the effort to gain information on this head has not been successful.

General Liprandi visited our wounded prisoners about

Casualties in the Light Brigade.

Return of the Light Brigade for the 25th October, 1854, carefully compiled from the Regimental Records, and verified as far as possible by the statements of some of the survivors (prisoners included). All Combatant Officers are accounted for in this Return, except Lord Cardigan, Colonel Mayow, and Captain Maxse.

REGIMENTS.	On parade in the morning.		Killed.		Wounded who returned to the Lines.		Prisoners.		Horses.		Remarks concerning the Wounded and Prisoners.				
											Mortally wounded of those who returned to the Lines.		The Prisoners.		
	Combatant Officers only.	N.C. officers and men.	Officers.	N.C. officers and men.	Officers.	N.C. officers and men.	Officers.	N.C. officers and men.	Killed.	Shot for wounds.	Officers.	N.C. officers and men.	Mortally wounded and died in the hands of the enemy, N.C. officers and men only.	Returned from Russia on the exchange of prisoners.	
														Officers.	N.C. officers and men.
4th Light Dragoons	11	115	2	16	2	9	...	16	52	9	...	2	6	...	10
8th Hussars.........	11	104	2	19	2	17	1	7	37	9	...	3	...	1	7
11th Hussars.........	7	135	...	25	3	27	...	8	72	not known	1	...	2	...	6
13th Light Dragoons	8	120	3	11	...	30	...	12	said to have been 84 in total loss.		...	...	1	...	11
17th Lancers.........	11	136	2	22	4	33	1	13	said to have been 99 in total loss.		1	...	not known.	1	not known.

9 p.m. on the day of the battle, six of whom died during that night.

The Russian Cavalry were in correctly-dressed squadrons, like our own, but there was usually a certain number in detached or extended order, drawn up out of the way, ready to act according to circumstances. These seemed to work by signal rather than word of command, and perhaps it was troops of this class that swept in on our first line. In this loose order they could not prevent any resolute groups of ours, with intervals of only six inches from knee to knee, riding through them; but they followed, and when a man on a slow or jaded horse fell behind they closed round. If they had sent more Cavalry from their main body in pursuit, many of our helplessly wearied and wounded could have been shot down without even risking personal encounter; this may be set down as want of dash on the part of the Russians, but it is the only way of accounting for so many of our men getting back.

According to Todleben, the Russians had 20,500 effectives, thirty-four squadrons included, at the battle, but, he does not say if the artillerymen for the seventy-eight guns are included in this; he puts their killed and wounded at 550.

The allies are said to have lost about 600 in killed, wounded, prisoners, and missing. A great many Turks, as they were leaving the farthest redoubts, must have been killed by the Russian Cavalry, who swept over the ground about Canrobert's hill in pursuit. The losses in our Heavy Cavalry from their own charge could not have been great, at any rate there was no perceptible diminution in their strength, and in a few minutes afterwards they looked as quiet and as formidable as if no encounter had taken place.

CHAPTER IX.

CAMP AT THE COL.—INKERMAN.—WINTER, SPRING, AND SUMMER AT BALACLAVA.

SOON after the battle, the Troop and all the Cavalry moved inside the Col, and encamped on the left-hand side of the road as it led to the French Head-quarters; 'I' Troop R.H.A. was also encamped here. A few tents had been brought over from the old camp, while the Troop was outside the Col, and the remainder, together with the men's things, were now brought by a non-commissioned officer, who had only one ammunition waggon with the boxes off, and a couple of drivers allotted to him for this duty; all the other drivers and horses left at the right attack were used throughout the day-time and part of the night also for siege purposes, and no one from the Headquarters of the Troop was allowed to leave the Col, so the removal was a long job, for the tents on the old ground had to be struck and packed by this noncommissioned officer and his two drivers. The men found that some of the gun buckets, camp kettles, etc., as well as many other articles, were missing. About the 2nd of November, the Troop was together once more, except Bombardier Lockwood and his party, who were still with the siege train. Second Captain Hon. McD. Fraser, and Assistant-Surgeon Prothero joined about this time. On the 2nd of November, the regiments composing the

Light Cavalry Brigade went towards Inkerman, and were encamped there. A great many men who had been failing, were now laid up altogether, and the Hospital Marquee and some tents were filled. Cholera also set in, and there were some deaths; the men who died here were buried on the side of a low hill which was behind the Troop encampment;. there is nothing to mark their graves. It may be interesting to observe that of all the men who, from first to last, were once fairly attacked with cholera, only one, Gunner Campbell (not the Limber Gunner Campbell), recovered.

One thing that struck every body at this camp was the state of readiness for any duty exhibited by the Zouaves and French generally. They had a delightful and powerful band, which used to play an hour or so before daylight; when clear morning, it would be found that the whole force had moved away to their appointed rendezvous, somewhere on the line of circumvallation, and not a single straggler of any sort would be left on the ground; Bandmaster, Drum-major, musicians, ambulance men, every one with a rifle over his shoulder, except the vivandières and the officers.

On the morning of the 5th November, the Troop turned out at the usual hour; it was a very damp, dark, foggy morning, and rain had fallen on and off for some hours; all however appeared to be pretty quiet, but about the time it ought to have been clear daylight, if a fine morning, some musketry was heard in the distance to the left (the front of the camp was towards Balaclava); the Troop at once moved to its left, crossed the road leading to Headquarters, and went to where the Zouaves were encamped; the position taken up would be about half a mile from the Col, where the line of circumvallation bends well into the plain. The Zouaves were in a trench which had been cut in the cliff a few feet below its brow;

the guns were unlimbered and run forward as close to the edge as possible, the Zouaves being underneath and firing occasional shots into the darkness in Balaclava plain to let the Russians see they were on the alert. The Heavy Cavalry were between the Troop and the Col, and 'I' Troop was also near this position. The cannonade and musketry at Inkerman now became terrific. The morning was so dark, that the discharges of musketry up there could be seen from the Col like streaks of fire, and the sparks from the Zouaves' muskets, underneath the Troop, could be seen falling to the ground at each discharge. There were one or two heavy guns in an earthwork at some distance to the left of the Troop, which were fired occasionally into Balaclava plain. Soon after this there was another fierce cannonade and musketry firing in the rear, in the direction of Sevastopol; this arose chiefly from a sortie directed by the Russians against the French left, so as to prevent them sending any succour to Inkerman. Lord Lucan was close to the Troop, and he sent Captain Fellowes, Assistant-Quartermaster-General, towards Inkerman to gain information of what was going on; when the latter returned, he reported that the battle was rather worse than at the Alma, that General Strangways had had his leg shattered by a shot, and that he had met Colonel (afterwards Major-General) Gambier, R.A., with some men, trying to drag up two huge guns to the battle. Lieutenant Strangways got permission to fall out, and go to General Strangways, who was his uncle. After a time the fog partially lifted, and then only a few parties of Russian Cavalry could be seen in the inner plain; they were in small groups, and extended from about the middle of it, on towards the ridge, between Nos. 2 and 3 Redoubts.

The musketry firing in the rear against the French had slackened, and when it was apparent there was no attack to be made in the direction of the Col, or on Balaclava, the Zouaves drew away to the left and went towards the battle, and the force of Heavy Cavalry and both Troops of Horse Artillery went to their lines; but after a short time 'C' Troop was ordered off to the front, and they were accompanied by a troop or a small party of the Scots Greys. 'C' Troop guns were not actually in action, indeed it was considered that after the arrival of the reinforcement of French, the fortune of the day changed in our favour. The fighting space on Inkerman ridge was so contracted, and the allies so packed in, that it appeared as if there was no way of getting more guns to the front, no matter what had been the intention.

The Troop halted in a very advanced position, and close to their left were a great number of Russian wounded lying on the ground; some were in the last throes of death, and others shivering with pain and cold; one, an officer, a very fine handsome man, was badly shot through the backs of both thighs, with the flesh terribly torn, and he lay on his back unable to move; he signed to some on the left of the Troop, and opened the skirt of his long coat to show the injury and the pool of blood he was lying in. He had superior underclothing, but wore the same dress as the privates, except that he had a peak to his forage cap, and some tiny metal stars or ornaments on his collar or shoulder-straps. The men, however, had not a drop of rum or even water to offer him, nor could they do a single thing except put a few stones under his head. An officer of Infantry, who happened to come up, sent one of his men to try and find a doctor, but without success; they were all engaged elsewhere. The ground just behind the Troop was like a slaughter-house. Dr. Prothero and all available doctors at the Cavalry camp had gone quite early to the fight. Many poor fellows must have died that night from exhaustion, for it was quite late when the Troop left the battle-field, and they were not likely to get attended to afterwards. Some who fell in the high brushwood would not be seen for days, and numbers of Russian corpses down the slopes, and on ground which was actually under the enemy's fire, had to be left unburied for a considerable time. Sir George Brown was taken to the rear wounded, and lying in an araba; and as he passed he raised himself on his elbow, and waved his hand at his Rifle Troop, as he used to call it. General Canrobert also passed close by, with his arm wounded and in a sling. The Troop at this time heard with sorrow that their grand old Artillery Chief General Strangways had succumbed to his wounds. The drivers and horses of a working party of 'C' Troop at the right attack that day were ordered into the battle, under fire, for various duties.

It was noticed that the French carried away their dead officers by placing the body across three muskets; then two ranks, of three men each, took the rifles at their extremities on their shoulders. One rifle supported the back with the arms and head hanging downwards outside; the middle rifle supported the body near the waist; the third rifle was behind the knees, with the legs and feet hanging down. In this way the men stepped together behind their regiments, and bore the body away to their distant camps for interment; and really they looked as much at home as if they were at that work every day in the year. As night was setting in, the Troop returned to their encampment near the Col; they had been without food all day.

At the time of the battle it was thought by the English that the fog favoured the Russians, by giving their most advanced columns the opportunity of ascending the heights unperceived by our picquets; but this view of the case was afterwards much modified, as it became known that great numbers of the enemy were altogether unacquainted with the ground, and therefore the fog must have been disadvantageous to them in many ways. What would tell against the Russians was the great height of the position, its narrowness on the top in some places, the very few roads to get up by, and these of a winding description. No one who has not experienced it, can imagine what confusion is possible with long Artillery trains, in a dense fog, on a difficult and unknown road, from which there is no getting off sideways, particularly if other troops get mixed up with them, where silence is a necessity, and no lanterns can be permitted. When once there is a halt, or any conflicting orders are given, an hour or so soon passes away, getting messages from front to rear, messengers often passing those they are seeking through being on the opposite side of the column. According to Todleben, "extra draught horses had to be added on account of the height," and room for all these teams had to be found in the dark on the limited space of workable ground—no easy matter to arrange after the firing had begun. Then, having once got their Artillery into action in any sort of line, the ravines and hollows, running right and left, forbade the regular advance of their outermost guns, whether few or many; indeed, their Infantry must have been puzzled to get through some of the brushwood at the heads of these ravines, for much of it was almost as high as the men themselves.

The English laboured under so many disadvantages that it is useless to try to enumerate them; besides, others have ably endeavoured to do this. Owing to the nature of the ground and the impossibility of our generals and superior officers moving the troops about or having recourse to tactics, Inkerman was said to be in great measure the Soldiers' Battle. The men considered that at one particular period in the early part of the fight things were getting desperate. They believed that what conduced primarily to their success was the tenacity with which they held on to their ground at the beginning of the action. They further thought that here there was full play for their rifle muskets, much more so than at the Alma; that the bullets found their way into columns far in rear, and that, owing to the fog, the enemy entertained the impression that they had more troops opposed to them than was the case. This is hearsay, and may be taken for what it is worth; but it was, nevertheless, the then *bonâ fide* opinion of our troops that were actively engaged.

Artillerymen and others who were enabled to take advantage of the low breastwork that had been erected were unanimous in pronouncing it as of great value. A French Field Battery that had to go into action in the open space near this slight shelter in a few minutes had nearly all their horses and many of their men shot down by the Russian Artillery, and the survivors had to lie on the ground unable to do anything to help themselves. One of these French guns was removed out of action past 'C' Troop a complete wreck, the parts being piled up on a carriage in a similar way to what was practised at Woolwich when drilling at removing disabled guns, etc.

It may help to give an idea of the time the two 18-pounders were got into action if we say that Brigadier-General Strangways was mortally wounded, and Colonel Carpenter, of the 41st, killed, and the news of this and other details of the fight taken to the rear before Captain Fellowes got to Inkerman; and that he, as he was returning, met Colonel Gambier trying to get the guns dragged up; so, if the distance, etc., is taken into account, an estimate might be made of the time they would open fire. Indeed, the morning was so far advanced when Captain Fellowes got back, that Lord Lucan was sitting down in one of the intervals between the unlimbered guns of 'C' Troop, having his breakfast of steaming broiled ham, etc., etc. The Zouaves, in particular, were at a loss to understand where this savoury smell was coming from, and they were cracking jokes with each other over it in the trench underneath.

After Inkerman fight the English troops entertained the belief that too much information regarding our positions, numbers, and condition generally, found its way to the enemy through the medium of the press.

From the 10th to the 14th November, 1854, the time was spent as usual, the guns and detachments being in a state of constant readiness; all other drivers and horses that could be spared, with one of the Lieutenants and two non-commissioned officers, were at work with the Siege Train, turning out at daylight and not getting back till after dark. The number of sick kept increasing. The weather, which had been dry for some time, now began to be cold and damp, with occasional rainy days and nights. The camp at the Col was very exposed. On the morning of the 14th a terrific storm broke over that part of the country, and in a short time every tent in the Heavy Cavalry was blown down except Lord Lucan's, which happened to be pitched in a sort of gully. Helmets, forage-caps, cocked hats, cork mattresses, air pillows, etc., were blown away through the air like feathers. Many horses got loose, the picket posts of a whole squadron of the Greys gave way, and the animals started off still fastened to the lines and stumps of posts, going before the wind, to all appearance, as if they had no control over themselves, and were blown away in company with any amount of small stones and loose earth. They made off in the direction of Sevastopol.

So great was the force of the wind that it was impossible to stand or walk upright, and the men had to go about on their hands and feet. Owing to the picket lines of 'C' Troop passing through the waggon wheels, none of the intervening picket posts broke, so the horses of the Troop were kept secure, but the tents were quickly blown down; only one belonging to the men, and the Commanding Officer's, remained standing. The captured Russian military cart was run close on the weather side of the latter, and it partially broke the fury of the storm. The only living things that seemed at all at home were Lord Lucan's pair of free-and-easy mules which he had for drawing his cooking-cart, etc., and which, according to custom, gave themselves up to plunder. These animals were not at all shy; when loose at night, as they usually were, they would silently poke their heads, ears, and all into any tent not properly secured, and make free with the men's biscuit or anything else that came in their way. During the storm the men had to sit or lie down on their things to keep them from being blown away, and it was evening before it abated sufficiently to admit of the tents being put up, or of any food being got ready, for fires could not be lighted before. The hospital marquee was blown down first; it was full of sick men. Some were dying, and there were one or two dead bodies in the araba alongside waiting interment; the marquee was blown over the latter.

Some time between the 20th and 25th of November the Troop moved a mile or so farther back from the Col in the direction of the Monastery of St. George, and they there made an effort to dig out excavations for hutting purposes. The officers and men worked with a good will, Second Captain (now Major-General) the Hon. McD. Fraser being the best navvy of all. In red night-cap and leathern belt he used to pick out and turn up tons of earth with the greatest ease and in masterly form. He was, however, only a fortnight or three weeks with the Troop, until he was sent away to take over some command or other. It was rather an ill-advised thing to attempt to hut at this place, for it was high up on the plateau, and exposed in every way, and there was no road or track to it. The only wood obtainable for roofing in was some saplings that grew in a plantation four or five miles off, towards the coast. Over these saplings mud was laid; the men put forth all their strength, but to no effect. They could not make headway, and the weakly ones were only laid up all the sooner. These green twigs, they were nothing else, had also to be used for cooking; only one hut and part of another was covered when the supply was exhausted, as the French troops were carrying them away also.

On the 5th December there was an alarm in the direction of Kamiesh, and both Troops Horse Artillery moved down there together, but their services were not required. Between the 6th and 12th December the Troop moved down to Balaclava, and encamped about 500 yards from the head of the harbour. The exact spot is slightly elevated, on the slope, and contracted in space, and is on the right as one leaves the harbour, passing close in to the foot of the hills. The rude cart track ascending the heights on that side, and by which the left half-Troop made its way up on the day of the capture of Balaclava, passed through the camp. There was also at this place a depôt or detachment of about 100 sick horses belonging to the Field Batteries at the right and left attack, but these animals were dying daily, some being destroyed as incurables.

The hunger of the horses during the first part of winter was very great; several spokes in the wheels were eaten through, and the body of the rocket carriage in particular was eaten so much that large pieces of leather had afterwards to be nailed over the openings to keep the contents from falling out. Whenever the poor animals had an opportunity, they set to work to eat each other on the necks, withers, and tails.

The routine was much as usual here; the daily working parties for the siege had hitherto been confined, as far as possible, to the waggon drivers and horses, adding as few of the gun drivers and horses as would make up the number of the working party which was daily demanded by requisition from the Artillery Headquarters, keeping two, three, or four guns in readiness throughout the day, as the numbers left in camp might admit of; but after arrival at this camp it usually took the whole strength of the Troop to meet the demands made on it for the siege. The hospital marquee was full, but as it was such a short distance to the harbour, the worst cases were easily conveyed on board ship. A great many died and were buried at sea on passage to Scutari, or after arrival at the latter place. Some recovered, and afterwards rejoined for duty, and some were sent on to England. Strange to say, all who were left in the hospital marquee at this particular time recovered, and no one actually died in the Troop camp after arrival at Balaclava until the ensuing fine weather had set in. Lieut. Earle, who had been ill for a long time, was now invalided. Three of the Nos. 1 were prostrate, and finally laid up: that is, of the then establishment of five sergeants, two had to be invalided—one to England, the other to Scutari, where he died. Another sergeant had been very sick indeed, but after severe illness in the hospital marquee, he recovered. The fourth sergeant was a great sufferer from dysentery, accompanied by rheumatic pains in his legs; but towards the end of December he was sufficiently convalescent to be able to perform the clerical duties of Quartermaster-sergeant. The Troop had all this time been without the services of the latter non-commissioned officer, and consequently all the necessary returns as to pay, etc., were in arrears: indeed, no successor was appointed till nearly midsummer. With the Lieutenant and non-commissioned officers, a large portion of the men were also prostrate. The non-commissioned officers and men who managed to stick to duty were more or less affected with bowel complaints and scurvy, consequent on the privations and hardships they were undergoing. So great was the mortality amongst the troops that Hart's Quarterly Army List, dated 1st January, 1855, shows that 158 officers of the Eastern Expedition had died or were killed in action, but it is believed that this does not include all the deaths occurring up to 31st December, 1854. The clothing, the overalls especially, was nearly all worn out. The drivers used to turn out with pieces of sack tied round their calves and loins for warmth, the great point being to keep the men effective by any means. No boots of any sort had yet arrived, and the supply the men took from England was quite used up, the soles having been dragged off by the mud.

On the evening of 17th December, on the occasion of some Russian festival, the Troop was ordered up again to the right attack before Sevastopol, as a sortie was expected. When all the drivers and horses had returned, after dark, from a weary day's work at the siege, the Troop at once got ready without a murmur, and moved off. They were able to take up their full fighting force of guns, and a fair number of waggons.

Nothing could better show the estimation in which the Troop was held by Lord Raglan and the authorities than the demand that was made for its services on this very night, for 'C' Troop was then farthest off of all the

Field Artillery, or any other field force; and it was known their working party would be the last to get back to its camp.

The Troop proceeded by way of the plain, where the mud (for road there was none) was knee deep, and up through the Col. It was a terrible pull of about six miles and a half, and the draught horses had done at least twenty miles that day. The night was far advanced when the Troop reached the ground behind the Picket-house ruins on the Woronzoff height, where it was ordered to remain till daylight. There appeared to be great festivities or religious services going on in Sevastopol. The monks or choristers could be heard chanting the whole night; bells were also ringing. The English Infantry were all on the alert, and staff officers moving about the whole night. There was, however, no sortie, and when the morning was well advanced the Troop returned to its camp at Balaclava. This was the last time Captain Brandling took the Troop into the field. A day or two afterwards he assembled as many of the men as happened to be left in from the duties of the siege, only about twenty-five in all, and told them he had just received orders to join his company in the Siege Train at once, and that he was sorry the whole Troop was not present, to bid them good-bye. He was a good deal affected, and said, amongst other things, that he could never have any desire to serve with better men, and that during the time he had been with them he found them earnestly willing to carry out his orders and wishes to the utmost of their power. These few men cheered him heartily as he left their little parade.*
A few days afterwards Captain Thomas rejoined, and the Troop were glad to have their own chief back again, and to see him in restored health.

* Lieut.-Colonel J. Brandling, C.B., died at Leeds 16th April, 1860.

As if in derision of the wants of the men, the first things that happened to arrive, about the beginning of January, were some casks containing dress jackets in material: that is, the breasts were laced, but the lace for the other parts, which were unmade, was loose inside in hanks. These jackets were just what could have best been spared, even if there had been tailors, a tailor's shop, thread, etc. So having conveyed them to camp, the men had the grim satisfaction of taking them to the ship again for re-conveyance to Woolwich. After this, some Infantry regulation highlows were served out, to which the men fitted their spurs. They were a very useful and acceptable covering for the feet. During the most telling part of the cold season—that is, from about the middle of November to the middle of February, when they were all hutted—nothing could exceed the devotion of the men to their duty, and the thoroughly good and comrade-like feeling which existed amongst them. If a faithful record could be obtained of each day's work done by the Troop, and of the various ways in which they contributed towards the duties of the siege during the dreadful winter, it would be most interesting, and would certainly prove that a heavy share of knocking about and hard labour fell upon them. There was an entire absence of insubordination or crime of any kind. It is true that one of the Foot Artillerymen, attached to the Troop, when engaged in carrying drinking water from a little well in the rocks at the harbour, pushed a Turkish officer, who was washing his face in it; but the officer had a private's overcoat on, and the man did not know him to be an officer. The man was, however, tried by General Court-Martial for the offence; but Osman Pasha, the Turkish Commander, feeling there was an entire absence of intentional disrespect to his officer, wrote a letter praying Lord Raglan for the man's pardon, acknowledging that every reparation had been made, and begging that, for the sake of the friendship existing between the English and Turkish armies and their Governments, the soldier might be forgiven. This letter, which was gracefully expressed in English, is no doubt in the records of the regiment, or at the office of the Judge Advocate-General. The pardon was granted at the time the sentence was read out on parade. The few effective men who were daily in camp, sometimes not more than a dozen, worked with all their might grooming the horses left in, and trying to make such of them as were sick as comfortable as possible. Many of the latter had bad sinuses in the back and withers, which had remained open from the early days of the siege, and were now frost-bitten. The men also worked at road-making, attending to their sick comrades, getting up huts, covering up the dead horses left near the camp, going great distances to grub up a handful of brushwood, roots, etc., so as to endeavour to even half cook the food.

During all this time, and for months afterwards, there was no abatement of the demands on the Troop for the duties of the siege. In December and January particularly, it fell especially hard upon the drivers; hungry, and in mud and misery, they toiled on, turning out in the morning often without breaking their fast, and not returning till after dark, when, having taken, standing round the camp-kettle, whatever food was ready for them, they set to work to groom their horses, frequently till late hours of the night. The fondness of the thoroughgoing Horse Artillery driver for his horses is proverbial, and even under these harassing conditions there was no diminution of it with the drivers of 'C' Troop; they could be seen trying to coax, as it were, their done-up horses to eat, holding the feed for them, rubbing their ears, etc., and staying by them until they themselves went to lie down in mud in a tent frowzy within, probably unwholesome from sick comrades unable to move, and covered in ice and snow without; not having any chance of removing their clothes, or opportunity of washing themselves; tormented with dysentery and diarrhœa during the hours of night, and rising with aching bones in the darkness to begin their toil again; and so it went on from day to day, some of the weaker ones having to give in, but the majority holding on like brave men. They deserve to have their names handed down to future members of the Troop, but at this distance of time it is impossible to remember all who were able to go unflinchingly through the campaign, and it is therefore better not to mention any in particular. Drivers at that time had no hope of promotion, or of bettering their condition, and the most they could look forward to, if very steady, was to become some officer's second bâtman towards the close of their services. Gunners of the Troop had occasionally to perform duty as drivers, whenever the latter's "effectives" fell short of the number required for siege duties.

Some time in January a few sailors from a war vessel anchored in Balaclava harbour erected a very fine and simple covering for the horses of the Troop. It was put up about 100 yards farther away from the harbour, and close in behind the large and high conical hill which is there. It consisted of four very stout ship's spars placed upright, about eighteen or twenty feet high, and in a row as a middle line, the lower ends being well sunk in the ground, and the upper ends or tops hollowed out in semicircular form, to receive other spars horizontally as a ridge pole; stout bolt-like nails were then driven down through the latter into the uprights. On each side of this middle line a row of shorter spars, about eight feet high, were put up to form the sides of the stable, the tops being hollowed out and strongly connected lengthwise by horizontal spars, exactly as the middle line was. Then eight spars, four on each side, were placed as rafters, their upper ends meeting the ridge pole exactly at the tops of the middle uprights, and their lower ends resting on the side uprights and their horizontals. The ends and joints were strongly secured by being shaped out as well as by having the stout nails driven in. Two long spars were inclined against the ends of the stable: that is, their tops were secured close up under the ends of the ridge pole, and their lower ends, which stood out, were well embedded in the earth; shorter pieces were fixed at the incline against the side uprights. This skeleton framework, though it looked fragile, was of great strength, and as the spars were all round and smooth, there was very little friction. Some part-worn canvas sails were then prepared for the roof and upper parts of the ends, all in one piece, with long stay ropes sewn on right across the upper side; it was then drawn quietly over the framework, and the ends of the stay ropes fastened to the ground with enormous pegs, which stood well away from the sides. The lower halves of the ends or gables were then built up with mud and stones; there were two doorways or openings on each side, and the remainder was filled up with a canvas wall. The eave or edge of the canvas roof projected about four feet beyond the side-walls, and a good deep trench was dug out to carry away the rain from the roof, and also the torrent that in bad weather came down from the conical hill, as well as from the Marine Heights, which were close at one end. In the space between the trench and canvas side-walls a low mud wall was thrown up, which helped to break the cold winds, save the canvas, and keep the stable warm, and a few flat stones were placed over the trench at the doorways to form culverts. The framework and canvas was designed and carried out by two or three intelligent sailors, and a few men of the Troop, in the course of a fortnight or so. Then a wooden stable was erected for the officers' horses, so that in the month of February every horse in the Troop had a covering of some sort overhead. In the canvas stable the horses' heads were inwards, with a passage one yard wide between, and there was just room enough behind the horses for the men to pass along singly. There was plenty of shingle and small stones about, so the floor was soon consolidated and made good. The night sentries had to keep the horses standing, on account of the cramped space; the harness and horse appointments were kept in tents close by. The stable was looked upon as a curiosity, and was unlike all others, which, as a rule, were dug out against some bank, and then covered over on the top with boards. Some time at the end of December or beginning of January, Colonel (later General Sir John) Dupuis, commanding R.H.A., and his Adjutant, Captain M. S. (now Lieut.-General Sir Michael) Biddulph, came to live in 'C' Troop camp. Towards the end of January one hut was issued to the Troop, and that was put up for the sick; a day or two afterwards, another, and so on till about the middle of February, when all the men were hutted. Captain Thomas and the Lieutenants stuck to their tents, making them double by placing one over the other. The excavations for both huts and tents were all dug out of the side of the conical hill. The before-mentioned sick depôt of Field Battery horses, or rather what was left of them, had been removed, but great numbers had died or were destroyed as incurables, and their carcases were left on the ground only about twenty paces from one end of the canvas stable, and with but a slight covering of earth over them. It was a perpetual labour for the men of 'C' Troop to carry earth in pieces of sack or on spades (for they had nothing else with which to carry it), and throw it over these heaps of carcases in order to try to keep down the smell. Lieut. (now Colonel) A. H. King joined the Troop some time about the beginning of 1855, vice Earle.

The mortality amongst the Turkish troops at this time was very great; their camp was beyond the conical hill, and fronting the plain, and their nearest way to the harbour was by 'C' Troop camp. Numbers of them actually lay down on the ground and expired, while they were being supported by their comrades to the shipping. They were so wasted that any who got on board ship must have died at once, and could only be taken out to sea to be thrown overboard. There is a large Turkish graveyard on the right-hand side of the main road from Balaclava quite filled with the bodies of those who died in camp. This burial-ground stretches half way across to the foot of the conical hill. There were great numbers of dead horses, and camels also, lying about the approaches to Balaclava, in fact, all the way up to the Plateau, and the air was quite tainted with the smell of decaying carcases. The horses had belonged to both Cavalry and Artillery, and had fallen down from weakness and exhaustion to die.

It should be stated that the Cavalry also had to carry up shot and shell for the siege during the early part of the winter, as well as their own forage. They placed the shot and shell in sacks, two or four in each, according to size, and tied up the mouth; then, equalizing the weight to the extreme ends, the sack was lifted across the saddle seat, and the men walked on foot, leading their horses from Balaclava to the Right and Left Siege Train Depôts before Sevastopol. This very soon told on the horses' backs, for they were in such poor condition that the wooden arch of the saddle-tree was quite down on the backbone and withers; so after a time it had to be discontinued with the Cavalry. The Infantry also, who were off duty in the trenches, had to make daily journeys and carry up one or two shot each.

On the night of the 18th February a reconnaissance was ordered for the following morning. The Troop was quite able to have taken out their own six guns, but from some cause or other, an order came from the Artillery Headquarters that two of the guns were to be horsed and manned by 'I' Troop. At midnight these men and horses came over in charge of an officer, but Lieutenant Strangways, who had charge of the 24-pounder howitzers, which were ordered to be so horsed, took his own Nos. 1, his coverers, lead and wheel drivers, and such numbers as were thoroughly conversant with the duties of fixing 24-pounder shells: for 'I' Troop was still a 6-pounder Troop.

The Troop then moved off (before 1 A.M.) to feel their way into the plain, where the small force for the reconnaissance was assembling under Sir Colin Campbell (later Lord Clyde). The men and horses of 'I' Troop not required followed in rear as far as Kadikoi, where they left, and went to their own camp in charge of their officer. The night, so far, was tolerably fine for the time of year; but as soon as the Troop reached the plain (probably about half-past one), the cold became intense, and a most terrible snow-storm came on. The small force of English Cavalry was indeed a mixed one. One Light Regiment seemed to be represented by the Colonel, a Captain, and two in the ranks, one of these being mounted on a piebald. The Heavies were a little more numerous, but it is doubtful if there were above two squadrons out of the remnants of the whole ten regiments.

There was a very small force of English Infantry, and they appeared to belong to the Highland Brigade. A French force was to have assisted; but in consequence of the weather, they were countermanded, and a messenger was despatched to stop the English, but he could not find his way, owing to the cold and blinding storm.

When Sir Colin Campbell had assembled his little force just in front of Kadikoi, they proceeded cautiously towards Canrobert's Hill, making frequent halts, so as to keep together. There was the greatest difficulty in making the horses face the storm, which blew against them, and, whenever they had the least chance, they turned about from it like human beings. The force went by their own left of Canrobert's Hill, in the opening between it and the next of the old redoubts. On the latter a Cossack vidette had been kept ever since the battle of 25th October; but on this particular morning his feelings were too much for him, for neither the man nor any of the picquet were there, and so the force passed on to the bottom of the outer plain. One of 'C' Troop ammunition waggons was horsed by six Spanish horses. Some of these animals had been recently handed over to the Troop as augmentation horses, but they could not draw Artillery waggons except on level and hard ground; and in a short time they had to be sold by auction to any one who would buy them. However, this waggon stuck in soft ground close by the foot of Canrobert's Hill; the officiating Quartermaster-Sergeant was ordered to remain by it with the drivers, as the force had passed on, and no help could be given to drag it out. After some little time this non-commissioned officer could see the outline of a solitary horseman coming stealthily down the slope of Canrobert's Hill. The latter could make out that there was something wrong at the bottom of the hill; he was helped to this by the white appearance of the ground. The non-commissioned officer, who was also on a Spanish horse, made a rush up at the solitary horseman, but the latter was too quick, and cut back over the hill towards Kamara. Who it was was never known, but in all probability it was the Cossack vidette, who, having left his post, was coming back now that the storm had moderated.

The Force soon reached the ground near the Aqueduct, where it halted till daylight began to show itself. Large close columns of Russian Infantry could then be seen standing with shouldered arms and fixed bayonets upon the Fedioukine Hills close by, but they did not open fire nor make any attempt to come down. Some French Infantry now arrived on the ground. Their Commander, having found that Sir Colin Campbell had started, thought it better to follow, notwithstanding that he had received the order countermanding the reconnaissance. After a short consultation of the Commanders, the Force commenced to withdraw, and they were allowed to do so without being molested by the Russians.

As 'C' Troop was passing over the ground on the Balaclava side of Canrobert's Hill, they came across the remains of one of the Russian Cavalry soldiers who was killed by the guns from the Marine Heights on the 25th October, with the grey overcoat and sky-blue overalls still on. The body was reduced to quite a skeleton, the boots were gone, and the bones of the instep were as white as if they had been boiled and bleached. The skull had rolled a few feet away from the body, but there was no flesh left on any of the bones. A chaplain, who, with a good many others, came out sight-seeing after daylight, dismounted and broke off one of the finger-nails, which he took away as a souvenir. There were several cases of frost-bite amongst the Force, as a consequence of this morning's work.

'C' Troop lost very few horses during the winter. None were actually left to perish, for if a horse fell from exhaustion while at work at the duties of the siege, and had to be taken out of the team and left in the mud, there was always an effort made to recover the animal by sending a party out at night to seek for it, or at least as soon as the news was brought in by the men who had had to leave it behind. Two or three horses had to be destroyed on account of the action of the frost on bad sinuses in the back or withers, and three or four more for diseased hoofs, that is, an ulcerated sore at some part of the coronet, from the effects of which the animal would have cast the hoof off altogether.

During the time Captain and Adjutant M. Biddulph was in 'C' Troop camp, he was much occupied in taking sketches of Sevastopol, at which he worked most unweariedly, leaving the camp as the evening came on and not returning until the next morning.

Towards the end of March the Troop was greatly reinforced in men and horses: some of their own men returned from Scutari, and a draft arrived from Woolwich. Many of these were volunteers, and two of them were non-commissioned officers, who cheerfully resigned their position to become gunners in the Troop. Brigadier-General Dupuis explained to them that there was no vacancy on the establishment of non-commissioned officers, and one of them in particular answered, "that when he volunteered he perfectly understood that he would have to join the Troop as gunner, and that he did not even wish or expect to have his claims considered with those of the men who had gone through the campaign." The General was much pleased, and complimented the man for having, as he said, "spoken so handsomely." The name of this non-commissioned officer, it is believed, was Cracknell. During the winter some very fine horses had been drafted into the Troop: a few of them had been chargers of Cavalry officers killed in action or invalided. The animals were sold by auction at Head Quarters, and bought in by the Artillery authorities, so in this way were posted to the Troop. One of them, a very fine bay, which had belonged to Assistant Quartermaster-General Fellowes, was put in the lead of No. 3 Gun. Some captured Russian horses were also posted to the Troop: two of these (chestnuts) had been officers' horses, and were very fleet; they were allotted to the Trumpeters, and when at home, long afterwards, not many Troop horses could keep up with them, or were handier.

During the spring the Troop was employed on some few occasions, with the Brigade under Sir Colin Campbell and the Cavalry, in reconnoitring the rear of the enemy's position towards the neighbourhood of Tchorgaun, and there were at times slight skirmishing engagements.

When the weather got fine, one of 'C' Troop howitzers (No. 3) had a most remarkable upset in Balaclava plain. Drafts of men and horses had joined from England for all arms of the service, and 'C' Troop was now largely reinforced. The calls on the Troop for the siege duties were at this time not very heavy, so quiet, easy drills, mounted and dismounted, were carried out as far as they could be. One morning Captain Thomas thought he would try one of the slowest of gallops, just to gradually get the horses into condition. It was the first attempt at anything exceeding the trot since the day the Battle of Inkerman was fought. The front of the Troop was towards Canrobert's Hill, and the left towards the ridge, from which it was distant about five hundred yards. Captain Thomas explained, when at the halt, that the gallop would be slow. The Troop moved off in the usual way, and the trumpet then sounded "Gallop!"

They had settled into a collected pace, when suddenly all, except the two off-leaders, of No. 3 team went down, the rearmost horses going right up over those in front as they fell in succession, the four drivers being underneath; the two limber gunners were thrown into the air towards the right front like footballs, and the howitzer and limber turned clean over, vent and ammunition boxes downwards, being at about an angle of forty-five degrees to what they were when advancing; both shafts had broken off, the proper near shaft leaving a fine-pointed piece, three-quarters of a yard long, sticking out of the splinter-bar, the point resting against the uppermost flank of the shaft horse. The wheel-driver had a most miraculous escape. When his horse fell, he passed in some way under the shaft horse, and he had the proper near limber wheel, after it had gone over, resting on the left side of his waist, and the hind feet of the shaft horse (then on its side) against his stomach, pinning him under the wheel. It was fortunate the horses were stunned for a few seconds, or it would have gone hard with the drivers. Had the shaft horse struggled, he must have staked himself on the broken piece of shaft, and have killed the wheel driver. The other five guns had gone on some distance and were not aware of the extent of the accident, and there were only the mounted men of the detachment and one or two others available to hand. However, the drivers were soon released, and the horses quickly put upon their legs. As soon as the shafts could be replaced, all were enabled to mount and return to camp in proper form, no man or horse bleeding or marked in any way. The pintail was bent and fractured very nearly through, and there was great difficulty in getting the howitzer unlimbered at all. The Russian Cavalry picquet used to ascend the little hill on which their vedette stood, near No. 2 Redoubt, and apparently watch these drills with great interest. They were looking on attentively, and pointing with their arms at this particular mishap, being distant about four hundred yards. They never fired; had they done so, they would have been shelled off the position every morning before the drills began, for the whole inner plain was used for this purpose by the mounted arms, both French and English.

The upset which has been described arose in consequence of a deep trench, about a foot wide and six or eight feet long, lying fair end on, in the track of the lead riding horse, and so covered and hidden with the grass which grew at the edges and met across, that it formed a perfect trap, and would disarm all suspicion even at a walking pace. The lead driver said he thought his horse had jumped or got over it in some way, and was then pulled down by the horse behind, which galloped right into it, and there fell. Had it been a lighter gun, it would probably have been stopped by such an impediment as the six horses and four men lying in a heap; but, although the pace was so slow, the immense weight of the 24-pounder howitzer overcame all resistance, and as it could not very well tumble over fair to the front, it went over in this way towards the right, snapping the shafts as if they were lucifer matches, and pulling round the thrown-down horses, which were still attached to the splinter-bar, as if they were mere kittens.

On the 14th April, 1855, Assistant-Surgeon (now Surgeon-Major) Park was appointed to the Troop, vice Prothero promoted.

A reconnaissance was made on the 19th April in the direction of Tchorgaun by 'C' Troop and some English Cavalry, under the command of Colonel Parlby, 10th Hussars, and by some Turks under Omar Pasha; there were also some French Cavalry and a French Rocket Troop, and a mixed Force of Infantry. Omar Pasha had chief command. The Rocket Troop came into action near the Aqueduct at the foot of the Fedioukine Hills, and made some good practice against the Russians, who were on the top and who retired out of range in the direction of the Tractir Bridge. 'C' Troop then crossed the Aqueduct and the Tchernaya River, proceeding towards Tchorgaun and the high ground beyond it. Colonel Parlby accompanied, but no opposition was met with, and only a few shots were exchanged by the patrols. After the requisite observations by the senior officers, the troops gradually returned to their camps, closely followed for some distance by the Russian Cavalry and Cossacks; the latter managed to make prisoners of some of our Commissariat Drivers, who did not keep with the column.

The ground at and beyond the Tchernaya was very beautiful, the road was nicely gravelled, and reminded one of a carriage-drive through some private park at home. There were plenty of trees, and an abundance of good grass growing everywhere, which, with the pure water of the river, must have helped to keep the Russian horses in good condition.

On 14th May, 1855, Second Captain (now Major-General) Hoste joined the Troop; he had been appointed in February, in succession to the Hon. McD. Fraser.

As the fine weather was setting in, a gunner of 'C' Troop, who had recently come out with the draughts from Woolwich, was kicked by his horse and badly injured internally, from the effects of which he died in a few days. The man was grooming outside the stable, and the horse was a very quiet one, but the flies were annoying it, and hence the accident. This was the first death that actually took palce in the Troop camp in 1855, but immediately after this cholera again set in, and some were carried off very quickly, amongst them Capt. King, 32nd Regiment, A.D.C. to General Markham. He was staying in 'C' Troop camp with his brother, Lieutenant A. H. King, at the time. After the death, Lieut. King succeeded to the vacancy of A.D.C., and quitted the Troop camp to reside with General Markham on the plateau. Amongst those who died at this time was a well-known old 'C' Troop gunner, named Cook. He had filled in the grave over a dead comrade late one afternoon, and, as he finished, he drew on the ground with his spade, saying, "There is just room enough here for me." Poor fellow! he was attacked by cholera during the night, and, rather before the same time next day, he was laid in the ground he himself had marked out.

It was astonishing the number of cases in which the men of the Army had a sort of presentiment that something was about to happen to them. Driver Perkins told some of his comrades, while the Army was waiting at the Bulganak, after moving out of bivouac, that he could not make out what was the matter with him, although he was in good health. A corporal of the Rifle Brigade, who attended to the cholera cases on board the "Monarchy"—staying by them and hand-rubbing them until they died—afterwards, at the Right Attack, and before any bombardment opened, insisted on going round his comrades and bidding them good-bye, saying he would not see them again, as he knew he could not come out of the trenches alive. He was a fearless, well-educated man, had been brought up to the medical profession, and was well known to the Troop from his serving out the medicines on board the "Monarchy." The daily casualties just then were almost *nil*, and there was not such heavy firing on the

Russian side as to cause him to think much about it. However, he was sitting in company with others in the trench, and on his rising, though still out of view of the enemy, a shot came through the earth that had been thrown up as a screen, and killed him instantly. A shoeing-smith named Bland, of 'C' Troop, a powerful man, who remained at work throughout the severe winter, said he knew he would not die then, but that he would as soon as the fine weather set in, and that the smell of the dead animals would certainly kill him. True to his saying, when the fine weather did set in, he wasted away, all his teeth fell out, and he died.

The narrow road from Balaclava to 'C' Troop camp led nearly straight past, and close to, the left of the conical hill on the low ground, but just before it reached 'C' Troop camp there was another narrow road which branched off to the right front and led up past the right of the conical hill, that is, it led through a sort of pass between the hill and the Marine Heights. The graves of the men who died here are about 20 paces up the hill, on the right-hand side of this latter road, just before it enters the pass. Capt. King's grave is the farthest up-hill, and is lengthwise across the heads of the others. In the triangular-shaped bit of low ground formed by these two roads and the foot of the conical hill on that side, stood the Troop stables and gun park.

Soon after the death of Captain King, 32nd Regiment, in 'C' Troop camp, Lieut. Grylls became very ill. When his promotion took place on 13th August, 1855, he was succeeded by Lieut. (now Major-General) J. E. Ruck Keene.

On the morning of the 25th May a considerable force, of which 'C' Troop formed a part, assembled in the plain near Kadikoi, with a view to establish the Sardinian Army on the Fedioukine Hills and Line of the Tchernaya generally. The troops moved on over the ridge to the outer plain, and the object was effected without any great opposition, the Russians withdrawing on the advance, and the Sardinian Army was left in possession: they were supported by some French and Turkish Troops. The English Troops returned to their camps at the close of the day. On the following morning 'C' Troop exercised in the outer plain, and had a good opportunity of examining the ground where the Light Cavalry charge took place, near the position supposed to have been occupied by the Russian guns, which the Light Brigade charged in front. Splinters of shells, and circular plates of iron with spiral stems attached, round which the Russian grape-shot had been packed, were lying everywhere about.

The bodies of our men seemed to have been buried with their horses, or at least, with some of them; that is, a large number appeared to have been drawn close together on to the ground in front of where the Russian guns probably stood, without any graves or hollows being made to receive them. Only a very little earth could have been shovelled on by the Russians, and this had packed itself and sunk close, for leg- and arm-bones, and portions of rotting uniform, were sticking out in all directions. The white collar and stripes of the 17th, the buff of the 13th, the red collars and cuffs of the 4th, the crimson overalls of the 11th, and the blue-and-yellow uniforms of the 8th, were all to be seen intermixed, and gave one melancholy feelings about the loss of so many gallant men.

The place of interment was a long, irregular-shaped sort of bed, only a foot or two above the surface of the earth, except where the carcases of horses lay. The ribs of these would not go down, and so made it higher at such places: there was a very disagreeable smell.

The burial of horses would have given some trouble, but the Russians, with their immense army, might easily have made graves of a decent depth for the officers and men.

The Troop came across the unburied body of a private of the Royal Dragoons, killed on the 25th October, lying in the long rank grass on the inner side of the ridge, near No. 2 Redoubt. The following day, Sergeant Beardsley and a few men got leave, went out with spades, dug a proper grave, and interred it: they brought away one or two of the coat buttons, but could not make out the name or number on his clothing. The body was decomposed, and almost a skeleton, but still not so much so as the body of the Russian found some months previously. This might be accounted for by the fact that the post of the Cossack vedette was not far away from the Englishman's corpse, and the vultures would be shy of approaching.

An assault was made on the Malakoff and Redan on the 18th June, at daybreak. It was said that Lord Raglan wished to bombard the place for some hours, beginning at daylight, and then deliver the assault probably about noon, but that General Pelissier considered that he could not conceal in daylight the number of troops he required for the storming of the Malakoff; and he so impressed Lord Raglan with this, that the latter, much against his inclination, agreed to the arrangement to assault in the early morning. The Russians were thoroughly on the alert, and the moment the attacking columns left the advanced trenches they were received with a most deadly fire, against which they could make no headway; so the attempt failed, with great loss of life. The Russians ran up an enormous black flag on the Malakoff, and on this occasion, as well as at the subsequent assault on 8th September, their troops, when once they ran from cover to their posts at the breastworks, were not moved about: that is, those in the front rank remained there, and, having discharged their muskets, passed them over their left shoulder to their comrades behind for re-loading, and took others all ready loaded and at full cock, which their comrades had passed over the right shoulder. In this way they sent a continuous leaden hail through the air from their old smooth-bores. This appears not to have been generally noticed by writers and historians, but it is another instance of the praiseworthy way in which the Russians made the most of everything they had. If the men were eight or ten deep, those behind the front ranks did all the loading and capping. One of 'C' Troop was an eye-witness of these proceedings on the part of the Russians on this particular morning.

On the night of the 23rd June a terrific thunderstorm, accompanied by a deluge of rain, broke over the country. Great numbers of rats were drowned in their holes in 'C' Troop camp, and their bodies afterwards washed out all over the ground. Some of the men's things in the Cavalry camp were carried quite away; a pouch belt of the Scots Greys found its way down to 'C' Troop camp, a distance of about a mile and a half. Even some of the metal rails of the railway were displaced, and removed to a distance by the force of the rushing water.

The death of Field-Marshal Lord Raglan took place on 28th June, and the 3rd July was fixed for the removal of the body in funeral procession from Headquarters to the steamer for transit to England. 'C' Troop was ordered to furnish one of its 9-pounder guns, complete in men and horses, on which to convey the coffin. This was a very grand sight; the pall-bearers were General Pelissier, Omar Pasha, General Della Marmora, and

Sir James Simpson, who were the Commanders-in-Chief of their respective armies, and all branches of the allied armies and navies were represented in the procession.

The death of Lord Raglan was deeply deplored by the Army, and by none more so than by the non-commissioned officers and men who had served from the beginning of the war, and who were present in action with him at the different battles, for they could form some idea of the difficulties he had to contend with, and of the way in which his temper was tried. They had every faith in his abilities as a commander, and were satisfied that nothing but stern fighting could suffice to make headway in such a war; also that he was perfectly blameless for the shortness of men, the want of clothing, the insufficiency of rations, medical comforts, and forage; and that the number of deaths from privations and hardships could not in any sense be left to his charge. He had tasks to perform and an extent of ground to defend out of all reason for the number of troops that was allotted to him. Though a one-armed man, and of good age, not many could get over the ground on horseback quicker, and he was perfectly equal to his work. The old soldiers liked him, and spoke kindly of his memory, and they felt proud of him for having stuck to his command till the last.

In the early morning of the 16th August, the English Cavalry and all the Field Artillery in and about Balaclava assembled in the inner plain long before daylight. The Russians had been observed to be in great numbers in the direction of MacKenzie's Farm and thereabouts for some days previously, and an attack was expected. The morning was very calm and fine, and just as it was grey dawn three signal shells were fired perpendicularly into the air from the top of Canrobert's Hill, being the signal determined on to show that the Russians were advancing, and very soon afterwards a fierce Artillery and musketry fire began at the Tractir Bridge and along the line of the Fedioukine Hills, facing the Tchernaya. The French and Sardinians were chiefly engaged here; the former had some of their Horse Artillery of the Imperial Guard, which had recently come out, in action. Their showy uniforms made them very conspicuous as they moved about on the Fedioukine Hills. There were two Sardinian guns close into the foot of the Fedioukine Hills, near the Aqueduct, but from this for a considerable distance to the right was left open. 'C' Troop was left rather independently by itself, and fronted this opening, but with orders to remain from a quarter to half a mile back from the Aqueduct. 'I' Troop, R.H.A., and it is believed 'A' Troop, R.H.A. also, together with the English Cavalry, except the 6th Dragoon Guards, were in the inner plain, and partially hidden out of view of the Russians. The English Heavy Batteries of position, one of which was drawn by teams four horses abreast, after crossing the track of 'C' Troop, went away from about Canrobert's Hill towards their right front, and took up position on high ground in that direction. The 32-pounder Howitzer Battery was brought into action, and did good service. The 6th Dragoon Guards were in the same direction also. General Dupuis had command of all the Artillery on the ground, and having given orders for the disposition of the various Batteries, he went towards the Tractir, and could be easily seen with the French and Sardinian Staff in the thick of the fight, as he wore the full uniform of the Horse Artillery. Towards the close of the battle he came and ordered Captain Thomas to take 'C' Troop down to the Aqueduct and come into action, which they did. Only a very few rounds, however, were fired, as the range was great. The Russians suffered severely in this engagement; the loss of the French and Sardinians was comparatively small, owing to the advantages of their position and the way in which they were entrenched. The two Sardinian field guns before mentioned, posted at the foot of the Fedioukine Hills, were stationary in action during the battle. Strange to say, they had no casualties, as there was good cover for them on their left. The ground occupied by 'C' Troop when in action would be about three hundred yards to the right of these Sardinian guns. The Russian Cavalry could be seen in great force close in under the heights which bend away from MacKenzie's Farm towards Inkerman; and about midway in this line, and in a sort of angle, the Russians had constructed a splendid battery with siege guns, only a few feet below the summit of the cliff, and consequently had so great a range that they could very nearly reach the Tractir Bridge, and would have played havoc with any troops attempting to follow up the retreat of the Russians after the battle. Towards evening the English troops withdrew to their various camps. Numbers of prisoners, great quantities of arms and accoutrements, as well as entrenching tools, were captured from the Russians.

The Malakoff was captured by the French about noon on the 8th September. The Russians were resting at the time, and the French got into the work without very much loss, but there was some desperate fighting afterwards inside it. In bringing up their Reserves to try and re-take it from the French, the Russians suffered enormous losses from the English Siege Batteries, in one of which Major H. F. Strange (afterwards Commanding Officer of 'C' Troop) served that day as a volunteer. At the assault on the Redan on this date, Lieut. King, A.D.C. to General Markham, greatly distinguished himself, and actually got into the work with some of the storming party, but our people were unable to retain possession of it. When the town was occupied by the Allies, it was found that the Russians had made some of the finest specimens of defence in mantlets, traverses, places of cover, and fortifications generally, that the world ever saw. They had indeed made good use of their time.

Soon after the 8th September, Lieut. King went to England. He was succeeded by Lieut. (now Colonel) William Stirling, whose appointment dated 11th August, 1855.

CHAPTER X.

Expedition to Eupatoria.

EARLY in October, 1855, it was decided that a Brigade of English Cavalry was to be sent to Eupatoria, and 'C' Troop was ordered to accompany it. On the 8th and 9th October the Troop embarked at Balaclava Harbour, one portion of them in the transport "Deva," and the remainder in the large clipper transport "Pride of the Ocean." Only a few men were left behind, amongst whom was the Trumpeter. Captain Forster's Troop, 6th Dragoon Guards, was also on board the latter vessel. The steam transport "Medway" took both the "Pride of the Ocean" and a Commissariat ship "The Bloomer" in tow. It was night when they passed before Sevastopol Harbour, and nothing could be seen except some camp fires on the north side. About two o'clock in the morning, when still some miles from Eupatoria, the "Pride of the Ocean" grounded slightly, but was got off again; the "Bloomer," however, remained fixed and had to be left. A war vessel was sent next day to protect her, as she was rather near the coast, and after throwing a great quantity of firewood and other things overboard, she was floated off. The disembarkation on the 13th and 17th October was effected in the usual horse boats, and the Troop moved into a sort of large yard, enclosed with high stone walls, and close to the sea. There were three or four of these yards leading one into the other. The bottom was of soft sand, which was a great boon to the horses, as they were able to lie down at night and get rest. The chief object in sending the English Cavalry Brigade to Eupatoria, was that they might assist the French and Turkish Troops in some rapid expeditions that were to be made, with a view to harassing the communications of the enemy.

The English Cavalry Brigade consisted of the 6th Dragoon Guards, Col. Jones commanding; the 4th Light Dragoons, Col. Low commanding; the 12th Lancers, Col. Pole commanding; and the 13th Light Dragoons. The 12th were from India, and had four squadrons. They were mounted on grey Arab geldings, quiet, useful little animals; the other three Regiments were in reduced numbers, two squadrons each. The Brigade was upwards of 1000 strong, exclusive of dismounted men.

In 'C' Troop there were: Captain H. J. Thomas, Lieuts. W. A. Fox Strangways, J. E. Ruck Keene, W. Stirling, and Assistant-Surgeon T. Park; 169 non-commissioned officers and men; 208 officers and troop horses; 6 guns; 17 ammunition waggons and carriages.

The French had a large Cavalry force, their 6th and 7th Dragoons and 4th Hussars, making in all twelve strong squadrons. They had a Troop of Horse Artillery, one or two slow Batteries, and a large Infantry force.

The Ottomans had a large force of Cavalry, and were able to turn out sixteen squadrons of sorts. They had a Troop of Horse Artillery, one or two slow Batteries of old-fashioned guns, and also a large force of Turkish and Egyptian Infantry.

There was also a force of Bashi Bashouks, who were cunning and useful for outpost work, and for ferreting out information regarding the enemy. Their commander was a venerable-looking man, who was usually followed by a standard-bearer, carrying an enormous cream-coloured standard with various characters worked on it, and fastened to a lofty pole, and there was also a man beating a pair of small tom toms attached to the front of his saddle; then the main body followed, in irregular order like a mob, dressed in any sort of dirty garments, such as pieces of sack tied on with twine, rope, etc. Some had long guns, suspended by a string round their necks, and resting across their backs; others carried lances of great length, with some trophies attached near the top, and all had daggers or knives of some sort stuck about their girdles. They had not the sedate appearance of the Turkish soldier, but were impudent-looking fellows, and would come grinning round the ranks whenever they had an opportunity, always on the look-out for what they could get. They were not very brave, and if ever they brought themselves up to the fighting point, so as to give chase to any parties of Cossacks, the latter were sure to be in the minority. It was said they were very cruel also whenever they had the mastery, and that on one occasion, after the English had left, they surprised and scalped a Cossack picquet when there was no authority at hand to prevent the atrocity.

The French and Turks were all quartered or encamped in the town, or on the land or fortified side of it, while the English Troops were quite away by themselves on the beach beyond the right of the town as it faces the sea.

Major Jenyns, 13th Light Dragoons, was Brigade-Major, and Major (now Lieut.-General) J. Conolly was Deputy-Assistant Quartermaster-General to the English Troops. Captain the Hon. C. Keith, 4th Light Dragoons, acted as A.D.C. He spoke French fluently, and there was a corporal of French Dragoons, who was equally good and quick at English, and who rode with the Staff. A driver of 'C' Troop, who had lived in France, was also useful in this way; so that all emergent orders in the field were conveyed with great clearness and precision. While at Eupatoria, all orders connected with the reconnaissances, and every other duty, were copied daily into the Troop Order-book, and therefore retained—thus differing from other operations in the Crimea, in which the orders were usually verbal, and kept secret as much as possible.

Eupatoria was a rather poor and straggling place; there were some two-storied houses, but the majority were one story, with long sloping roofs, something like the larger pitmen's cottages in the North of England. They lay in a semicircle round the inner part of the bay or harbour; there were fifteen or twenty rude windmills in a row on the left side near the sea, and these were the most noticeable objects when the town was looked at from any considerable distance. The place is very flat, and the streets only a few feet above the level of the sea, except actually in the streets, the soft sand is ankle-deep everywhere. Some strong earthworks had been thrown up on the side farthest from the harbour, but the right side of the town facing the sea was rather open. There were, however, a couple of war-vessels usually at anchor ready to search that part with their fire in case of an attack by the Russians. The water, which is procurable from wells, is brackish, and some of it so salt that it will not make tea. There is a quantity of sand in it; in fact, it is impossible to disturb or draw it from the shallow wells without at the same time drawing up the sand. Many of the French horses, which had been there before the arrival of the English, died from the amount of sand they had swallowed with their water.

A General Order, dated Eupatoria, 15th October, was issued, intimating that the French General D'Allonville was in supreme command of the place, and that the troops of the different nations were commanded as follows:

The English Cavalry Brigade	By Brigadier-General Lord George Paget.
The French Infantry—4th Division of the 2nd Corps	By General of Division De Failly.
Division of French Cavalry of the 2nd Corps	By General of Brigade Walsin d'Esterhazy.

The Muchir Achmet Pasha was in chief command of the Ottoman Troops.

General D'Allonville was a most active officer, and appeared to superintend everything connected with the reconnaissances himself. He was very careful in his turn out, and was usually followed by a non-commissioned officer carrying a small bright-looking tricolour, but he dispensed with any escort or numerous staff

The country for many miles round Eupatoria, or at least as far as the reconnaissances were ever carried out, is generally arid and desolate. There are vast salt lakes and marshes, and large stagnant pools with the salt in crystals round the edges, nothing growing near them but the coarsest and scantiest vegetation, and in many places the sand is ankle deep. It is very flat, but there are occasional conical mounds to be met with, from ten to twenty feet high, and five or six feet across the top, said by some to be tumuli; but, at any rate, they are very useful for the lonely shepherds or cattle-drovers in times of peace, from which to watch their flocks, and they were well suited for the purposes of reconnoitring. There are no trees, and drinking-water for man or beast is only procurable from wells in the neighbourhood of the very few hamlets that are about. All outside Eupatoria there were numerous packs of the largest and fiercest wolf-like wild dogs, twenty or thirty in each pack, and in such a state of starvation that a dead horse or camel was eaten up all but the bones in a few hours.

At a distance of sixteen or eighteen miles from the town the land in some directions loses its extreme flatness, and the vegetation is better, but there is still the same want of water and trees.

By the 20th October the Brigade had completed its disembarkation, and orders for a reconnaissance were immediately issued. The first expedition started from Eupatoria in two columns on the 22nd October at 6 A.M.

One column under the chief Ottoman General Achmet Pasha comprised a very large mixed Infantry force, a Regiment of Turkish Cavalry, three Batteries, and some Bashi Bashouks. They assembled outside the postern, in the direction of the strip of land between the Salt Lake and the Black Sea.

The other column, under General D'Allonville, comprised about four thousand mixed Infantry, thirty-four squadrons of allied Cavalry, three troops (English, French and Turks) of Horse Artillery, and some Bashi Bashouks. Ambulances for the wounded always attended these expeditions.

One of the Ottoman Generals was left in command at Eupatoria.

The assemblage of such a large mixed force in the dark was always exciting, and it was amusing and puzzling to hear the different languages.

There was a small commissariat, but the troops themselves carried two days' rations cooked, and one day's barley for the horses. The men also took their water canteens full at starting, as it was intimated that drinking water would be scarce.

D'Allonville's column proceeded to reconnoitre the forces of the enemy on a part of the route between Simpheropol and Perekop, and they at first marched in a northerly direction, and afterwards bore towards the east near the lake Sasik Guilore, until they arrived at the village of Karagurt, about eighteen miles from Eupatoria, where they bivouacked for the night, and destroyed the village. An advanced force of Russian Cavalry had shown itself in front during some part of the march, but the French Horse Artillery opened fire on them, and they retired as the allied column advanced. Orders were issued at this place, that, in case of any sudden alarm during the night, the men were to fall in dismounted, with carbines, in front of their lines, having previously, as far as time would permit, saddled their horses. This order held good for all subsequent occasions.

The other column, under Muchir Achmet Pasha, had proceeded from Eupatoria in the direction of Sak, by the strip of land between the sea and the lake.

On the morning of the 23rd at daybreak, the column under General D'Allonville proceeded in a rather southerly direction towards the village of Temesch, near to which there was a strong Russian force; they, however, retired, and the column continued its advance on the village of Towzla. On a rising ground near this village 'C' Troop was ordered to go into action against the enemy, which it did with good effect. On this occasion the configuration of the ground was such that the result of the firing was well seen. Some Russian Cavalry were driven from their position, the last shot that was fired going right into the middle of a Troop, which was cutting away at a gallop rather across the front. Lord George Paget was close by at the time, and observing the effects of the fire. He was never lavish of praise, and seldom indulged in laughter or merriment on parade, but this last shot so tickled him that he broke out with a loud " Ha ! ha ! " and addressing Captain Thomas, said, " By Jove, you deserve a step of brevet rank for that shot alone." During the time 'C' Troop was in action, it was fired at by the enemy's Artillery, from the direction of its left front, but sustained no loss. The ground occupied by the Russians seemed to be sandy and very uneven, and had all the appearance of low earthworks. No Artillery horses or limbers could be seen, in fact nothing but the smoke after each discharge of their guns. 'C' Troop was supported by the 6th Dragoon Guards. There was a slight hollow between the opposing forces. As the afternoon wore on General D'Allonville formed a junction with the other column under Muchir Achmet Pasha, near the village of Sak. This village was destroyed, and the allied Troops bivouacked close by for that night. During the 24th the expedition returned to Eupatoria by the sea-coast road. Some horses and mules died from exhaustion and want of water. There was very little of the latter in the few wells that were met with, and these were soon emptied, so that great numbers of horses had to go without any. A French war brig, and an English transport, upon which guns had been placed temporarily, co-operated with the troops on this occasion, firing on the enemy's flanks and on some of their outlying picquets. There were a great many hares started when on these expeditions, and the chase at times was very amusing. A Colonel of French Dragoons had a fine hound that was continually running them down, sometimes close in on the line of Russian scouts, and it was often a wonder that the animal got back to his master.

On the 27th October the second Expedition left Eupatoria in three columns. The orders as to rations, etc., were much the same as before, except that the ration of barley was reduced, also the ration of meat, but there was an extra allowance of coffee.

The first column under General Achmet Pasha comprised a large force of Ottoman Infantry, some slow guns, and half the Turkish Cavalry with their Troop of Horse Artillery.

The second column under General de Failly comprised a large force of French Infantry, and some slow French guns.

The third column under General D'Allonville was made up of the other half of the Turkish Cavalry, the whole of the French and English Cavalry, with both Troops of Horse Artillery.

Orders were issued that only perfectly effective men and horses were to be taken.

The columns assembled in succession outside the postern leading towards Sak, and by 11 A.M. they had all moved off.

The expedition proceeded in the direction of the ruined village of Sak, and having reached a point not far from there, they halted for a short rest. The Cavalry and Artillery were dismounted, and orders were given quietly to prepare for a rapid advance for a long distance. Capt. Thomas then selected three of the best-horsed waggons, two for the nine-pounders and one for the howitzers, to keep up with the guns as closely as they could. He also selected a few pairs of the best spare horses for the same purpose, and then gave orders for the Quarter-Master Sergeant to take all the remaining waggons and carriages and join the French and Turkish Infantry, and remain with their column. Previous to dismounting, the French Cavalry with their Troop of Horse Artillery were placed at a good distance, probably eight hundred yards, to the right front of the English Cavalry and 'C' Troop, the English were in the centre. The Turkish Cavalry with their Troop of Horse Artillery were on the left of the allied forces, and there was an interval of about seven hundred yards between them and the English Cavalry, with which they were very nearly in line. The whole allied Infantry and the slow guns were as it might be in the right rear of 'C' Troop, which was on the right of the English Brigade. The Cavalry were not in extended lines, but in columns of sorts or echelons. The time occupied by the "dismount" was about the same as at an ordinary Field-day.

General D'Allonville now ordered "mount" and "advance" to be sounded, and there was an instant rush away from the Infantry, the French giving the pace, which was a rapid "trot out." 'C' Troop was in "double column of subdivisions from the centre." There was no galloping except occasionally for a few yards to correct any distance that was lost owing to irregularities in the ground. The path of 'C' Troop lay more or less in a slight hollow, with gentle ups and downs in it, and the 12th Lancers on their left rear was the nearest Regiment. The ground was such as to prevent those in 'C' Troop seeing everything that was going on in front, and they at times lost sight of both French and Turks, and even their own English Regiments, except the 12th Lancers; but it was well understood that General D'Allonville knew there was a considerable body of Russian Cavalry out, and that he wished to push these in on their reserves at such a pace as to create a certain amount of confusion, make them unmask their guns, and otherwise show the numbers and disposition of what was supposed to be one of their covering armies.

But the Russians appeared to get back at a very good pace. There was no check of speed on the part of the Allies for a distance of perhaps four miles, and only then when the shot from the Russian guns of position actually came through the French Cavalry, and the shells were bursting over them. They then sounded "halt," and the bugle call was passed along the low hill tops to the English and Turks, who now halted in conformity to the French. The French, English, and Turks were thus nearly in the same relative positions they occupied before the advance began, except that the French were not so far in front. The French then instantly diminished their front by shifting squadrons in rear of their right, so as to take a portion of them from under fire. The French Troop of Horse Artillery came into action at the same time. The spot upon which 'C' Troop was halted was a sort of wide recess, having high ground in front, and rather high ground on the right and left. Very little could be seen in the direction of the French except the shells which were bursting over them; and towards the left none of the troops could be seen except the 12th Lancers, who had now formed line, and were about 120 yards to the left of the Troop. There was not a straggler of any sort about, and the day was quite calm. This short halt gave breathing time to the gun horses, and after a few minutes Captain Keith, A.D.C., came from the left, and, saluting Captain Thomas, said, "You are to take your Troop, Sir, over that hill in your front, and come into action," but he did not add one word as to what was likely to be met with on the other side, nor as to what they were to open fire upon : merely turned his horse's head and galloped off again. There was therefore no time for reconnoitring the ground or pre-arranging anything before starting. As there was no efficient trumpeter with the Troop, Captain Thomas gave the command, "Trot—march!" and instantly "Form line to the front," which was done as "on the move," the flanks coming up at a gallop ; therefore not a moment was lost. From the spot on which the Troop stood at the halt to the top of the rising ground in front would be about 200 yards, so that the horses were all fairly at a rapid gallop before they reached the crest, the Commanding Officer being about twenty yards in front. No shot of any sort had so far been fired by the Russians in this direction, but they must have had some excellent officers reconnoitring the advance of the Allies, or some other means of conveying to their gunners what was likely to take place, for the instant that even the very top of Captain Thomas's busby was seen by them ascending the hill, they let go their first gun, the heavy shell from which struck the ground a few feet in front of his charger, and sent such a quantity of earth against the head of the animal that it reared into the air and swerved round, and the men of the Troop who saw it thought that both officer and horse were killed. This shell flew over the Troop, and burst amongst the waggons. Owing to this momentary check of the Captain's speed, the " gun of direction " had almost come up to him by the time his charger was fairly fronted and at the gallop again, and he signed with his arm, which was understood to put on speed. The ground was now favourable, with a gentle descent towards the enemy; there seemingly being a moderate hollow between the opposing forces, and the Troop being in full view, the Russians let go at them from large guns of position. After a short advance the Troop came into action; the range, however, was too great to be fully effective, so " Front, limber-up," was ordered, and a further advance made. Here, as at the Alma, fortune favoured the Troop, for in a few seconds they had passed within the range for which the Russians were firing, and immediately afterwards came into action with splendid results.

If a line were drawn across from the French to some advanced Turkish Lancers on the left, the position of the Troop would be about 400 yards in front of it, but they were rather more than this distance in front of the 12th Lancers.

General D'Allonville and others, who were wide of the smoke, could no doubt see the results better than those immediately behind it. Having remained in action as long as was deemed advisable, the Troop retired. In the act of limbering-up, or at the beginning of the retire, one of the detachment horses had its hock broken away by a shot, and before reaching the crest another detachment horse had a large splinter of shell driven flatways up through the sole of the foot, breaking away the bones. The appointments were taken off, and the animals destroyed as soon as they could be got from under fire. A mounted gunner was also wounded while retiring. In the French there were many casualties, but in the English Cavalry there were none, as they were a little farther back than the French, and the ground gave them more cover. Some Turkish Lancers may be said to have behaved admirably; they were at the halt, and never wavered while they were being fired into. Altogether the Allies had about thirty men killed and wounded in this affair. The services of the Troop this day were very much praised by the French, but the full effect of the firing was not thoroughly known until it was heard of from the Russians themselves in conversation after the signing of the Armistice. The credit of selecting the position for action was entirely due to Captain Thomas; Lord George Paget did not come near the Troop.

After coming out of action, the Allied Cavalry and Horse Artillery retired on the Infantry. During the retreat they were followed by a considerable body of Russian Cavalry, who, however, did not show any disposition to fight. When the junction of Cavalry and Infantry was effected, the whole allied force went into bivouac for the night in the neighbourhood of Sak, and long chains of Cossack picquets were immediately placed by the enemy to confront those of the Allies. The next day the wounded were sent under sufficient escort to Eupatoria.

In the early morning of the 28th, the whole of the Cavalry and Horse Artillery left bivouack, and proceeded in a direction rather more inland. After a few hours' marching, they came upon a considerable force of the enemy's Cavalry, in front of which they manœuvred for some hours, but no engagement ensued. This was a very grand sight; it was probably the largest force of Cavalry that had got within striking distance of each other during the entire war. On the Russian side the land, for a great distance, lay in a very gentle slope, and it enabled the Allies to see that the country for miles was chequered with the enemy's squadrons; these appeared to go about, move to their right or left, halt, etc., as one man. There was a moderate breeze blowing from the direction of their right flank, and the jets of dust caused by the movement of the horses' feet seemed to begin at the one moment when they moved and to be shut off at the one moment when they halted. It looked as if they had at first been formed up in two or three long lines, and had then advanced in echelon of squadrons from the right or left of regiments. There were about thirty-eight squadrons of the Allies, and certainly double that number of the Russians, without counting irregulars, and the forces were generally within from three-quarters of a mile to a mile of each other. So large a force of Cavalry in two such compact bodies, manœuvring in opposition in real warfare, can seldom have been seen; indeed, it would require a similar waste of country to admit of it, and they would have to be, by chance or otherwise, miles away from their Infantry. Towards noon the Allied Cavalry drew off, and retired to bivouac near Sak, followed, as usual, by some of the Russian Cavalry. There was no water to be had this night, and the horses suffered very much in consequence.

On the morning of the 29th the expedition set out on its return to Eupatoria, and the troops reached their camps just before noon. The war-vessel "Diamond" co-operated from the sea-coast on this occasion.

These expeditions were perhaps as bold and risky as anything that was attempted in the open field against the enemy during the war. From the time of quitting the defences of the town, numbers of Cossacks usually hung around the Allied force, sometimes far off, sometimes quite near; and the whole unemployed Russian Army thereabouts could at once have been put on the alert by signalling. As night set in, and the force prepared to bivouac, long chains of Cossack vedettes gathered round, so close that their swords, carbines, or lances could be distinctly seen. They effectually prevented the Allies from pushing patrols well out to gain information, and any morning the reconnoitring force might have had to confront a powerful army in overwhelming numbers, which had been marched against them during the night.

About this time there was great mortality amongst the Ottoman troops; they had a large steamer at anchor in the harbour, and their sick used to be taken on board, but it turned out afterwards that many were removed there merely to die. The steamer occasionally went to sea for a short trip, supposed to be for the benefit of the sick, but in reality to throw the dead overboard; for one morning, after a storm, the sea-shore for miles was covered with their corpses that had been washed up by the swell. The General commanding was very much annoyed about this, as was every one else, and he gave orders that all the bodies were to be collected by the Turks, and buried on land.

On the 2nd November the third Expedition left Eupatoria. A small column, of which two squadrons 12th Lancers formed a part, assembled at 5 A.M. They were instructed to march towards the village of Chotai, about fifteen miles distant, and endeavour to capture some commissariat cattle, etc., belonging to the enemy, which was said to be collected in that neighbourhood. The greatest secrecy was enjoined. By daylight this force was some considerable distance on their journey, and complete success attended the expedition, for they captured a great number of cattle, sheep, horses, vehicles, and camels; also a Russian officer, a Cossack, and a number of villagers. A large quantity of hay was set on fire and destroyed. The operation was necessarily of a slow character, and the column did not reach Eupatoria till very late at night. The whole of the captured animals were distributed by allotment amongst the troops of the different nations. The mutton, which proved to be very good, was a great treat to the English troops, who had been for some time on salt rations.

The remainder of the troops assembled at 5·30 A.M. on this morning, under the command of General De Failly, carrying one day's provisions, cooked, and one large feed for each horse. This column proceeded considerably to the right of Chotai and far inland, making a demonstration with a view to drawing off the attention of the enemy from the other column. After many hours' manœuvring, the troops returned to Eupatoria, reaching their camps late in the evening.

The weather soon began to get cold, and the cutting winds told upon the horses of the English Brigade, particularly those that were at picket out on the beach away from the enclosures; these were within a few dozen yards of the sea, and had no protection. The sand was so loose that it would not hold the picket-posts, and there was great difficulty in keeping the animals secure at night. The horses' rations ran short, and hay had to be borrowed from the French.

The English Brigade had now in use the ordinary long, loose Chesterfield pilot coat, as worn by civilians at home in winter: very comfortable to walk about in, but when worn on horse-back in the military saddle, it remained in folds about the wearer's waist, and did not admit of falling down to afford any protection to the thighs. It was of woolly, thick cloth, and consequently rather cumbersome.

The French Cavalry had a useful sort of garment served out to them; it was a very loose and shapeless kind of pelisse, reaching below the hips, with a hood, but without any ornament; four buttons only down the front, and a slit up as far as the waist behind, so as to sit easy when worn mounted. It fitted loosely over the uniform, and the cloth was only of the same thickness as that of the coat or jacket, so that the soldier could use his arms freely, and he was sufficiently warm during day-time. They wore their pouch-belts outside, and their long carbines slung over the shoulder. Altogether they looked very picturesque, particularly the Dragoons, who had leopard or tiger skin round their helmets. The hood was comfortable at night in bivouac. Their officers wore the same pattern, so there was complete uniformity.

Fourth Expedition.—A reconnaissance was made on the 12th November, starting at 7 A.M., under the command of General of Brigade D'Esterhazy. The English force, under Colonel Jones, 6th Dragoon Guards, was composed of one strong squadron from each of the four regiments, and two guns of 'C' Troop. One day's rations, cooked, and one large feed of corn for each horse was taken. This reconnaissance extended over one day only, and no casualty occurred. A general order was issued on the 12th November, giving instructions as to where commanding officers should rally their men in case Eupatoria was attacked, and requesting Captain Thomas to examine and decide on the points from which his guns could best take the works of the Ottoman entrenched camp in reverse.

Fifth Expedition.—A force, of which 'C' Troop and five squadrons of English Cavalry formed a part, left Eupatoria at 5·30 A.M. on the 16th November, under command of General De Failly, taking one meal, cooked, and one feed for each horse. The object was to bring in all the fire-wood that could be secured, and set fire to whatever they were unable to remove. This expedition was also a success; a quantity of wood was carried away, and what could not be removed was set on fire. The column returned to Eupatoria in the evening, without seeing any of the enemy, except a strong detachment of Cossacks.

Sixth Expedition.—A Reconnaissance.—On the evening of the 19th November, a Russian force made their appearance before Eupatoria, and a reconnaissance of French Cavalry was ordered for the following morning (the 20th). All the other troops were to be in readiness at daybreak. As the morning wore on, and the French Cavalry were still out of sight, the English troops were ordered to move out as a precautionary measure, and the whole afternoon was spent in manœuvring about. On the retreat to Eupatoria the enemy followed up as far as the bridge near that place, bringing guns with them. 'C' Troop unlimbered on this occasion, but there was no firing.

Some time in November Lord George Paget assembled the whole of the English troops on a foot parade, and informed them it had been decided by the authorities that the Brigade should winter at Scutari; and he read out some very complimentary letters and despatches which had been forwarded from General D'Allonville, through Marshal Pelissier, to the English Headquarters, speaking in high terms of the Cavalry Brigade and

Services of 'C' Troop during the Campaign. 257

Troop of Horse Artillery attached to them. Lord George on this parade specially alluded to the good conduct of 'C' Troop. No crime whatever had been committed by any one belonging to the Troop during the time it was employed at Eupatoria. Nearly all the men preferred leaving their pay for deposit in the savings bank, rather than spend it on the bad liquor obtainable from the few sutlers that were about the place.

On the 24th and 25th of November the Troop embarked in the transports for Scutari. On arrival there on 1st December they were quartered, the men in huts close to the large white barracks, and the horses in a large Turkish Cavalry stable near the landing-place.

On leaving the shores of the Crimea, all ranks in the Troop had just cause to feel proud of its having been selected for the following posts and duties.

When the Army sat down before Sevastopol, the camp ground of the Troop was the nearest of all to the Fortress; it was therefore felt to be a post of honour.

In response to a call on its resources, the Troop furnished a substantial detachment of *bonâ fide* Horse Artillerymen for working at the siege guns and in the trenches in the first bombardment, beginning on the 17th October, which detachment remained with the Siege Train for many weeks; and though of necessity it weakened the Gun Detachments, it did not otherwise impair the efficiency of the Troop for the battles which took place at that time, notwithstanding the exceptional difficulties they had to contend with, as narrated in these pages.

It was ordered by the Commander-in-Chief that the Troop was to be on the ground at Inkerman an hour before daylight every morning, on the watch, and prepared to resist any attack in that quarter; no other Field Artillery accompanied the Troop on these occasions, while at the same time it was ordered that the first alarm was to be sent to the Troop in case of an attack on the position at Balaclava, which was some miles in an opposite direction.

Owing to the good services of the Troop at the Battle of Balaclava, the Commander in-Chief ordered that they were not to leave the ground even for that night to get any portion of their food, necessaries, or tents.

On the 5th November, as soon as it was found that no attack was intended on the position at the Col de Balaclava by the Russians, the Troop was ordered to the Battle at Inkerman.

On the occasion of the Russian Festival in December, 1854, the Troop was ordered up to the plateau, to assist in resisting the anticipated sortie from Sevastopol, though at that time its camp-ground was a great distance off.

They took part in the reconnaissance under Sir Colin Campbell on the 19th February, 1855.

At the battle of the Tchernaya, when an additional English Battery was required to go into action, 'C' Troop was ordered for that duty.

The Troop was honoured by being ordered to furnish one of its guns, upon which to convey the remains of Field-Marshal Lord Raglan, in grand funeral procession of the allied armies, to the place of embarkation for England.

When the expedition to Eupatoria was decided upon, 'C' Troop was ordered for that duty.

Finally their guns were the oftenest in action against the enemy of any field guns in the English Army, and it is confidently believed that they were also oftener in action than any other six field guns of the French, Turkish, Sardinian, or Russian Armies, counting from the outbreak of the war until its conclusion.

It should be added that other Field Artillery on the plateau also furnished detachments for the bombardments and siege duties; but it fell hard upon 'C' Troop, owing to the way they were split up, and the extra labour that was thrown upon the old hands by the large augmentation of horses.

In December, 1855, Assistant-Surgeon Park left the Troop on promotion, and he was succeeded by Assistant-Surgeon E. Bowen.

During the winter evenings at Scutari a night school was started for the men, where they were taught mental arithmetic and writing, as far as it was possible to carry it out. At this time the Troop was presented, through Major Grylls, with a flag which had been worked specially for them by the ladies of Cornwall.

On the 18th or 19th March, 1856, the Troop fired the salute in honour of the birth of the Prince Imperial of France, and on the 31st fired one to celebrate the conclusion of peace, news of which was received by telegram.

On the 6th of April Captain Thomas embarked for England on promotion, and was succeeded by Major H. F. Strange, who joined on the 20th April.

On the 7th April the Troop was inspected by the Sultan Abdul Medjid.

CHAPTER XI.

RETURN TO ENGLAND.—CHANGES OF QUARTERS.—EMBARKATION FOR INDIA.—INDIAN SERVICE.—RETURN HOME.—IRELAND.—CONCLUSION.

ON the conclusion of peace between the allied powers and Russia, arrangements for the return home of the English Army were commenced. All unserviceable horses of mounted corps were cast and sold, and some animals were handed over to the Turkish Government to be used for breeding purposes; thus most regiments, troops, and batteries returned to England considerably below their proper establishment of horses.

On the 30th May, 1856, Major H. F. Strange, Lieutenants W. Fox-Strangways, J. E. Ruck Keene, and Assistant-Surgeon Essex Bowen, together with 125 non-commissioned officers and men, and 124 horses, embarked and sailed for England on board the transports "Brandon" and "Sydney." They were followed, on the 8th June, by Lieut. W. Stirling and seventy-four non-commissioned officers and men, who brought home the guns, stores, and other carriages in the transport "Alster." On arrival at Portsmouth, the Troop was sent by rail to Woolwich, where it was complete on the 28th June. By the middle of July, 1856, all the Field Artillery from the Crimea had arrived there, and on the

14th July the force, consisting of 'A,' 'C,' and 'I' Troops, and thirteen Field Batteries, was reviewed by the Queen. In August there appeared in regimental orders the names of the non-commissioned officers and men upon whom the French war medal had been conferred by the Emperor Napoleon III. Sergeant Henry Bacchus was selected from 'C' Troop; he had served throughout the campaign; he was present at Alma, Balaclava, Inkerman, Sevastopol, and with the Expedition to Eupatoria, and on all occasions was distinguished for his zeal.

The following summer, on the 25th June, 1857, the Troop was present at a review in Hyde Park, when the Queen decorated with the newly-instituted order of the Victoria Cross sixty-one officers, soldiers and sailors of the Army and Navy. On the 25th July, 1857, the Troop left Woolwich for Aldershot. It was moved again on the 21st August to Ireland, where it was quartered five years, and was stationed at Cahir, Newbridge, the Curragh, and Dublin, making numerous moves between the last-named three places.

The manner in which the number of Horse Artillery guns was tripled between 1848 and 1853 has already been described. About the same time the regiment was largely increased. The 11th and 12th Battalions were formed on the 1st November, 1848, and the 13th and 14th Battalions on the 1st February, 1854, and 1st April, 1855, respectively. In consequence of these augmentations, instructions were issued in April, 1859, for a reorganization of the Regiment, to come into effect on the following 1st July. Among other changes the term "Battalion" was replaced by "Brigade," and "Troop" and "Company" by "Battery." Accordingly 'C' Troop became *'C' Battery Royal Horse Brigade.* Medical Officers now became regimental, and were regularly posted to Brigades and Batteries, and this system obtained till 1873.

About 1861, a more important regimental alteration was effected—namely, the change of the armament of the Artillery from smooth-bored to rifled guns. Rifled ordnance had been used at the siege of Sevastopol, but owing to defective construction, it produced but little effect. Not long afterwards Mr. (now Sir William) Armstrong invented a breech-loading rifled gun, which was so superior in range and accuracy to the pieces hitherto in use, that it was adopted into the service. The smooth-bored muzzle-loading field pieces became obsolete, and their places were supplied in the Horse Artillery by a 9-pounder gun of about six cwt. of the new pattern, calculated to fulfil the requirements of field service. 'C' Battery, on the 29th April, 1862, at Newbridge, received the new equipment, which consisted of six 9-pounder breech-loading rifled guns, with six ammunition waggons, a forge, and a store waggon.

The reorganization and rearmament just mentioned were followed on the 19th February, 1862, by the amalgamation of the Indian, with the Royal, Artillery. Four Brigades of Horse, and ten of Field and Garrison, Artillery were then added to the Regiment; and the Indian Artillery, which had sprung in 1748 from the Royal Artillery, thus rejoined it after a varied but distinguished career of 114 years. The old Royal Horse Artillery now became the 1st, the late Bengal the 2nd and 5th, and the Madras and Bombay the 3rd and 4th Royal Horse Brigades.

On the 30th August, 1862, '*C*' *Battery*, 1*st Horse Brigade*, marched from Newbridge, crossed over to England, and proceeded to Aldershot, from whence, on the 9th March, 1863, it marched to Windsor and fired the Royal salute on the occasion of the marriage of the

Prince of Wales. Shortly afterwards, on the 30th May, 1863, it moved to Woolwich, where arrangements were to be made the following year to enable the relief of the old Indian Brigades to be commenced. With this object, on the 1st April, 1864, the 1st Horse Brigade was divided into two, making a total of six Brigades of Horse Artillery, which were lettered from 'A' to 'F.' The Batteries of the old Royal Horse Artillery formed 'A' and 'B' Brigades; the former comprised 'A,' 'B,' 'C,' 'G,' and 'K,' the latter 'D,' 'E,' 'F,' 'H,' and 'I' Batteries. All those of 'B' Brigade had served in India during the mutiny, excepting 'I' Battery. From the date of this organization the Batteries of each Brigade were relettered from 'A' downwards, 'C' Battery still retaining its original letter. In August the relief began by the two junior Batteries of 'A' Brigade, 'D' and 'E,' proceeding to India to relieve two Batteries of 'C' Brigade Royal Horse Artillery. The following year the remainder of 'A' Brigade was held in readiness to complete the relief which had been begun, and accordingly on the 10th August, 1865, '*C*' *Battery* '*A*' *Brigade*, with 'A' and 'B' Batteries, left Woolwich, and embarked the same day at Gravesend on board the hired steam transport "Hydaspes." With 'C' Battery were Captain and Brevet-Colonel the Hon. E. T. Gage, C.B., Lieuts. C. S. Harvey, T. Burnett, Assistant-Surgeon A. Chester, Veterinary Surgeon J. B. W. Skoulding, with 10 Staff Sergeants and Sergeants, 1 Trumpeter, and 136 Gunners, Drivers and Artificers. On the 11th, the "Hydaspes" sailed for India, and, although an auxiliary steamship, she sailed nearly the entire voyage, which lasted 120 days. On the 24th October, she touched at the Cape of Good Hope, and reached Calcutta on the 10th December, 1865. The following day the Battery disembarked and encamped on the "Maidán" outside Fort William. The non-commissioned officers and men were here supplied with white helmets and clothing and other articles of personal outfit for Indian service. The Battery was inspected by the Commander-in-Chief, Lieut.-General Sir Hugh Rose (now Lord Strathnairn), who expressed his satisfaction at everything connected with it. On the 22nd December it left Calcutta by rail, travelling by night only, the days being spent in standing rest camps. On the morning of Christmas Day it reached Benares, where all ranks were most hospitably entertained by 'C' and 'F' Batteries of 'C' Brigade Royal Horse Artillery (now 'C' Battery 'B' Brigade, and 'N' Battery 'B' Brigade, respectively). 'C' Battery took over from the former Battery, which was under orders for England, its native establishment, horses, bullocks, camp equipage, etc. (see Appendix XIX.). This establishment remained unchanged during the time the Battery was in India, with the exception of some alterations in the numbers of the bullocks and bullock drivers, and of the second line of ammunition waggons.

On the day of arrival at Benares the Battery unfortunately had its first experience of cholera in India. The Farrier Sergeant died after a few hours' illness, and the wife and two children of the Armstrong Armourer Sergeant a few days afterwards, of the same disease, and in an equally sudden manner. About the second week in January, 1866, the Battery marched for Lucknow, and en route, at Allahabad, took over the guns and carriages (see Appendix XIX.). On the 17th February it reached Lucknow, and a few days afterwards Major J. S. Tulloh took over the command, having exchanged with Colonel Gage, who returned to England. This exchange was followed by others which have caused some confusion in the succession list of Commanding Officers; Captain C. R. Hill is shown as one, and was taken up on the muster-roll of the Battery, though he never joined or did duty.

Coincident with the introduction of Armstrong field pieces into the service great attention had been devoted to the construction of rifled guns, and gradually a strong feeling was manifested that these breech-loading guns were not the best description of weapon the Field Artillery could be armed with. In consequence, towards the end of 1866, a committee of thirteen senior Artillery officers was assembled to report whether it was desirable or otherwise to continue the use of the then existing breech-loading system of rifled ordnance for field service. Without attempting to go into the *pros* and *cons* of this much vexed question, it may be briefly stated that the committee came to the conclusion that the balance of advantages was then in favour of muzzle-loading field guns, and it recommended that they should be manufactured in future. This report was approved, and by degrees muzzle-loading rifled guns were introduced, the breech-loaders becoming obsolete. 'C' Battery, as will be seen hereafter, received the new pattern armament on its return from India in 1876.

During nearly four years spent at Lucknow little of any interest happened. There was a Grand Durbar for the Viceroy to receive the native Princes and nobility of Oude, and the Battery annually carried out its gun practice at Koosaihree, a camp half-way on the road to Cawnpore.

An accident happened on an occasion when the garrison of Lucknow was being reviewed by Lord Napier of Magdala, after his return from Abyssinia. The particulars are given to show the falls and perils to which Horse Artillerymen are liable in the field. In galloping past at "close intervals" a detachment horse in the rear rank of No. 5 subdivision fell after passing the saluting point.

The gun-drivers of No. 5 gun had neither time to pull up, nor room to clear the fallen man and horse, and the leading horses fell over them, followed by the centre and wheel horses. The limber gunners were thrown from the limber, which, with the gun, was heaped on the top of all, the result being a struggling mass of six men and seven horses, from which with some difficulty three of the former were extricated more or less injured, though none fatally. It was at first thought that the centre driver, Adams, who was underneath everything, was killed. He was picked up insensible and taken to hospital. On examination, however, it was found he had experienced no fracture of his limbs or internal injury, and he was curiously enough the first man of those hurt to resume his duty. His nerve was, however, so shaken by his severe fall, that he was removed from the gun team to an easier post in a waggon. Of the horses, three were so injured that they had to be destroyed on the ground. Galloping past at "close intervals" was afterwards, in 1873, abolished as dangerous, there being no room for the centre guns of a Battery, as in this case, to avoid a fallen man or horse.

On the 18th December, 1869, the Battery marched for Meerut, arriving in January, and it remained there till the 1st November, 1871, when it marched *via* Delhi for Peshawur, where it arrived on the 11th January, 1872.

During this year an alteration took place in the regimental rank of the two senior officers of the Battery. The great results produced by the German Field Artillery during the Franco-German War of 1870, drew attention to the increased importance of Batteries in modern warfare, and the then Secretary of State for War, Mr. (now Lord) Cardwell, recognizing the great responsibility of such a command, decided that it should be held by a field officer. Accordingly on the 5th July, 1872, all

Captains of the Royal Artillery were gazetted Majors, and the second Captains ordered to be styled Captains.

The Commander-in-Chief in the cold season, before going to the camp of exercise at Hassan Abdul, visited Peshawur, and inspected the regiments there. After seeing 'C' Battery, the following communication was made to it :—

"Peshawur, 17th December, 1872.

"Sir,—The Brigadier-General has been commanded by Lord Napier of Magdala to express his Excellency's satisfaction with the excellent appearance and general efficiency of 'C' Battery, 'A' Brigade, R.H.A., and I have to request you will communicate this to Major Whinyates, his officers, non-commissioned officers, and men.

"Signed,
"A. V. WAUCHOPE, Captain.
"(Brigade-Major.)"

During the two years passed at Peshawur the non-commissioned officers and men suffered very much from the fever peculiar to the place, notwithstanding that large drafts were sent at the commencement of each hot season to the hill stations of Cherat and Murree. The casualties were, however, few, and in the severe outbreak of cholera which occurred in the autumn of 1872, when both the European and Native regiments in the station suffered severely, the Battery had the good fortune to escape with but one fatal case, and that a child. On the 5th December, 1873, it marched out of Peshawur on its way down country to Umballa. An officer with it, writing at the time, thus describes the routine of the daily marches :—

"At a quarter to five 'Reveillé' sounds, and before that hour no motion or sound of any kind is allowed in camp, as it would disturb the men's rest, and nothing in the world wakes you like the sound of knocking out a tent-peg. The moment 'Reveillé' sounds there is a general clatter; all the men turn out, the tents are struck and packed on the camels, and sent off. Half an hour suffices for this, and then 'Boot and saddle' sounds; the men go to their horses and get them ready, while the spare men roll up and pack the picket ropes to which the horses are fastened. A quarter of an hour after 'Boot and saddle,' 'Squad parade' sounds, the horses are taken to the guns and hooked in, the men mount, and the Battery is ready for inspection. A quarter of an hour after 'Squad parade,' we march off, a rear-guard of four men being left behind, who see that the native sweepers clean up the camping ground and burn all the spare litter, etc.; they also see all the baggage clear of the camp on the road. In the meantime your khidmutgar has prepared, and you have drunk, a cup of hot tea. It is now a quarter to six, quite dark and bitterly cold—so cold, that with the thickest winter clothes and a cloak over them, it is all you can do to keep warm. After you have been marching for an hour and a half, the sun rises and your spirits rise too, and, when you have been going two hours, the latter reach the highest point they attain during the day, for 'coffee-shop' appears in sight. This is a most excellent Indian arrangement. A gunner and his wife are in charge of the 'coffee-shop,' and make a small profit by it. They are sent on over night, half-way to the next halting-place, and when you march up every man in the Battery gets a cup of hot coffee, for which he pays about $1\frac{1}{2}d.$, and which he generally supplements with some bread. We have coffee and sandwiches at the same time, and we are all agreed that the happiest moment of the day is when you have had your coffee, lighted your cheroot, and are just beginning to get warm in the bright morning sun. The marches are from nine to fourteen miles in length, and you arrive in camp at from half-past eight to half-past nine o'clock, and are formed up; the camp having been previously marked out by numerous pegs and strings, the men dismount, the drivers unhook, and the gunners lay down the picket ropes. The picket rope is about forty yards long, fastened to the ground by long wooden pegs, and there is one to each subdivision (gun), and consequently six in the Battery. Each horse is fastened by his head to the picket rope, and by heel ropes to a peg, to keep him from kicking, and to keep him in his place. As soon as all is ready, the horses file on the picket lines, the trumpeter sounds 'Stable hour,' the harness is taken off, and the horses groomed, watered, and fed, and in about an hour and a half 'Turn-out!' sounds; the men pitch their tents and eat their breakfasts, and we go to ours. After you have had breakfast, your servants have generally got your tent up, and you go and change your clothes, dress, etc."

On the 17th January, 1874, the Battery marched into Umballa, having made the forty-two marches, about 432 miles, in forty-four days, the horses arriving in excellent condition, and without any casualties.

In 1873, a reorganization of the Medical Department took place, and medical officers ceased to form part of the Regimental establishment. In consequence, Assistant Surgeon W. W. Quinton, to the regret of all ranks, after seven years' service with the Battery, left it very soon after its arrival at Umballa.

In 1875, the year of the Prince of Wales's visit to India, the Government decided to assemble at Delhi a force of some 20,000 men to receive him. 'C' Battery was detailed to form part of the force, and accordingly marched in company with 'A' Battery 'A' Brigade from Umballa on the 19th November, 1875, and encamped at the Lahore Gate of the city of Delhi on the 1st of December. On the 4th December the Battery marched to the Artillery Camp at Bussunt, where ten Batteries were assembled for Artillery manœuvres. These lasted until the 22nd December, upon which day the several divisions of the Army intended to take part in the general manœuvres were formed. 'C' Battery joined the Cavalry Brigade of the Second Division, composed of the 11th Hussars, a regiment of the Central India Horse, and 4th Bengal Cavalry. Constant divisional parades occupied the time till the 3rd January, 1876, when the Battery joined the Third Division, which, with the Fourth Division and five other Batteries of Artillery, was ordered to carry out some experimental field firing on a spot that had been selected near the Kootub.

On this ground a dummy force equal to about two divisions of an Army Corps was placed on an elevated defensive and entrenched position. The Infantry, who were in shelter trenches, were represented by figures of baked mud ; the Artillerymen by stuffed scarecrow-like contrivances ; the guns, which were in gun-pits or behind slight epaulments, by bundles of sticks on crossed posts; the reserves of Cavalry and Infantry by canvas screens of proper height and width stretched between sticks. The attacking force consisted of twelve Battalions of Infantry, or about 6000 men, and six Batteries of Artillery. The operations began by an attack by the Artillery: a steady fire was maintained for two hours at ranges varying from 1200 to 2000 yards; the effect was good, and as a spectacle it was very fine. The continuous roar of the guns, the scream of the shells flying through the air, and the columns of dust and smoke thrown up in the enemy's position, was the nearest approach to a real battle that could be imagined without being fired at in return. When the enemy's guns were considered to be pretty well silenced, four Brigades of Infantry were sent against the position in the new attack formation. The first line of skirmishers opened fire at 700 yards, and these were reinforced as they approached the enemy, until within about 200 yards of the advanced shelter trenches, when the reserves closed up and the final rush was made. The effect of the Infantry fire was disappointing; for though the rattle of 2000 breech-loaders was appalling, yet it was ineffective until within 300 yards of the position. Periodically "Cease firing" was sounded to enable the ground to be examined, and the hits counted, marked and recorded. The Infantry appeared to have overestimated the range, but at the closer distance the fire began to take effect, and the result was terrific. These experiments were the most interesting event during the camp.

On the 6th January, 1876, the whole of the troops closed in on Delhi to receive the Prince of Wales, who arrived on the 11th. On the following day a grand parade and march past took place, there being present twelve Batteries of Artillery, thirteen Regiments of

Cavalry, and twenty-four Battalions of Infantry. On the 14th and 15th manœuvres took place, one-half the force attacking the city, which the other half defended.

On the 29th January the Battery moved from its camp at Daheepore down to the Delhi Railway Station to carry out some experiments. This was a very hard and hot day's work for the men. The horses, guns, carriages, tents, baggage, and native establishment were packed on a train, the object being to ascertain the time and accommodation necessary to move a Battery of Horse Artillery complete by rail, broad gauge, and by end loading. The operation was performed twice. The time occupied in embarking was fifty-four minutes, in disembarking twenty-four minutes, and eighty-four trucks and carriages were required (see Appendix XX.). The Commander-in-Chief was present on the second occasion, and when all was completed, Lord Napier complimented the non-commissioned officers and men on the efficient manner in which the work had been accomplished.

On the 31st January, 1876, the Battery marched to return to Umballa, which it reached on the 12th February. Nothing of consequence occurred during the remainder of the time spent there, but in August, upon the anniversary of the Brigade having been twelve years from home, some athletic sports were held, and it may be not uninteresting to quote the result of one of the events contested, as a proof that 'A' Brigade in general, and 'C' Battery in particular, had not deteriorated in smartness and efficiency at drill during that period in a hot climate. A prize of twenty rupees was given for the shortest time taken in " Dismounting and Mounting " gun and carriage. Six detachments competed, three from 'A' Battery, and three from 'C.' All were picked men, save one detachment, No. 4 subdivision, 'C' Battery, under Corporal Orchard, who took his men as they stood on parade, and with them beat all the others, the time from the command, "Dismount gun and carriage," to the command "Fire!" being forty-five seconds. An officer inspected each gun when it had finished, to see that all the side-arms were properly buckled on, ties in linch-pins, etc., as any defect in this respect would have been disqualifying. Artillerymen will recognize the smartness of this performance with a breech-loading gun, which is so much more difficult to manipulate than a muzzle-loader.

Preparations were now made for the move home at the end of the year, as then 'A' Brigade was to be relieved by 'B' Brigade, when the Battery experienced a great loss in the death of its excellent farrier, William Church, who died on the 28th October. The behaviour of the Battery during its service in India was uniformly good, and on more than one occasion it received special commendation from the Commander-in-Chief for its conduct and efficiency.

On the 20th November, 1876, 'C' Battery left Umballa, and on the 5th December, together with 'E' Battery, 'A' Brigade, and the 16th Lancers, embarked on board H.M.S. "Jumna." With 'C' Battery were Captain J. Burnett (attached), Lieuts. Barry Domvile, and J. D. Legard, with two staff-sergeants, seven sergeants, and 124 non-commissioned officers and men. The "Jumna" reached Portsmouth on the 7th January, 1877; on the 8th the Battery disembarked and proceeded by rail to Woolwich. On the following day it was inspected by the Commandant, Major-General (now Lieut.-General Sir Charles) D'Aguilar, who had been Second Captain of 'C' Troop in 1853. After the inspection the non-commissioned officers and men were granted the usual furloughs given on return from foreign service. In about a month, on their return, a complete new equipment was taken over at the Royal Arsenal (see Appendix XXI.), including six 9-pounder muzzle-loading rifled guns. The horses received were the browns left by 'C' Battery, 'B' Brigade, and thus the colour of the Battery was changed from bay, which it had been since its formation. During the summer it went through the usual phases experienced on return from India, the transfer of many of the oldest and most efficient soldiers to the Coast Brigade, the loss of batches of volunteers anxious to return to India, and the drilling and forming of recruits.

At a previous part of this history reference was made to a reorganization of the regiment, which took place about now. It was as follows: On the 1st July, 1877, 'A' and 'B' Brigades, the old Royal Horse Artillery, again became one Brigade, which remained lettered 'A,' and to each Battery in it was assigned the letter it was originally formed under. To 'E' Battery, 'B' Brigade (originally 1st Rocket Troop), was given that of 'D' Troop, which was reduced in 1816. The confusion caused by changing the letters of the various Troops in 1816 has already been explained. The new 'B' Brigade was formed of the batteries which had composed 'C' and 'D' Brigades.

By the end of the summer, the Battery had pretty well settled down, and was ordered in August to march to the newly-acquired land range near the town of Hay in Wales, to carry out the annual practice. It left Woolwich on the 8th August, 1877. *En route* all ranks were most hospitably entertained on two occasions. The first was on the march, between Bicester and Chipping Norton, at Westcote-Barton, the Rev. E. Lockyer being the host, whose son, between 1872 and 1875, had been a subaltern in the Battery. As no body of soldiers had passed through the village within the memory of the oldest inhabitant, the appearance of a Battery of Horse Artillery was quite an event to the people, who welcomed all ranks most cordially. Again, between Ledbury and Hereford, the whole Battery was entertained at Stoke Edith Park by Lady Emily Foley, who was good enough to extend the same kindness to them when returning on the 10th September.

On arrival at Hay on the 18th August, the encampment was formed in a field midway between the town and the top of the Black Mountain, upon which the practice was to be carried out. 'B' Battery, 1st Brigade arrived on the 18th also, and encamped on the same ground. The weather proved unfortunately very wet during nearly the whole of the practice, which was however successfully carried out, and was of an interesting nature, being against wooden dummies daily placed in positions to represent troops in different formations, and at unknown ranges. The arrangements were made by Lieut.-Colonel W. Fox Strangways, who took much pains to make the work of a practical and instructive character. The practice was finished on the 7th Sept., and the following day the Battery marched on its return to Woolwich, where, after a wet journey, all hands were glad to find themselves on the 18th September.

In the spring of 1878 the Battery was ordered to Aldershot, and left Woolwich on the 17th May. On arrival it was quartered in the Permanent Barracks. Little out of the ordinary routine occurred during the two years passed here. Quarter-Master Sergeant J. F. Cossey, after a service of upwards of fifteen years with 'C' Battery, received as a well-earned reward a commission in the Commissariat Department on the 1st June, 1878. In the spring of 1880 orders were received to proceed to Ballincolig. The Battery accordingly marched to Avonmouth, and on the 22nd April embarked there on board H.M.S. "Assistance." On nearing Queenstown, however, a counter-order was received to proceed to Dublin, where on arrival the Battery remained at Porto Bello till removed on the 14th May, 1880, to Newbridge.

Among the volunteers for India who left the Battery after its return home, some joined 'E' Battery, 'B' Brigade (originally fifth Troop first Brigade Bengal Horse Artillery), the Battery under Major G. F. Blackwood, who was killed, which so highly distinguished itself with Brigadier-General Burrows' column at the battle of Maiwand on 27th July, 1880, and which under Captain J. R. Slade, later the same day, so gallantly covered the retreat of the remnant of the force into Candahar. On this day the men late of 'C' Battery, in the words of the last-named officer, "acquitted themselves to the satisfaction of one and all." Gunners Mathewman and Swinnerton were killed. Gunner Ryan, who was sick at the time, during the retreat had his thigh broken through falling off a gun limber and being run over; he died and was buried within the walls of Candahar. Gunners Murray and Reilly escaped.

A reorganization of the Royal Artillery took place on the 1st April, 1882, the main object being to improve the recruiting for the Regiment. With regard to the Horse Artillery, the three then existing Brigades, 'A,' 'B,' and 'C,' were consolidated into two Brigades, 'A' and 'B,' each composed of thirteen Batteries: of the old 'A' Brigade, 'K' Battery was reduced (the second time this misfortune had befallen it), and 'A,' 'E,' 'F,' and 'G' Batteries of 'C' Brigade were added, and became 'L,' 'N,' 'K' and 'M' respectively. At the same date certain Batteries, not among those first for foreign service, were placed on a reduced establishment. 'C' Battery was one of them, and was placed on a four-gun strength (see Appendix XXII.).

At the commencement of this work it was explained how essential mobility was to produce an effective Field Artillery, and how much that mobility depended upon skilled Drivers. The public have recently become acquainted with the excellent driving of the Royal Artillery at the assaults of arms at Islington and elsewhere. Especial attention was always paid to driving in 'C' Battery, and an account of the competition during the athletic sports on 29th July, 1882, at Porto Bello, where the Battery moved to from Newbridge on the 17th May, 1881, is as follows:—On that occasion prizes were given for trotting and galloping a gun with a team of six horses round a figure marked out by pegs and posts driven into the ground at intervals. A certain number of points were given for a faultless passage round the course laid out, but marks were deducted if either horses' hoof or gun-wheel touched any of the boundaries, the width between which was slightly greater than the track of the gun wheels. For the trotting competition eleven teams entered, and 'C' Battery won the two prizes given for this event. For the galloping trial two prizes were also given, and eight teams competed. 'C' Battery won the first prize, and its other three teams tied with a team of another Battery for the second prize. The following day the ties were galloped off in the Phœnix Park, when 'C' Battery won.

In the spring of 1883, the Battery was ordered to be in readiness to move to England, and accordingly the Head Quarters and right half Battery sailed on the 6th May from Dublin in H.M.S. "Assistance" for Liverpool, from whence, on the 7th, they marched for London, and on arrival, on the 22nd, were quartered in the Barracks, St. John's Wood. They were joined on the 25th May by the left half Battery which had sailed from Dublin on the 18th May for Portsmouth, and from thence on the 21st marched to London.

This brings the history of 'C' Battery, 'A' Brigade, Royal Horse Artillery up to the present time. With it we have passed from the period when slow moving trains of Artillery crawled painfully after an Infantry, armed with smooth-bores, and when Artillery and Cavalry were safe from Infantry fire at all but the shortest distances. We leave the Battery when it is equipped to move at the fullest speed that Cavalry can attain, and when, itself armed with weapons of extraordinary range, it has to meet the fire of Infantry at the furthest extent of the field of battle. We have seen something of the trials and victories of the past. If the writer turns with regret from the record that forms his last work in common with the Battery with which so many of his hopes and interests were bound up, he is at least more fortunate than ordinary biographers. If he comes to praise his Cæsar, he has not to also bury him.

Other triumphs have yet to be told. The coming years, bringing with them other changes and other trials, will bring with them fresh opportunities of distinction. The British soldier, less fortunate than those of Continental armies, can never tell in what climate or in what country he may be next called on to meet a foe. But in looking on the past, he can be sure that whatever dangers, whatever difficulties have to be met, the same qualities that have carried the Battery through its former trials, long and steady preparation in peace, cool but rapid determination in war, self-sacrifice, devotion to duty, and ready obedience to discipline,—these, if they do not always lead to victory, will always insure the Battery having a history to which the past and future members may look with pride, the pride which a soldier feels at duty to the country done, distinction for the Battery won.

APPENDIXES.

No. I.

Translation of Frederick the Great's authority to the Minister of State von Schlabrendorf, for incurring the expense necessary to equip the first raised Troop of Horse Artillery.

21st April, 1759.
Camp Landshut.

My dear Minister of State von Schlabrendorf,—

Because in accordance with the enclosed, it requires that which is therein specified to equip six 6-pounder guns, I cannot otherwise but that you should pay the necessary monies with 2227 Thalers 12 Groschen out of the military chest under you; also thereupon you must correspond with Colonel Krusemark, because all has to be made, and he shall got that and the rest. But all this presses much.

I am your well-affectionated King,

FREDERICK.

The in the enclosure estimated requirements for equipment with cost are thus.

3 under officers.
42 gunners.
—
45 men total.

To make these mounted it would cost:

45 Horses at 40 Thalers . . .	1800 Thalers.	
45 Saddles with belongings at 6 Thalers	270 ,,	
45 pairs of boots at 3 Thalers 12 Groschen	157 ,,	12 Groschen.
	2227 ,,	12 ,,

The following account of the formation of the first Horse Artillery in the French Army by General Mathieu Dumas is taken from the "Souvenirs" of that officer, Tome i. pp. 514-9 (Paris, Gosselin, 1839).

"The object which most occupied me while I commanded at Metz (in 1791) was the first formation of a company of Horse Artillery. I was very anxious to succeed, and I knew that I should meet with great obstacles, even from the chief Artillery officers. The advantages of Light Artillery were too evident, and too well proved by the evidence of the Prussian Army, to be contested; but opinions differed on the manner of forming it. Ought the Wurtz system to be adopted, as the most distinguished of the older officers proposed, or ought the gunners to be mounted, as I had always believed, in order that they might easily follow the movements of their pieces, at full speed and without serious accidents? Sure that this last plan was preferable, I had obtained from the Minister of War (Duportail) authority to try it at Metz, while at Strasbourg they attempted the Wurtz system. The contractor, Lanchère, had just brought to Metz eight hundred horses obtained in the Vosges and in Switzerland; and I was allowed to select two hundred from them. After taking the hundred strongest draught horses, I chose out of all the remounts another hundred of the handiest, lightest, or, perhaps it may be said, the least heavy, horses. I asked the regiment of Artillery to supply fifty horsemen, volunteers; and I also took fifty Chasseurs from the Twelfth Regiment of Chasseurs, commanded by Le Comte de Latour-Maubourg. Then I organized this company of one hundred men, giving the command to two Artillery officers, Captain Barrois and Lieutenant Debelle, who, notwithstanding the opposition of their superiors and of many of their comrades, answered to my invitation, and offered themselves as volunteers. Their example was followed by some sous-officiers of Artillery and of the Chasseurs. Having distributed the horses, and supplied all the details of armament and of equipment, I established a real school of mutual instruction in which the gunners and the chasseurs taught one another equitation and gunnery. After six weeks' drill, the brave officers who supported me, and who have since acquired so much renown in this new arm, informed me that the company of Light Artillery was sufficiently instructed to manœuvre in line. I made the trial of them in a grand manœuvre on the ground known as the Camp de Richemont, between Metz and Thionville. I was astonished at the promptitude and precision of the movements of the two batteries, whether in taking up different positions on the roughest ground, or in passing from right to left of the line of battle, in order to support the wings in changes of front. I was no less satisfied to obtain the approval of those Artillery officers who had the most disbelieved in success, and especially of Colonel Senarmont. If I insert here all the details of the formation of the first company of Horse Artillery which existed in the French Army, it is only to claim and preserve for my memory the honour of having rendered a useful service to my country."

The Wurtz system spoken of by Dumas was one in which the gunners were not mounted, but were carried on a sort of Irish outside car, sitting back to back, the ammunition in the centre between them. Dumas, having only spoken of the raising of one battery, goes on to say that he was astonished with the drill of two. His work gives no explanation of this; but in the following extract from the life of General Pajol, it will be seen that two companies of Horse Artillery were raised at that time, 1791, so that Dumas may only refer to the company raised by himself, personally, while another was raised alongside, or else his company may have acted as two batteries :—

"The two first companies (of Horse Artillery) were formed on 20th November, 1791. This number was increased to nine in 1792, and thirty in 1793. Regiments were organized, the number of which, varying according to creations and reductions, was nine in 1794, seven in 1795, eight in 1800, six in 1802, seven in 1810, and six in 1811."—" Pajol, General en Chef," Paris, 1874, tom. i, p. 150.

"Histoire de la Guerre de la Péninsule," par le Général Foy, Paris, 1827; tome i. pp. 118-9: "Many guns were at that time (1792-3) brought into the field. Those of a calibre of 'quartre' were attached to battalions of Infantry. Howitzers, the 'Huit,' and the 'Douze' calibres, and even the Seize calibre specially intended for sieges, then formed batteries of from six to twelve pieces, called batteries of position. For Field Service, an improvement suitable to French impetuosity had been recently borrowed from the Prussians. This consisted in mounting a certain number of gunners, who, by this means, arrived on the ground at the same time as the best-horsed guns, were always ready to work them, and being able to more easily escape from assailants, could fire longer and at closer quarters. The Horse Artillery at its creation was composed of the most active Artillerymen, and was afterwards recruited from the best Grenadiers. It performed marvels. In the campaigns in Germany simple captains of this arm acquired a reputation throughout the Army. Generals soon wished to have no other Artillery, because this being lighter and more efficacious, less of it was required, and the length of the columns on the march was proportionately shortened.

No. II.

To Major-General St. Leger.

Fort William,
11th April, 1797.

My dear General,—I send you back the memorial respecting the Light Artillery. Without being regularly bred to Artillery, it is not difficult to perceive the advantages which would attend such an establment as it proposes in this country. There are certain principles in Artillery, the truth of which is undeniable in all countries, and which the Light Artillery would bring into effect in this. One of these is, that the more speedily and the greater ease with which the gun is transported the better, provided there is equal weight of metal and equal strength of carriage. The want of speed in the Artillery of this country has been the cause that many advantages have been missed. Many opportunities of bringing the enemy to action have not been taken because the Artillery could not be brought up in time; and for some unaccountable reason the native armies, having had better draught-bullocks and larger establishments, have been able to draw off their Artillery when that of the British Army could not be moved. The only objection to Light Artillery is the scarcity of horses in India. I put the expense out of the question, as, if the establishment is necessary, the expense of it is not to be considered. I am afraid that scarcity will be fatal to what is proposed in the memorial, although I think that an establishment adopting some of its great principles may be had without difficulty and at a trifling expense, and that it will render as effectual service in this country as that proposed, which I think must be rejected on account of the want of the necessary supply of horses.

Everybody is aware of the difficulty which attends the movement of Artillery by means of horses even in Europe, where the roads are comparatively excellent, where forage is comparatively plentiful, and the climate so favourable to them. The largest establishment of horses that can be supposed necessary for a park of Artillery is never equal to transporting it for any length of time or distance, and the only method of supply that can be adopted is that of pressing horses from the country in proportion as it is found that those belonging to the

Artillery are knocked up. That is the universal practice in all the armies of Europe, and however improper, it cannot be dispensed with.

(During the Mysore War I am informed that Lord Cornwallis had some light guns drawn by horses; but I believe before—I am sure very shortly after he ascended the Ghauts—long before he was near the enemy, the horses were knocked up and the guns were drawn by bullocks.)

Recourse cannot be had to such a measure in India; and therefore, supposing that it was possible to establish a train of Light Artillery drawn by horses, which would be attended with some difficulty, the want of the supply of horses in the countries in which it is intended it would be used is an objection to the establishment which must be fatal.

However, to have some Artillery which can be moved with celerity will be attended with such advantages, that I cannot readily give up the idea merely because there is a difficulty attending the original purchase of horses, and because their future supply would be impracticable. I should therefore propose that there should be an establishment of horses for eight guns and four howitzers, with harness, etc., at all times ready at the park, in addition to their usual establishment of bullocks, etc. It is unnecessary at present to enter into a detail of all that would be necessary for such an establishment; but my idea is that the horses should never be used excepting when it is desirable, on account of being near the enemy, to move the Artillery at a quick rate; and that all the ordinary duties of transport should be done as usual by bullocks.

I likewise think that the artillerymen might ride upon the horses and upon the carriages of the guns. I am aware that the latter is liable to objections, but in my opinion, not to those to which it is liable in Europe, as it is not intended that the Artillerymen should be upon the carriage for a greater length of time than during that which the horses are drawing it, and it cannot therefore be supposed that they will strain it to the same degree as it is strained in Europe, where the horses being at all times to the gun, and generally going at an advanced rate, the Artillerymen are obliged to sit on them and upon the carriage, which by constant use becomes strained.

I think the long and heavy brass 6-pounders, and the $5\frac{1}{2}$ in. howitzers, would answer best for this purpose. The former I know to be of as great use in the field as any gun can be. Being lighter than the 12-pounders, they are more easily transported; and carrying both grape and round shot as far, they ought to be preferred for all field purposes. I have not yet had an opportunity of examining the Artillery here, but I imagine the mechanism of the carriage good, and well calculated for quick movements; if so, it ought not to be altered for the sake of a few light guns, as, in my opinion, the carriages of all guns, light or heavy, should be upon the same construction, and all should be liable to have horses put to them and moved at any rate that may be thought necessary.

If the gun carriages are not so constructed as to be easily moved, they ought all to be altered, whether they are to be drawn by bullocks or horses. Thus, then, by this plan you would gain the great advantage of being at all times prepared to move twelve pieces of cannon at an advanced rate; the horses being but little worked (for, by all accounts, the enemy in this country is not generally very close) would at all times be able to do the work required from them, and the establishment would require additional supplies but seldom. I should propose to attach to these guns, when they are in use, a party of Light Dragoons; they would answer the double purpose of escort, and they could assist in holding the horses when the guns were unlimbered. Part of the 15th Dragoons and of Rohan's Hussars attended some British Light Artillery for a length of time, and did besides the patrol duty of the post to which it was attached,

I think that if more is attempted at present, all will fail; and, as I stated above, I really think that it is utterly impracticable to find horses in India to supply the loss and waste of them which would be occasioned by an establishment of Light Artillery.—Believe me,

ARTHUR WESLEY.*

* *Lord Mornington's family adopted the ancient spelling of their name "Wellesley" about May, 1798.*

No. III.

MUSTER ROLL *for November*, 1793. *The Troop Commanded by Captain Edward Howorth in the Brigade of Royal Horse Artillery.*

Captain . . . Edward Howorth.

Captain Lieutenant.

First Lieut. { 1. William Millar.
{ 2. Frederic Griffiths.

Second Lieut. Thomas Fenwick, on command.

Sergeants. { 1.
{ 2.
{ 3.

Corporals. { 1. Thomas Gardiner.
{ 2.
{ 3.

Bombardiers. { 1. George Jessiman.
{ 2. Joseph Schofield.
{ 3. Robert Miller.
{ 4.
{ 5.
{ 6.

Farriers. { 1.
{ 2.

Collar Maker.

Wheeler.

Trumpeter.

Gunners. { 1. James Henry.
{ 2. John Barr.
{ 3. Archibald Bell.
{ 4. William Cunningham.
{ 5. Michael Cain.
{ 6. John Smith (Hospital).
{ 7. Simon Lilley.
{ 8. Alexander Goodall.
{ 9. Robert Harrygary.
{ 10. William Cree.

Drivers.
1. Richard Hill.
2. Richard Howden.
3. John Mance.
4. Benjamin Branscomb.
5. Richard Sharp.
6. Samuel Lees.
7. William Jacobs.
8. Thomas Smith.
9. James Virgin.*

* Enlisted 15th October, 1793, attested 30th Nov., 1793, 47 days.

Woolwich, 15*th November,* 1793.

Mustered then, Captain Ed. Howorth's Troop in the Brigade of Royal Horse Artillery, commanded by His Grace the Duke of Richmond, Master-General of the Ordnance, being one Captain, Captain-Lieut., two First Lieutenants, one Second Lieutenant, Sergeants, one Corporal, three Bombardiers, Collar Maker, Farriers, Wheelers, Trumpeter, Ten Gunners and eight Drivers for 30 days from the 1st to the 30th November, 1793, inclusive. Also 1 second Gunner or Driver from the time mentioned against his name to 30th November, 1793, being 47 days. We do certify for those being present in No. 25.

(Signed)
J. COCKBURN.
J. B. WILSON,
E. HOWORTH, Capt. R. H. Artillery.

No. IV.

Return of Detachments of 'A' 'B' 'C' and 'F' Troops R.H.A., embarked for service in Ireland on the 26th November, 1797, at Woolwich.

STRENGTH.										ORDNANCE, &c.			
Captains.	Subalterns.	Assistant Surgeon.	Staff Sergeants.	Non-com. Officers.	Gunners.	Drivers.	Artificers.	Trumpeter.	Horses.	6-pounder Guns.	12-pounder Guns.	5½in. Howitzers.	Ammunition Waggons.
2	3	1	2	12	92	51	6	1	177	4	2	2	13

The division from 'C' Troop comprised 1 Captain, 1 Staff Sergeant, 1 Corporal, 1 Farrier, 1 Collar Maker, 1 Trumpeter, and 38 Gunners and Drivers.

No. V.

Dublin Castle, 9th June, 1798.

[*Extract of a Letter from* MAJOR-GENERAL JOHNSON *to* LIEUT.-GENERAL LAKE, *dated at Ross, 7th June,* 1798.]

I send you a return of the killed, wounded, and missing of the troops engaged on the 5th instant. Their numbers you will, I trust, find not great, when you take into consideration the numbers they were opposed to. This must be imputed to their gallantry. I likewise send a return of the ordnance, ammunition, and standards taken from the rebels. The numbers killed cannot be ascertained. We are busy in burying those killed in the town. Those in the country will be attended to when we are more at leisure. In my former letter I was prevented, by a pressure of business, doing justice to the merits of several officers to whom I am highly indebted for their extraordinary exertions. I cannot say too much in favour of Captain (afterward Lieut.-General Lord) Bloomfield, British Horse Artillery, and Captain Thornhill, commanding the Royal Irish Flying Artillery, whose great exertions contributed very effectually to our success. We had a great loss in Lord Mountjoy. Captain Tottenham's Yeomanry Cavalry, and Captain Boyd with the *débris* of his corps, have rendered me every possible assistance. In making mention of these particulars, I would not wish you to suppose I do not feel myself much indebted to every individual, a very few excepted.

[*Extract from a return of the killed, wounded, and missing, of the Troops engaged at Ross on 5th June, 1798.*]

British Horse Artillery.—1 rank and file and 9 horses killed; 2 rank and file and 4 horses wounded; 1 rank and file and 1 horse missing.

Irish Flying Artillery.—1 rank and file and 11 horses killed; 2 rank and file wounded; 12 rank and file missing.

Total of all corps.—90 killed and 54 horses; 59 wounded and 5 horses; 81 missing and 4 horses.

HENRY JOHNSON, Major-General.

Return of Ordnance, Stores, etc., taken from the Rebels in the Action 5th June, 1798.

5½-inch howitzer . . .	1	Iron 4-pounder	1
Swivels	14	Iron 3-pounder	1
Iron 2-pounder . . .	1		

An immensity of pikes, which were broken as soon as taken; also muskets, likewise destroyed: a variety of standards and colours. From the best private accounts which have been received, the number of the rebels killed is stated to be upwards of 2000. Their wounded must have been very considerable, but the number cannot be ascertained, as they were carried off by the rebels.

No. VI.

Encampment for a Troop R.H.A. 157 men, 135 horses, 6 guns. 1806.

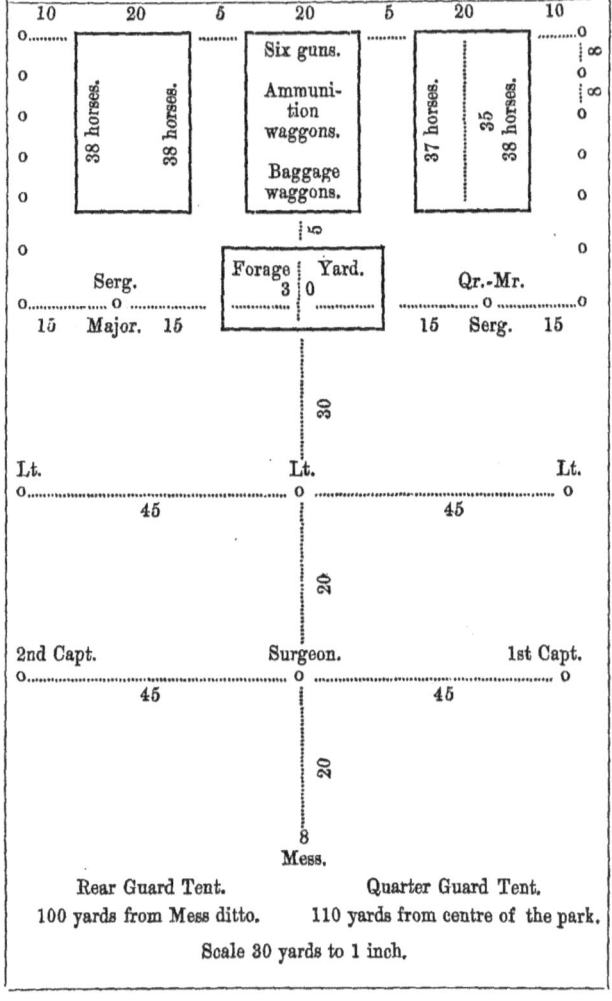

No. VII.

Embarkation Return of 'C' Troop Royal Horse Artillery embarked at Northfleet on 5th October, 1808, for Spain.

STRENGTH.													EQUIPMENT.					
Officers.	Staff Sergeants.	Sergeants.	Corporals.	Bombardiers.	Gunners and Drivers.	Farrier.	Collar Makers.	Wheeler.	Trumpeter.	Women.	Child.	Officers' Horses.	Troop Horses.	6-pounder Guns.	5½in. Howitzer.	Ammunition Waggons.	Baggage Waggons.	Spare Wheel Carriage.	Forge Cart.	Baggage Cart.
6	2	3	3	6	131	1	2	1	1	4	1	12	148	5	1	6	3	1	1	1

No. VIII.

[*Letter from Lieut.-Colonel Bull, C.B.K.H., commanding R.H.A., in Ireland, to officer commanding 'H' Troop (originally 'I' Troop, and now 'I' Battery, 'A' Brigade).*]

Island Bridge, 9th June, 1834.

My Dear Whinyates,—In respect to the roster of troops for Ireland. I consider it was decided in 1819 by Sir Augustus Frazer, and sanctioned by Sir John McLeod, at the urgent request of several captains of Troops, that as a regular roster for service had not been found possible during the war, and as the only duty for Troops of Horse Artillery during the peace, out of Great Britain, would be Ireland, that a roster should be formed for that country, beginning with 'A' Troop, whose regular turn for Ireland it might fairly be considered (that Troop never having been there since its formation), and continued by letters, and this was at that time acted upon, and I believe has been strictly conformed to ever since.

The detachment of Sir Alexander Dickson's Troop was, however, ordered to Scotland subsequently to the roster being established, which I think it right to remind you of; but still I do not see how it can, or ought to interfere with the Irish roster, nor do I think it does with the Cavalry. Most surely I should be happy to see you and my old Troop here, but I would much rather, if I had any voice in it, see the roster kept inviolate, at least during peace, as established in 1819, and therefore I hope this letter may be useful to you.—Yours truly,   R. BULL.

No. IX.

Embarkation Return of 'D' Troop Royal Horse Artillery, at the Dockyard, Portsmouth, on the 12th February, 1810, for Lisbon.

DISTRIBUTION.														AMMUNITION.						
Captains.	Subalterns.	Staff Sergeants.	Sergeants.	Corporals.	Bombardiers.	Gunners.	Drivers.	Trumpeter.	Collar Makers.	Wheeler.	Farriers.	Shoeing Smiths.	6-pounder Guns.	5½in. Howitzer.	Ammunition Carriages.	Forge.	Spare Wheel Carriage.	Curricle Cart.	Baggage Waggon.	Horses.
2	3	2	3	3	5	78	60	1	2	1	2	4	5	1	6	1	1	1	1	160

No. X.

From CAPTAIN ANDREW CLEEVES *to* MAJOR HARTMAN, *King's German Legion.*

Camp near Albuera, 20th May, 1811.

Sir,—According to your request, to explain the loss of the howitzer in the battle of the 16th instant, I have the honour to state as follows: The enemy began the battle with a pretty sharp cannonade on our left, which the Battery of Artillery under my command opposed. The action getting warm on our centre and right, the 1st Brigade of General Stewart's Division (Colonel Colborne's) was ordered to the scene of action with four guns of my Brigade, to the right of the head of the column, and the remaining two followed the rear. Getting near the enemy, I formed line, and came into action on the top of a hill, about eighty or ninety yards distance from the enemy's column (which I imagined was just going to deploy), to cover the formation of our Infantry, which formed in the rear of my guns, making the hill nearly the centre of his front.

The left of our line discharged a volley of musketry and charged the enemy, but were repulsed; the right did the same, and would have been successful, had not, in this critical moment, our soldiers descried the enemy's Cavalry, which tried, *ventre à terre*, to turn our right flank, and our line gave way. I had no other chance than to cover our soldiers and save the guns (the men ran through our intervals, which prevented our limbering-up), but to stand firm, and to fight our ground. We prevented the Cavalry from breaking our centre, but finding no opposition on our right, they turned us, and cut and piked the gunners of the right division down. The left division limbered up, and both guns were saved; but the shaft horses of the right gun were wounded and came down, and the leading driver of the left gun got shot from his horse. Corporal Henry Finche had presence of mind enough to quit his horse, to replace the driver, and then galloped boldly through the enemy's Cavalry. His own horse, which ran alongside of him, secured him from the enemy's cuts and saved the gun, which I made immediately join the fight again. At this moment I was made prisoner, but had the good luck to escape unhurt.

Two guns were nearly immediately retaken, but the howitzer was carried off. Lieutenant Blumenbach was taken and wounded with the left division. Lieut. Thiele and myself were taken with the right, the former badly wounded by the Polish Lancers.—I have the honour to be, Sir, ANDREW CLEEVES,
To Major Hartman. Captain, King's German Legion.

No. XI.

Establishment and Distribution of a Troop of Horse Artillery of four pieces of Ordnance as ordered by Master General, 25th February, 1819, serving in Great Britain.

	Strength.																Equipment.
	Captains.	Lieutenants.	Staff Serjeants.	Serjeants.	Corporal.	Bombardier.	Gunners.	Drivers.	Tr. and Act. Tr. Farrier.	Shoeing Smith.	Collar Maker.	Wheeler.	Total.	Horses. Riding.	Draught.	Total.	Light 6-pounders.	Forge.
Two pieces of ordnance	2	3	2	2	1	1	16	4	2	1	1		35	22	8	30	2	
Detachment dismounted equal to two pieces				1	2	1	16	4					24					
Forge							2			1	1	4		4	4		1
Officers' Servants							4	1					5					
Officers' Batmen and Spare							2	3					5		2	2		
Total with the Troop	2	3	2	3	3	2	38	14	2	1	1	1	73	22	14	36	2	1
Head Quarters, etc.							9	4					13					
Total	2	3	2	3	3	2	47	18	2	1	1	1	86	22	14	36	2	1

Each Troop, except the Rocket Troop, found 1 Non-commissioned Officer, 9 Gunners, and 4 Drivers, to form the Adjutant's detachment at Woolwich. The forge horses of Troops quartered there formed part of the remount depot.

No. XII.

Establishment of a Troop Royal Horse Artillery in Ireland raised to a strength of 4 guns in 1828.

ESTABLISHMENT.									HORSES.		ORDNANCE AND CARRIAGES.				
Officers.	Staff Sergeants.	Sergeants.	Corporals.	Bombardiers.	Gunners.	Drivers.	Artificers.	Trumpeter.	Total.	Riding.	Draught.	Light 6-pounders.	12-pounder Howitzers.	Ammunition Waggons.	Forge.	Total.
5	2	3	3	2	49*	19*	4	1	88	39	31	2	2	2	1	7

* 2 gunners and 1 driver are lent to each troop in Ireland from those in England, also the 3 servants of the Field Officer Commanding Royal Horse Artillery. Total 7 gunners and 2 drivers to the two Troops serving in Ireland.

No. XIII.

Great pains was taken about this time, 1840, to obtain men of good character for the Horse Artillery, and the certificate to character of Arthur Eggar who joined ' C ' Troop about this is given as a specimen.

> Right Hon. Lord Bolton.
> Rev. G. P. Jervaise.
> Rev. Lovelace B. Wither of Herriard.
> Right Hon. Lord Sherbourne.
> General Sir Lowry Cole.
> Frederick Thrasher, Esq.
> Rev. Henry Austin, Rector of Ellisfield.

The above all gave an excellent character to Arthur Eggar, entered the Artillery in August last, Major Blachley's Troop.

No. XIV.

A brief account of the Field Artillery in the United Kingdom in the early part of 1848.

In England there were five 2 gun Troops of Horse Artillery without ammunition waggons. The Field Batteries consisted of 4 Batteries of instruction at Woolwich, each of 4 guns with 45 horses. At Leith Fort there were 2 guns complete, with 28 horses. At Chester and Weedon there were 2 guns with harness but without horses, the orders being to hire them if required. On return from foreign service, Companies were posted to one of the Batteries at Woolwich for about a year, after which they went dismounted to an out-station, and their place was filled by another Company on its return home.

In Ireland there were two 4 gun Troops of Horse Artillery. There was a Field Battery of 4 guns with 45 horses at each of the following places: Athlone, Ballincolig, Charlemount, and Dublin. The Companies attached to these Batteries were changed from time to time; but the Batteries never marched in relief, nor were there at this time any regular Drivers in the Regiment, excepting those with the Horse Artillery.

No. XV.

Establishment of 'C' Troop Royal Horse Artillery on being raised to a strength of 4 guns in November, 1848.

Strength.													Equipment.						
Captains.	Lieutenants.	Staff Sergeants.	Sergeants.	Corporals.	Bombardiers.	Gunners.	Drivers.	Trumpeter.	Artificers.	Total.	Riding Horses.	Draught Horses.	Total.	Light 6-pounder Guns.	12-pounder Howitzers.	6-pr. Ammunition Waggon.	12-pr. Ammunition Waggon.	6-pounder Rocket Carriage.	Forge.	Captain's Cart.	Total.
2	3	2	3	3	2	51	19	1	4	90	40	30	70	2	2	1	1	1	1	......	8

No. XVI.

Establishment of 'C' Troop on being raised to a strength of 6 guns in May, 1853.

Strength.														Equipment.							
Captains.	Lieutenants.	Staff Sergeants.	Sergeants.	Corporals.	Bombardiers.	Gunners.	Drivers.	Trumpeters.	Artificers.	Total.	Riding Horses.	Draught Horses.	Total.	Light 6-pounder Guns.	12-pounder Howitzers.	6-pr. Ammunition Waggons.	12-pr. Ammunition Waggons.	6-pr. Rocket Carriage.	Forge.	Captain's Cart.	Total.
2	3	2	3	3	6	79	54	2	6	160	56	80	136	4	2	5	2	1	1	1	16

No. XVII.

Embarkation Return of 'C' Troop Royal Horse Artillery, embarked at the Dockyard, Woolwich, on the 18th March, 1854, for Turkey.

Strength.											Horses.		Ordnance and Carriages.						Arms.		Ammunition.						
																					6-pr. Guns.			12-pounder Howitzers.			
																						Case.			Case.		
Captains.	Lieutenants.	Assistant Surgeon.	Staff Sergeants.	Sergeants.	Corporals.	Bombardiers.	Gunners.	Drivers.	Trumpeter.	Artificers.	Riding.	Draught.	6-pounder Guns.	12-pounder Howitzers.	Ammunition Waggons.	Rocket Carriage.	Store Waggons.	Forge.	Swords.	Carbines.	Round Shot.	Common.	Spherical.	Shells.	Common.	Spherical.	Carcases.	Carbine Ammunition.
2	3	1	2	5	2	6	80	77	1	9	57	135	4	2	9	1	3	1	105	36	718	84	122	196	24	236	16	408

No. XVIII.

Establishment of a 9-pounder Troop Royal Horse Artillery, as laid down in Adjutant-General's Circular, Woolwich, 29th November, 1855.

Strength.											Equipment.								
									Horses.										
Officers.	Non-commissioned Officers.	Gunners.	Drivers.	Trumpeter.	Farrier.	Shoeing Smiths.	Collar Makers.	Wheelers.	Riding.	Draught.	9-pounder Guns.	24-pounder Howitzers.	Gun Ammunition Waggons.	Howitzer Ammunition Wag.	Store Cart.	Rocket Carriage.	Spare Gun Carriage.	Forage Waggons.	Water Carts.	Hospital Cart.
6	20	97	133	1	1	6	3	2	92	180	4	2	6	5	1	1	1	2	3	1

No. XIX.

Equipment, etc., taken over from 'C' Battery 'C' Brigade (now 'C' Battery 'B' Brigade) Royal Horse Artillery, in January, 1866 (native establishment, harness, etc.). Guns, carriages, etc., received at Allahabad from the Arsenal in February, 1866.

Taken over from 'C' Battery 'C' Brigade R.H.A.															Received from Arsenal.						
				Grass Cutters.					Horses.*							Ammu. Waggons.					
Store Lascars.	Tindal.	Jemadar Syces.	Syces.	Double.	Single.	Bullock Drivers.	Bheesties.	Sweepers.	A number of natives connected with the Bazaar Establishment.	Draught.	Riding.	Bullocks.	Double Sets of Harness.	N.-C. Officers and Gunners' sets of Appointments.	9-pounder Armstrong Guns.	Horse Draught.	Bullock Draught.	Spare Gun Carriage.	Store Waggon.	Store Cart.	Hospital Cart.	* 10 spare, with neither harness nor appointments.
12	1	3	118	70	38	32	5	5		74	104	63	49	70	6	6	6	1	1	1	1	

No. XX.

Railway transport in India. End Loading—Broad Gauge. Horse Artillery. 29th January, 1876.

'C' Battery 'A' Brigade Royal Horse Artillery.

4 Officers, 2 Staff Sergeants, 5 Sergeants, 118 Gunners and Drivers, 124 Native followers.

Open Siding, Sindh, Punjab and Delhi Railway Yard.

11· 3 A.M.		Bugle to embark.
11·40	,,	Baggage and Camp equipage 267 maunds, loaded.
11·43	,,	Six 9-pounder breech-loading guns, 6 ammunition waggons, forge, spare gun carriage and store waggon loaded in 40 minutes.
11·57	,,	178 horses, 62 men, loaded in 54 minutes.
12·45 P.M.		Bugle to disembark.
1· 5	,,	Guns and waggons all out in 20 minutes.
1· 9	,,	Horses out in 24 minutes.
1·22	,,	Bugle to re-embark.
1·31	,,	Trucks run back, ramps fixed, first horse going in.
1·47	,,	Guns, etc., all loaded in 25 minutes.
2· 4	,,	Horses all loaded in 42 minutes.
2· 6	,,	Ramps in and trucks coupled on.
2·15	,,	Bugle to disembark.
3·17	,,	Battery ready to move off in 62 minutes.

Number of carriages and trucks used 84, viz. 1 first-class, 5 second-class, 5 third-class, 33 double horse, 16 cattle trucks, 6 covered goods, 12 open and 6 brakes.

The President of the Railway Transport Committee, Sir Charles Reid, in his report stated: "A Battery of Horse Artillery fully equipped for active service with first and second line of waggons, supposing 4 horse ramps and 2 sets of girders were available, would embark in one hour."

No. XXI.

Establishment of, and Equipment taken over by ' C' Battery, ' A' Brigade, R H.A., in January, 1877, on return from India.

Strength.																	Equipment.		
Major.	Captain.	Lieutenants.	Staff-Sergeants.	Sergeants.	Corporals.	Bombardiers.	Gunners.	Drivers.	Trumpeters.	Farrier.	Shoeing Smiths.	Collar Makers.	Wheeler.	Total.	Riding Horses.	Draught Horses.	Total.	9-pr. M.-L. R. Guns.	Ammunition Waggons.	Forge.
1	1	3	2	6	5	5	70	61	2	1	3	2	1	163	56	52	108	6	2	1

No. XXII.

Establishment of ' C' Battery, ' A' Brigade, Royal Horse Artillery, as sanctioned for Home Service for 1882-83.—Horse Guards, War Office, 1st April, 1882.

Officers and Men.															Ordnance.			Horses.		
Major.	Captain.	Lieutenants.	Staff-Sergeants.	Sergeants.	Corporals.	Bombardiers.	Gunners.	Drivers.	Trumpeters.	Sergt.-Farrier and Carriage Smith.	Collar Makers.	Wheeler.	Shoeing Smiths.	Total.	Guns, 9-pr. M.-L. Rifled.	Ammunition Waggon.	Ammunition and Store Waggon.	Total.	Riding.	Draught.	Total.
1	1	3	2	6	5	5	46	47	2	1	2	1	3	125	4	1	1	8	38	34	72

No. XXIII.—War Services of 'C' Troop, R.H.A.

Battles.	Sieges.	Actions.	Dates.	Remarks.
		Ross	5th June, 1798.	
		Wexford and Vinegar Hill	21st June, ,,	
		Benavente	29th December, 1808.	
		Cacabellos	3rd January, 1809.	
		Constantino	5th January, ,,	
		Heights of Bulganak	19th September, 1854.	
Alma			20th September, ,,	
		Capture of Balaclava	26th September, ,,	
Balaclava			25th October, ,,	
Inkermann			5th November, ,,	
	Sevastopol		8th September, 1855.	
		Eupatoria	23rd and 27th October.	Received the thanks of the French General D'Allonville, Commanding Allied Forces for actions of 27th October.

No. XXIV.—War Services of 'D' Troop, R.H.A.

Battles.	Sieges.	Actions.	Dates.	Remarks.
Albuera*			16th May, 1811	Specially mentioned in the despatch of Marshal Sir Wm. Beresford, commanding Allies.
		Usagre	25th May, ,,	Very favourably mentioned in the despatch of Major-General the Hon. Wm. Lumley, commanding Allied Cavalry.
		Fuentes Guinaldo	25th September, 1811.	
		Aldea-de-Ponte	27th September, ,,	
		Ribera	24th July, 1812	Very favourably mentioned in despatches by Major-Gen. R. B. Long.
		San Munos	16th November, 1812.	
		Ford of the Yeltes	17th November, ,,	
		Salamanca	22nd May, 1813. ,,	
Vittoria			21st June, ,,	
		Pyrenees	26th to 30th July, 1813.	
Orthes			27th February, 1814.	
		Aire	2nd March, ,,	Thanked in public orders by Lieut.-General Sir Rowland Hill, and for its conduct on the several recent occasions when engaged.
			10th April, ,,	
Toulouse			18th June, 1815.	
Waterloo		Capture of Paris	8th July, ,,	
		Engaged in many other affairs during the Peninsular War, being always in advance or rear-guards.		

* "The dispersion of our Cavalry scarcely left us 400 or 500 British at any point, and these, with two regiments of Spaniards, were all we had to offer by way of resistance to their numerous and overwhelming columns. The ground, however, favoured us, and the Horse Artillery did its duty with brilliant effect. The enemy lost a great number of men, and from 400 to 500 horses, by the operation of this arm alone."—Extract from a letter of Brigadier-General R. B. Long, Bivouac near Vicente, 26th June, 1811.

No. XXV.

List of Stations at which 'C' Battery 'A' Brigade has been quartered since its formation.

Woolwich				To Crimea	29 Aug.,	'54
To Canterbury	... Nov.,	'94		,, Turkey	26 Nov.,	'55
,, Lavant	... June,	'96		,, Woolwich	31 May,	'56
,, Brighton	... Jan.,	'97		,, Aldershot	24 July,	'57
,, Canterbury	... Oct.,	'98		,, Dublin	21 Aug.,	'57
,, Swinley Camp ...	... June,	1800		,, Newbridge	20 April,	'58
,, Canterbury	... Aug.,	'00		,, Cahir	23 Feb.,	'59
,, Woolwich	... Mar.,	'02		,, Curragh	14 Aug.,	'59
,, Sevenoaks	... April,	'03		,, Dublin	10 Oct.,	'59
,, Radepole	... June,	'03		,, Newbridge	31 May,	'60
,, Christchurch	... Dec.,	'03		,, Curragh	31 May,	'61
,, Weymouth Camp...	... July,	'05		,, Portobello Barracks	25 July,	'61
,, Wareham	.. Oct.,	'05		,, Curragh	10 Aug.,	'61
,, Woolwich	... May,	'06		,, Portobello Barracks	14 Aug.,	'61
,, Warley	... Nov.,	'07		,, Newbridge	23 Aug.,	'61
,, Spain	... Oct,	'08		,, Dublin	26 Aug,	'61
,, Woolwich	... Feb.,	'09		,, Newbridge	10 Dec.,	'61
,, Christchurch... ...	... July,	'14		,, Dublin	30 Aug.,	'62
,, Woolwich	... June,	'15		,, Aldershot	1 Sept.,	'62
,, Chatham	... Oct.,	'15		,, Woolwich	31 May,	'63
,, Canterbury	... Dec.,	'15		,, Bengal	10 Aug.,	'65
,, Athlone...	... Sept.,	'16		,, Benares	22 Dec.,	'65
,, Island Bridge ...	... Aug.,	'18		,, Lucknow	... Jan.,	'66
,, Woolwich	24 April,	'21		,, Meerut	18 Dec.,	'69
,, Manchester	30 April,	'26		,, Peshawur	1. Nov.,	'71
,, Island Bridge ...	15 Aug.,	'29		,, Umballa	5 Dec.,	'73
,, Athlone	30 Sept.,	'30		,, Delhi	19 Nov.,	'75
,, Island Bridge ...	... Oct.,	'31		,, Umballa	31 Jan.,	'76
,, Woolwich	26 Aug.,	'33		,, Deolalee	20 Nov.,	'76
,, Sheffield	18 Aug.,	'37		,, Bombay	4 Dec.,	'76
,, Leeds	... May,	'39		,, Woolwich	8 Jan.,	'77
,, Newcastle-on-Tyne	20 Aug.,	'39		,, Camp Hay	8 Aug.,	'77
,, Portobello, Dublin	30 Aug.,	'41		,, Woolwich	8 Sept.,	'77
,, Limerick	... July,	'43		,, Aldershot	16 May,	'78
,, Portobello, Dublin	... Aug.,	'44		,, Dublin	17 April,	'80
,, Woolwich	... Aug.,	'45		,, Newbridge	14 May,	'80
,, Leeds	... Aug.,	'51		,, Dublin	17 May,	'81
,, Woolwich	3 May,	'53		,, St. John's Wood,		
,, Turkey	18 Mar.,	'54		London...	23 May,	'83

No. XXVI.—SUCCESSION LIST OF OFFICERS AND STAFF SERGEANTS OF 'C' BATTERY, 'A' BRIGADE, ROYAL HORSE ARTILLERY, SINCE ITS FORMATION.

CAPTAINS.	From.	To.	SECOND CAPTAINS.	From.	To.
Edward Howorth, *l.c.*	1·11·93	1·10·99	George Cookson	1·11·93	·94
			William Millar	9 ·9·94	16 ·7·99
Edward [Stephens] Trelawney	1·10·99	1·6·1801	Fredric Griffiths	16 ·7·99	3 ·9·1801
(Sir) George Adam Wood	1·6·1801	3 ·9·01	Howard Douglas	·3 ·9·01	·01 or ·02
Fredric Griffiths	3 ·9·01	30 ·3·06	Edmund Curry	·01 or ·02	1 ·6·04
			William Jenny	1 ·6·04	·06
Henry Evelegh, *m.*	1 ·5·06	8 ·5·11	John Chester	·06	9 ·4·12
Edward Wilmot, *m.*	8 ·5·11	1 ·2·19	William Eyles Maling	9 ·4·12	·19
			William Miller	·19	1 ·5·21
Sir John May, K.C.B., *l.c.*	1 ·2·19	2 ·3·25	Thomas Dyneley, C.B.	1 ·5·21	13 ·7·25
			Alexander Macdonald, C.B.	13 ·7·25	11·12·26
John Chester, *m.*	2 ·3·25	3 ·9·31	J. Sinclair	1 ·1·27	20·11·28
Charles Blachley, *m.*	15 ·9·31	18 ·7·33	J. E. G. Parker	20·11·28	5 ·2·29
Thomas Dyneley, C.B., *m.*	18 ·7·33	19 ·6·35	Philip Sandilands	10 ·2·29	4 ·6·36
Edward Thos. Michell, C.B., *l.c.*	19 ·6·35	11 ·6·38			
			Francis Warde	4 ·6·36	15 ·6·40
Henry Blachley, *m.*	24 ·7·38	23·11·41	William Berners	15 ·6·40	·41
			Noel Thomas Lake	·41	5 ·4·45
William B. Ingilby, *m.*	28·11·41	7 ·5·47	Augustus Henry Frazer	5 ·4·45	1 ·4·46
			Collingwood Dickson, *m.*	1 ·4·46	2 ·9·51
			Hon. G. T. Devereux	2 ·9·51	23 ·2·52
			C. L. D'Aguilar	23 ·2·52	6 ·9·53
Edward Charles Warde	19 ·5·47	17 ·2·54	John Saltren Willett	6 ·9·53	20 ·6·54
George C. R. Levinge, *m.*	17 ·2·54	2 ·8·54	Hon. D. McD. Frazer	20 ·6·54	1 ·1·55
Henry John Thomas	3 ·8·54	23 ·2·56	Dixon Edward Hoste, *m.*	1 ·1·55	23 ·2·56
(Captain J. Brandling, attached from Sept. to Dec. '54, in command)					
Henry Francis Strange, C.B., *l.c.*	23 ·2·56	1 ·4·61	Charles Rowland Hill	23 ·2·56	24 ·3·60
Robert John Hay, *m.*	1 ·4·61	18 ·1·64	Ralph Gore	24 ·3·60	26·12·65
Hon. Edward T. Gage, C.B., *c.*	18 ·1·64	2·66			
*John S. Tulloh, C.B., *m.*	2·66	6.67	Arthur T. G. Pearse	26·12·65	6 ·7·67
Charles R. Hill	7·67	10·67			
*John S. Tulloh, C.B., *m.*	11·67	20·10·68			
G. Allix Wilkinson, *m.*	20·11·68	1·10·71	F. J. G. Hill	6 ·7·67	17 ·1·72
F. A. Whinyates	1·10·71	4 ·7·72			
			CAPTAINS.		
			W. W. Murdoch	20 ·1·72	8·10·73
MAJORS.			H. M. Robertson	8·10·73	13 ·3·78
F. A. Whinyates, *l.c.*	5 ·7·72	19 ·7·81	A. E. England	13 ·3·78	12 ·3·81
*E. D. Elliott, *l.c.*	20 ·7·81		E. A. Ollivant	12 ·4·81	16 ·9·83
			W. W. Smith	17 ·9·83	

LIEUTENANTS.	From.	To.	LIEUTENANTS.	From.	To.
William Millar	1·11·93	9 ·9·94	Fredric Griffiths	1·11·73	7·10·95
John Bentham	9 ·9·94	·11·94	Hon. W. H. Gardner	7·10·95	16 ·7·99
Edward V. Worsley	·11·94	·96			
Thomas Downman	·96	1·11·97			
William J. Lloyd	1·11·97	1800	Philip J. Hughes	16 ·7·99	12 ·9·03
George Jenkinson	1800	1 ·6·06	George Rodber	12 ·9·03	·05
			Edmund Yeamans Walcott	·05	23 ·3·09
Charles Parke Deacon	1 ·6·06	·06	Henry Mussenden Leathes	23 ·3·09	·11
William Webber	·06	17 ·4·12	William Eyles Maling	·11	9 ·4·12
John James Chapman	17 ·4·12	·16	Michael T. Cromie	9 ·4·12	·13
W. Cochrane Anderson	·16	5·11·27	William Henry Bent	·13	·15
			Basil Robinson Heron	·15	6·11·20
Henry Palliser	6·11·27	·29			
			Burke Cuppage	6·11·20	·30
			Edward Trevor	·30	23 ·6·32
Evan Morgan	·29	10 ·2·34			
			Robert Luard	23 ·6·32	·33
			William Wallace D'Arley	·33	10 ·1·37
Augustus Henry Frazer	10 ·2·34	7 ·5·41	Edward Charles Warde	10 ·1·37	·39
Edward Price	7 ·5·41	1 ·4·46	George Drought Warburton	·39	28 ·5·44
Henry Lemprière	1 ·4·46	1 ·7·47	Richard Blackwood Price	28 ·5·44	13 ·4·46
			J. Charles William Fortescue	13 ·4·46	·8·47
Charles Henry Morris	1 ·7·47	1·11·48	Augustus C. Lennox Fitzroy	·8·47	30 ·6·48
Henry Arthur Vernon	1·11·48	15·10·50	John George Boothby	30 ·6·48	5 ·8·52
D. Sarsfield Greene	15·10·50	17 ·2·54	J. E. Michell	5 ·8·52	20 ·6·54
S. M. Grylls	17 ·2·54	13 ·8·55	W. A. Fox-Strangways	20 ·6·54	20 ·8·57
J. E. Ruck-Keene	13 ·8·55	24 ·5·59			
Turner Van Straubenzee	24 ·5·59	1 ·2·62	G. A. A. Walker	20 ·8·57	1 ·4·60
Vincent F. Tufnell	1 ·2·62	22 ·8·65	S. P. Lynes	1 ·4·60	10 ·5·65
Seymour H. Toogood	22 ·8·65	30·12·67			
*H. J. Kinsman	30·12·67	16·10·69	T. Burnett	10 ·5·65	28 ·1·69
T. B. Tyler	16·10·69	13·12·71			
			B. F. Domvile	28 ·1·69	30 ·5·77
E. S. B. Lockyer	23 ·1·72	16 ·1·75			
G. T. Pretyman	16 ·1·75	1·10·77			
John Hotham	1·10·77	6· 4·81	J. K. Trotter	1 ·6·77	2 ·9·80
C. F. Hadden	12 ·4·81	6·10·82	E. F. Becher	15·10·80	12 ·7·81
A. Chambers	6·10·82		E. C. F. Holland	4 ·8·81	11 ·8·83
			W. M. Russell		

* Late Bengal Artillery.

LIEUTENANTS.	FROM.	TO.
Thomas Fenwick	1·11·93	·11·94
Henry W. Parish	11·94	6 ·3·95
Fredrick Walker	6 ·3·95	·97
Robert Pym	·97	3·12·1880
William Roberts	3·12·00	·02
John Marjoram Close	·02	25·11·02
Henry Onslow	25·11·02	·06
Edward Barlow	·06	24 ·1·13
John Sampson Rich	24 ·1·13	·19
William Smith	·19	·23
William Swabey	·23	15·11·24
John Alexander Wilson	15·11·24	·29
Robert Burn	·29	14 ·8·34
J. H. Cockburn	14 ·8·34	·34
E. F. Grant	·34	·35
W. Fraser	·35	18 ·3·36
G. Sandham	18 ·3·36	13 ·4·42
William Henderson	13 ·4·42	10 ·4·45
J. M. Adye	10 ·4·45	29 ·7·46
W. A. Middleton	29 ·7·46	30 ·6·48
F. W. Craven Ord	17 ·8·48	1 ·4·52
George Leslie	1 ·4·52	7·12·52
A. Y. Earle	7·12·52	6·11·54
A. H. King	6·11·54	11 ·8·55
W. Stirling	11 ·8·55	18 ·8·57
W. H. Watson	15 ·8·57	1 ·4·60
R. Handcock	1 ·4·60	23 ·7·61
G. S. Harvey	23 ·7·61	23 ·5·66
*James Loch	23 ·5·66	22 ·3·71
S. Gardiner	22 ·3·71	16 ·4·73
J. D. Legard	16 ·4·73	7 ·8·78
H. Knight	7 ·8·78	31 ·5·81
H. G. Weir	31 ·5·81	4 ·1·82
L. A. McClintock	1 ·4·82	27 ·1·83
E. A. Burrows	13 ·3·83	

ASSISTANT SURGEONS.	From.	To.	STAFF-SERGEANTS.	From.
			T. McLaren	1794
			T. Dewhurst : A. Brown	'94
			J. Bruce	'95
			W. Thomas	'96
			W. Talboys	'99
W. Harris	1803		G. Blackett	1801
			J. Caruthers	'04
			A. Dale	'06
Peter Venables	1808		A. Little	'10
			W. Howes	'11
J. D. Fraser	1815		G. W. Pattison	'15
E. D. Verner	1816		J. Alexander : R. Oliphant	'16
J. W. Frazer	1818		W. Unsworth	'23
E. Cannon	1819		J. Achindachy	'25
			T. Whitehead	'26
			S. Adam	'31
			C. McDougal	'32
			J. Lomax	'34
			J. Dickson	'37
			G. Oliphant : M. McGregor	'39
			G. Hunter	'41
			R. Spence	
			T. Green	'47
			H. Jefferson	'48
			J. Fenton	'49
			J. Stewart	'51
			W. Brown	'54
A. Rudge	1854		C. Dunbar	
E. S. Protheroe			W. Norton	
T. Park			A. Crawford	
E. Bowen			W. Lloyd	
G. Pain	1856		J. M'Loughlin	'56
			J. Dix	
			C. Reeves	
J. Wood			H. Bacchus	
H. C. Miles			R. Steven	'57
A. Chester	1858		F. Foster	
	1863		J. Guthrie	'58
W. W. Quinton	1865		J. Reed	'60
			J. Drummond	'61
	1868	1874	T. W. Kirkbride	'63
			G. Langrish	'64
By the ruling of a Warrant of 1873, Medical Officers became again departmental, and ceased to form part of the Regimental establishment.			P. Murphy	'66
			J. Scully	'67
			R. Nichols	
			J. F. Cossey	'68
			W. Higgs	
			T. Hearne	'71
			C. Deacon	'77
			F. S. Palmer	'78
			S. Brown	'79
			W. Graham	'80

GENERAL INDEX.

Adams, Driver, injured at review at Lucknow, 266.
Adye, Brigade-Major, 88, 129.
Aire, the engagement near, 67.
Airey, General, 112, 200.
Aladyn, camp at, 78.
Albuera, letter giving an account of the Battle of, 59.
Aldea de Ponte, "D" Troop at, 62.
Allahabad, 9, 264.
Allan, —., of 18th Hussars, 38.
Alma, Battle of the, 92, *et seq.*
Almeida, Affair of, 58.
Alten, Brigadier-General, 38.
Ambrose, Assistant-Surgeon J., 56.
American Colonies, revolt of the, 25.
Anderson, Captain J. R., 74.
Arbuthnot, Assistant-Adjutant-General, 38.
Arerias, 45.
Armstrong, Sir William, inventor of breech-loading rifled guns, 262.
Artillery, early attempts at progress in, 5.
Artillery returned from the Crimea, reviewed by the Queen, 261.
Artillery manœuvres in India, 269.
"Assaults of Arms," success of 'C' Battery in, 276.
Astorga, 29, 35, 42.
Athletic sports, 271.
Austria, Artillery of, at beginning of eighteenth century, 6; covered retreat of their Infantry at Sadowa, 15.

Bacchus, Sergeant H., selected to receive the French war-medal, 261.
Bad wine summarily dealt with, 80.
Baddeley, Captain, kindness of, 88; at the Alma, 94, 96.
Baird, Sir David, despatched to the Peninsula, 29; his remarks on the scarcity of transport and supplies during the Peninsular War, 32; wounded, 49.

Balaclava, Battle of, 124, *et seq.*; further remarks on, and recollections of, 149, *et seq.*
Balaclava, Charge of the Light Brigade, general review of the various accounts of the, 160, *et seq.*
Ballistæ, military machines superseded by cannon, 2.
Bantry Bay, arrival of the French Expedition at, 25.
Barlow, Lieutenant E., 29, 33, 38, 39, 45; reminiscences of, 53.
Bashi Bashouks, 240.
"Battery," first use of the term, 6.
Baylen, disaster of General Dupont at, 30.
Bazaine, Marshal, his retreat to Verdun, 9.
Bazelle, 31, 46.
Beane, Captain George, 47; joins 'D' Troop, 65; killed at Waterloo, 68.
Beardsley, Sergeant, 233.
Bembibre, 42.
Benavente, Affair at, 36.
Beresford, Marshal, 58; his despatch to Lord Wellington after the Battle of Albuera, 61.
Betanzos, 33, 48.
Biddulph, Captain M. S., joins 'C' Troop camp, 220; employed in making sketches of Sevastopol, 225.
Bingham, Major, brings the order for 'C' Troop to embark for the Crimea, 75.
Blackwood, Major G. F., 275.
Blake, a Spanish General, 30, 35.
Bland, Shoeing-smith, death of, 231.
Blayney, Driver, death of, 82.
Bloomfield, Captain, praised by General Lake, 27.
Bloomfield, Colonel John, 74.
Bonaparte, Joseph, nominated King of Spain, 29.
"Bonaparte never forgave the unfortunate," application of the saying, 42.

302 Index.

Bosphorus, an unpleasant trip on the, 77.
Brandling, Captain John, appointed to temporary command of 'C' Troop, 86; his remarkable uniform, 94; his services at the Alma, 99, *et seq.*; his readiness for action illustrated, 124; his reply to General Strangways, 129; narrow escape of, 138; discovers Captain Nolan's body, 142; complimented by Lord Raglan, 143; bids farewell to 'C' Troop, 215; his death, *ibid.*
Brown, Sir George, 78; at the Alma, 94; his coolness under fire, 121; wounded at Inkerman, 207.
Brereton, Lieutenant W., at Aire, 67.
Brereton, General, at the Alma, 94.
Brest, return of the French Expedition to, 25.
Briant, Sergeant, 37.
Brighton (Brighthelmstone), 'C' Troop at, 25, 28.
Bulganak, Affair of the, 89.
Bull, Lieutenant-Colonel, letter from, to Captain Whinyates, June 9th, 1834, 289.
Burnett, Captain T., 263, 272.
Burrows, Brigadier-General, 275.
Busaco, Battle of, 58.

Cacabellos, 42.
Cairncross, Major James, his praise of 'D' Troop, 67.
Cambarros, 36.
"Camp equipage," for Artillery, details of, 12.
Campbell, Gunner, 204.
Campbell, Limber-Gunner, 204.
Campbell, Sir Colin, 222, *et seq.*
Candahar, the retreat to, 275.
Cannon, invention of, in Europe, 2; unwieldy nature of, 3.
Canrobert, General, inspects the camp at Aladyn, 79; wounded at Inkerman, 207.
Canterbury, 'C' Troop at, 25, 28.
Canvas Stable, the, 218.
Cardigan, Lord, reconnaissance by, 79; Lord Lucan's instructions to, 157; hampered by his orders, 159; at No. 6 Gun, 167.
Carpenter, Colonel, killed at Inkerman, 209.
Carrion, attack on, 38.
Carter, Lieut. T., 56.
Castaños, a Spanish General, 30, 33.
"Castles of Asia," fort at, 76.
Cator, Brigadier-General, 74, 83.
Cebrones, mishap of the Alcalde of, 36.

Certificate of character for Horse Artillery, 292.
Charge of the Light Brigade, support given to the first line, 171; table of the casualties in, 201.
Charles VI. of Spain, abdication of, 29.
Chartists, 71.
Chasseurs d'Afrique, part taken by the, at the Battle of Balaclava, 143.
Chester, Assistant-Surgeon A., 263.
Chester, Colonel, death of, 103.
Chester, Second Captain, 29, 34, 38, 44.
Chivalrous feeling between the French and English Armies in the Peninsula, anecdote of, 64.
Chobham Camp, in 1853, 91, 103.
Cholera, first appearance in the English Army in the Crimea, 80; again appears, 81, 204, 230.
Cholera in India, 264.
Christchurch, 'C' Troop at, 28.
Church parade disturbed, 121.
Church. Farrier William, death of, 272.
Circassian archer at Balaclava, 143.
Cleeves, Captain Andrew, letter from, to Major Hartman, 290.
"Col de Balaclava," 125.
Colbert, General, death of, 44.
Commissariat difficulties in the Crimea, 77, *et seq.*
"Committee of United Irishmen," arrest of the, 26.
Confusion caused by the reduction of 'D' Troop, 68.
Constantino, 34; engagement at, 46.
Cook, Gunner, singular presentiment concerning his death, 230.
Cookson, G., the first "Second" Captain of 'C' Troop, 24.
Cookson, Colonel, 33, *et seq.*
Cossey, Quartermaster-Sergeant, receives promotion, 274.
"Coverers," duties of, 20.
Cracknell, ——, a volunteer for 'C' Troop, 225.
Craig, a Gunner, wounded at Constantino, 46.
Crawford, Captain, praised by General Lake, 27.
Crimean War, narrative of the, 73-289.
Cromie, Lieutenant M., killed at Waterloo, 68.
'C' Troop, formation of, 24; reduction of strength of, 28; departs for Spain, 29; Captain Evelegh's Diary of events connected with, during the Peninsular campaign of 1808-9, 32-51; in the action at Benavente, 41; at Villa Franca, 43; at Constantino, 46; arrival at Coruña, 48; embarks at St.

Lucia, 48; in extreme peril, 50; arrival home, 51; losses of, during Peninsular campaign, 53; reviewed at Hounslow Heath, 53; risk of being broken up, 54; on home service, 69; present at review in Hyde Park on 18th June, 1836, 70; marches for Ireland, 70; stations in Ireland, 71; returns to England, 71; under orders for the Crimea, 72; changes in, 73; embarks for the seat of war, 75; arrival in Turkey, 76; proceeds to Varna, 81; receives a 9-pounder equipment, 82; embarks for the Crimea, 83; lands at Eupatoria, 85; advances from Eupatoria, 87; crosses the Bulganak, 88; at the Affair of the Bulganak, 89; at the Battle of the Alma, 92, *et seq*.; marches to the Katchka and the Belbec, 111; arrives at McKenzie's Farm, 113; proceeds to Balaclava, 114; at the Battle of Balaclava, 124, *et seq*.; at Inkerman, 205; in the camp at the Col, 210; sickness amongst, 213; Lord Raglan's estimation of, 214; prepares for a sortie from Sevastopol, 215; in the reconnaissance of 19th February, 222; reinforced in men and horses, 225; an awkward accident to, 226; reconnaissance of 19th April, 228; death of a gunner belonging to, 229; graves of the men of, 231; at the battle of the Tchernaya, 236; embarks for Eupatoria, 239; engaged at Eupatoria, 245; specially praised by Lord George Paget, 257; returns to Scutari, 257; recapitulation of the services of, during the Crimean War, 257-9; presented with a flag from the ladies of Cornwall, 259; returns to England, 260; changes of quarters. 261; departs for India, 263; arrival in India, 264; changes of quarters in India, 264, *et seq*.; accident at Lucknow to, 265; complimented by Lord Napier of Magdala, 267; forms part of force to receive the Prince of Wales at Delhi, 269; returns to Umballa, 271; returns to England, 272; home service, 273; proceeds to Ireland, 275; reorganization of, 275; returns to London, May 21, 1883, 277.

Dacres, Colonel R. J., 76.
D'Aguilar, Major-General, inspects 'C' Troop, 272.
D'Allonville, General, in command at Eupatoria, 242.
Davy, Lieut., blown up at Betanzos, 48.

De Failly, General, 243.
De La Fayette, *Divisions* of Horse Artillery formed by, 8.
Delhi Railway Station, experiments at, by 'C' Troop, 271.
Della Marmora, General, pall-bearer for Lord Raglan, 234.
D'Esterhazy, Walsin, General of Brigade, at Eupatoria, 243.
"Detachment," description of a, 8.
Devna, camp at, 79.
Dickson, Colonel Sir Alexander, despatch to, 67; on the false economy pursued in regard to the Horse Artillery, 70.
Dickson, Major Collingwood, 120.
Difference in organization of ancient and modern Artillery, illustrated by operations in 1709 and 1811, under Marlborough and Wellington, respectively, 21.
Dinner party broken up suddenly, 47.
"Directory" of France, Expedition sent by the, to Ireland, 25.
Divisions of Horse Artillery first formed, 8.
Domvile, Lieutenant Barry, 272.
Doncos, 34, 45.
Don Joseph de Prado, 33.
Downman's Troop, 32, 41.
Driver Corps established, 16.
Drivers, duties of, 16.
Drummond's Brigade, 38.
'D' Troop, 55; embarks for Lisbon, 56; one portion ninety-four days in reaching Lisbon, 57; engaged at Albuera, 59; at the cavalry action at Usagre, 62; at Fuentes de Guinaldo, and Aldea de Ponte, 62; at Ribera, 63; at St. Muños, 65; inspected by Lord Wellington, 65; special praise bestowed on, by Major-General Long, 65; at Salamanca, 66; at Vittoria, 66; actions in the Pyrenees, 66; at Orthes, 67; at the engagement near Aire, 67; at Toulouse, 67; on home service, 67; proceeds to the Netherlands, 68; at Waterloo, 68; at the capture of Paris, 68; reduction of, Duke of Wellington's reasons for, 68; reorganization afterwards, 69.
Dublin, attempt of the rebels on, 26.
Dumas, General Mathieu, his account of the introduction of Horse Artillery into the French Army, 280.
Dunn, A. R., a subaltern officer of the 11th Hussars, special act of bravery of, 147; selected to receive one of the first of the Victoria Crosses, 148.
Dunn, Lieutenant W., 56.
Dupont, General, disaster of, at Baylen, 30.

304   *Index.*

Dupuis, Colonel, joins 'C' Troop camp, 220.
Dutch Republicans, 25.
Dyneley, General, 104.
Dyneley, Lieutenant, mortally wounded at the Redan, 104.

Earle, Lieutenant, 75, 83; on Lord Cardigan's staff, 79; invalided, 213.
Egan, the Rev. Mr., under fire, 121.
Egerton, Colonel, 116.
El Burgo, bridge of, 48.
Embarkation returns, 5th Oct. 1808, 289; of 'D' Troop, 12th Feb. 1810, 290; of 'C' Troop, 18th March, 1854, 294.
Encampment for a Troop, 1806, 288.
Equipment, etc., return for January and February, 1866, 295.
Establishment of a nine-pounder Troop, Royal Horse Artillery, 29th Nov. 1855, 295.
Establishment of a Troop of Royal Horse Artillery, 25th Feb. 1819, 291; ditto in 1828, 292.
Establishment of 'C' Troop, Nov. 1848, 293; ditto May, 1853, 294.
Establishment, etc., return of 'C' Battery, January, 1877, 297; ditto 1882-3, 297.
Eupatoria, English fleet arrives at, 85; Expedition to, 239; names of officers and enumeration of forces engaged in, 240; the military operations at, 244, *et seq.*
Evans, Captain, death of, 103.
Evans, Sir de Lacey, his kindness, 124.
Evelegh, Captain H., 28, 29; his *Diary* of events in the Peninsular campaign, 32-51.
Ezela, the bridge of, blown up, 40.

Fane, General, 66.
Fasson, Assistant-Surgeon, 86.
Fellowes, Captain, 145, 205.
Fenwick, the first "Second" Lieutenant of 'C' Troop, 24.
Ferdinand VII. of Spain, abdication of, 29.
Field Artillery in the United Kingdom in 1848, 293.
Field Batteries, description of, 11.
Fisher, Captain G. B., of 'G' Troop, 27.
Fitzmayer, Colonel, 92.
Flanders, composition of a Train of Artillery in, in 1727, 4.
Fletcher, Captain, kindness of, 48.
Foley, Lady Emily, entertains 'C' Battery at Stoke Edith Park, 274.
Foy, General, on Horse Artillery, 281.

Fraser, Bombardier, 81; in charge of the hospital marquee at Pravadi, 82.
Fraser, Second Captain Hon. McD., joins 'C' Troop, 203; makes a good "navvy," 211.
Frazer, Lieutenant-Colonel Sir Augustus, 54.
Frederick the Great, his improvement of Artillery, 6.
French Republicans, 25.
French, the, in Portugal, 29, *et seq.*
Fuentes de Guinaldo, 'D' Troop at, 62.
Fuentes d'Onore, Norman Ramsay at, 23.
Fuse, introduction of new-pattern, 74.

Gage, Captain the Hon. E. T., 263.
Gambier, Colonel, 205.
George III. commends Captain Griffiths, 28.
Graham, Sir Thomas, 54.
Grajal, 38.
Greatly, Colonel, 34, *et seq.*
Griffiths, First Lieutenant of 'C' Troop, 24; commended by George III., 28.
Grylls, Lieutenant, 75, 83; illness of, 231.
Grylls, Major, 259.
Guitiriz, 33, 47.
"Gunners," duties of, 19.
Gustavus Adolphus, the father of Field Artillery, 5.

Hamley, Captain, his adventures at the Castles of Asia, 76.
Harding, Colonel, 38, 46.
Hardinge, Lord, increase of guns by, 71.
Hardships of the Crimean campaign, 216.
Harold, Gunner, death of, 87.
Hartman, Major, letter to, from Captain Andrew Cleeves, 290.
Harvey Bagenal, a leader of the rebels at Ross, 26.
Harvey, Lieutenant C. S., 263.
Heavy Brigade, Charge of the, at Balaclava, 129.
Henry, Captain C. S., 74.
Henry of Prussia, Prince, 1759, 7.
Herreria, 34; Herrerias, 44.
Hill, Captain C. R., 264.
Hill, Sir Rowland, 58.
Hinojosa, French retreat to, 63.
Hoche, General, 25.
Hope, General, 38.
Horse Artillery, description of their special duties, 9.
Horse Artillery, first formation of, in the English Army, 8.
Horse Artillery, reorganization of, 261.
Hoste, Second Captain, joins 'C' Troop, 229.

Index. 305

Hounslow Heath, review at, in 1811, 53.
Howorth, Sir Edward, the first Captain of 'C' Troop, 24, 25, 57.
Humphrey, Captain Evelegh's friend, 47.
Hussars (8th), at Balaclava, 175; (11th), 165.
Hyde Park, composition of a Train of Artillery at a camp in, in 1723, 3; review in, June 18th, 1836, 70; review in, by the Queen, June 25th, 1857, 261.

India, employment of Horse Artillery in, 8, 282.
Indian, amalgamated with the Royal, Artillery, 262.
Indian Artillery, relief of, 263.
Indian Mutiny, an instance of Horse Artillery performing Cavalry duty during the, 8.
Inkerman, description of the Battle of, 205, *et seq.*; English Artillery at, 15.
Ireland, two guns of 'C' Troop sent to, 25.

Johnson, Major-General, at Ross, 26; at Vinegar Hill, 27; letter from, to Lieutenant-General Lake, 286.
Jones, Colonel, 38, 255.
Junot, General, generous treatment of, by Lord Wellington, 64.

"Kalter" guns, 5.
Keene, Lieutenant J. E. Ruck, 231.
Keith, Captain, 249.
Kennington Common, Chartist demonstration on, 71.
King, Captain, 32nd Regiment, death of, 230; his grave, 231.
King, Lieutenant A. H., 221, 230; distinguishes himself at the Redan, 237.
Kinglake's account of the Battle of Balaclava, reviewed, 152, *et seq.*
Kulali, the barracks at, 76-7.
Kunersdorf, Battle of, 7.
Krusemark, Colonel, 279.

La Baneza, 42.
Lake, Colonel, at the Alma, 94; his horse shot, 99.
Lake, General, at Vinegar Hill, 26; his commendation of the Royal Artillery, 27; letter to, from Major-General Johnson, 286.
Lallemand, General, acknowledges the loss inflicted by 'D' Troop, 62; his praise of Captain Whinyates, 64.
Lautour Maubourg, General, defeated at Usagre, 62.
Lavant, 'C' Troop at, 25.
Lawrence, Colonel, 93.

Lawrence, Gunner, 87.
Lefebure, Captain G., 56; receives the praise of Marshal Beresford, 62; praised by General Long, 63; death of, 64.
Lefebvre, General, taken prisoner, 41; Sir John Moore's considerate behaviour towards, 42; his subsequent fate, *ibid.*
Legard, Lieutenant J. D., 272.
Leipsic, Battle of, 1631, 5.
Levinge, Captain, in command of 'C' Troop, 73, 75; death of, 80.
"Light Artillery," adopted by the Austrians, 8.
Light Brigade, Charge of the, at Balaclava, 139.
Light Brigade, formation of the, 163.
Light Dragoons, unusual uniform for an officer of, 114.
"Limber Gunners," description of, 8.
List of Stations of 'C' Troop, 300.
Llewellyn, Dr., 82; prepared to follow his calling, 86.
Lockyer, Rev. E., entertains 'C' Battery at Westcote-Barton, 273.
Lockwood, Bombardier, 122, 203.
Londonderry, Lord, his observations on the retreat to Coruña, 52.
Long, General, at Ribera, 63.
Lucan, Lord, at the camp at Devna, 80; 205; his breakfast on the morning of the Battle of Inkerman, 210; his mules, 211.
Lugo, 34, 35, 36, 47.
Lumley, General, 61; his acknowledgment of the services of 'D' Troop, 62.
Lushington, Captain, and the Russian non-commissioned officer, 120.

Macdonald, Captain, thanked by Sir Rowland Hill, 67.
Macleod, Dr., 35.
Madrid, capitulation of, 35.
Mainwaring, Colonel, kindness of, 48.
Maiwand, Battle of, 275.
Majors, introduction of, into the Artillery, 266.
Malakoff, assault on the, 233; capture of the, 237.
Mallet, Lieutenant H., 56.
Maloney, Mrs., her sad fate owing to possession of too many dollars, 45.
Manners, Lord C., 41.
Manningham, General Coote, 36.
Markham, General, 230.
Marlborough's Artillery in 1709, description of, 21.
Marlborough's campaign in 1702, composition of his "Trains," 3.
Massena, at Wagram, 9.

20

Mathewman, Gunner, killed, 275.
Maude, Captain G. A., 88; wounded at Balaclava, 125.
Maxen, Battle of, 7.
Mayorga, 37.
Mayow, Colonel, at Balaclava, 189.
McKenzie's Farm, 112, et seq.
Mercer, Captain, at Waterloo, 15; incurs the displeasure of the Duke of Wellington, 68.
Michell, Lieutenant, 75, 80.
Millar, W., one of the first Lieutenants of 'C' Troop, 24.
Monasteria Aveza, 37.
Money abandoned on the retreat to Coruña, 45.
Moore, Sir John, in Portugal, 29; military operations of, 33, et seq.; his first meeting with Sir David Baird, 37; death of, 49.
Morris, Captain, eager for the fray, 122; wounded, 140.
Movements before the Heavy Brigade Charge, 152.
Muchir Achmet Pasha, at Eupatoria, 243.
Munseta, action at, 9.
Murray, Gunner, 275.
Muster-roll for November, 1793, 285.
Muzzle-loading field guns, 265.

Napier, Colonel, killed, 49.
Napier, Sir Charles, his order for the march to Ireland of 'C' Troop, 71.
Napier of Magdala, Lord, holds review of Lucknow garrison, 265.
Napoleon's use of Artillery, 9.
Napoleon gives up the pursuit of the English, 43.
Ney, Marshal, supports Soult's pursuit of the English, 43.
"No. 1," special duties of, 13.
Nogales, 44.
Nolan, Captain, death and burial of, 142; mentioned, 199.
Norcott, Major, 93, 97.

Omar Pasha, inspects the camp at Devna, 79; pall-bearer for Lord Raglan, 234.
Orchard, Corporal, 271.
Ordnance, Master-General of the, his duties, 3.
Ormes, Bombardier, 142.
Orthes, Battle of, 67.
Osman Pasha's successful intercession for a Foot Artilleryman, 216.
Otway, Lieutenant-Colonel, 41.

Paget, Lieutenant-General Lord, 39, 42; order of, after review at Hounslow Heath, 53.

Paget, Brigadier-General Lord George, and Lord Cardigan, 169; at Eupatoria, 243; his merriment at a good shot, 245.
Pajol, General, on Horse Artillery, 281.
Palafox, a Spanish General, 30.
Park, Assistant-Surgeon T., 228, 259.
Parlby, Colonel, 228.
Pelissier, General, 233; pall-bearer for Lord Raglan, 234.
Peninsular War, 1808-9, operations in the, 30, et seq.
Perkins, Wheel-driver, killed at the Alma, 99.
Peshawur, 'C' Troop at, 266; description of the march from, to Umballa, 267.
"Picquet-house Hill," 118.
Poland, war against by Gustavus Adolphus, 5.
Portars, 34.
Pozurama, 38.
Presentiments of death, instances of, 230.
Pretsch, a Battery of Horse Artillery raised at, 7.
Prince Imperial of France, salute in honour of, 259.
Prince of Wales's visit to India, 269.
Projectiles of Horse Artillery, weight of, 9.
Prothero, Assistant-Surgeon, 203.
Prussian Infantry overcome by Austrian Artillery, 6.
Puente de Vizana, 41.
Pyrenees, actions in the, 66.

Quintin, Colonel, 41.
Quinton, Assistant-Surgeon, leaves 'C' Troop, 269.

Radcliffe, Major-General R., reorganizes the Horse Artillery, 69.
Radipole, 'C' Troop at, 28.
Raglan, Lord, at the camp at Devna, 79; at the Alma, 94; compliments General Scarlett and Captain Brandling, 143; his high estimation of 'C' Troop, 214; death of, 234; character of, 235.
Railway Transport Return, in India, 29th Jan. 1876, 296.
Ramie, Gunner, wounded at Constantino, 46.
Ramsay, Norman, at Fuentes D'Onore, 23.
Rapid movements of Horse Artillery, instances of, 11.
Raynsford's Brigade, 38.
Reasons for writing this history, 1, 2.
Redan, assaults on the, 232, 237.
Reilly, Gunner, 275.

Index.

Retreat of Russian Cavalry, 151.
Retreat to Coruña, summary of the events of the, 52.
Return of Detachments embarked for service in Ireland, 286.
Return of killed, etc., at Ross, Ireland, 5th June, 1798, 287.
Rewards for service, former niggardly distribution of, 66.
Ribera, Affair of, 63.
Roche, Father, a rebel leader at Ross, Ireland, 26.
Rogan, Commissary, 82.
Romana, 39.
Romer, Colonel, 86.
Rose, Sir Hugh, inspects ' C ' Battery at Calcutta, 264.
Ross, Colonel, 20th Regiment, 42.
Ross, Lieutenant-Colonel Sir Hew, 54.
Ross, in Ireland, the victory at, 26.
Royal Artillery, farther reorganization of, 275.
Rudge, Assistant-Surgeon, 75, 82.
Russian bravery, instance of, 120.
Russian festival, preparations for an expected sortie from Sevastopol on a, 214.
Russian movements at the Battle of Balaclava, 155.
Russian retreat at the Battle of the Alma, 103.
Russian tactics, singular instance of, 234.
Ryan, Gunner, 275.

Sadowa, Austrian Artillery at, 15.
Sahagun, 38.
Salamanca, Affair at, 66.
Saladaña, 38.
Sandham, —., 38.
Scarlett, General, complimented by Lord Raglan, 143.
" Schemer," Captain Evelegh's horse, 33.
Sevastopol, first sight of, 117; precautions before, 118.
" Seven Years' War," Artillery in the, 6.
Sevenoaks, ' C ' Troop at, 28.
Shaw, Gunner, 80.
Shewell, Colonel, at Balaclava, 175.
Simpson, Sir James, pall-bearer for Lord Raglan, 234.
Skoulding, Veterinary-Surgeon J. B. W., 263.
Slade, Captain J. R., 275.
" Soldiers' Battle, The," 208.
Soult, Marshal, at Carrion, 38; continues the pursuit of the English, 43.
Spain, request of, to England, for assistance against Napoleon, 28.
Spanish Junta, facility of, in creating armies on paper, 35.

St. Arnaud, Marshal, 92.
St. Leger, General, Colonel Wellesley's letter to, 8, 282.
Stacey, Driver, 124.
Stewart, Brigadier-General, 39.
Stirling, Lieutenant, appointed to ' C ' Troop, 238.
Strange, Captain H. F., 93, 119; serves as a volunteer at the taking of the Malakoff, 237.
Strangways, Colonel, 74, 79, 81, 82, 83, 94; wounded at Inkerman, 205; death of, 207.
Strangways, Lieut.-Col. W. Fox, 274.
Strangways, Lieutenant, 80.
Stratton, Gunner, death of, 81.
Stuart, Mr., one of the British Commissioners, 34.
Succession List of Officers and Staff Sergeants of ' C ' Battery, Appendix XXVI., the folded table preceding this Index.
Sultan Abdul Medjid, inspects ' C ' Troop, 259.
" Sweet Waters of Asia," ' C ' Troop at, 78.
Swinley, ' C ' Troop encamped at, 28.
Swinnerton, Gunner, killed, 275.

Tamorama, 37.
Tchernaya, Battle of the, 236.
Texel, Dutch Expedition delayed in the, 25.
Thomas, Captain H. J., 74; appointed to ' C ' Troop, 81; illness of, 86; rejoins ' C ' Troop, 215.
Thrupp, Driver, drowned, 79.
Tilly at the Battle of Leipsic, 5.
Todleben's comparison of English and Russian Artillery at Inkerman, 15.
Tordesillas, Napoleon at, 40; his communication to Marshal Soult from, ibid.
Toro, the place where Sir John Moore first met Sir David Baird, 37.
Toulouse, Battle of, 67.
Trabadelos, 34, 44.
" Trains," a technical term, when first introduced, 3.
Trautenau Expedition of Frederick the Great, 6, 7.
Triple Alliance against Russia in 1854, 72.
Tulloh, Major J. S., takes over the command of ' C ' Battery, 264.
Turkish soldiers, instance of cruelty of, 145.
Turks, mortality amongst the, at the Crimea, 221.
Tweeddale, Marquis of, his eulogistic remarks on ' D ' Troop, 67.

308   Index.

"United Irishmen," a secret society, 25.
Usagre, cavalry action at, 62.

Valderas, 39, 40.
Varna, 'C' Troop at, 81; accident during the embarkation of 'C' Troop at, 83-4.
Venables, Assistant-Surgeon E., 29.
Victoria Cross, one of the first recipients of the, 148; distribution of the, by the Queen, 261.
Villada, 38.
Villa Franca, 34, 42.
Villatte, General, 66.
Vinegar Hill, escape of the rebels at, 26.
Vittoria, Battle of, 66.
Volunteers for 'C' Troop, 225.
Volunteers for Indian service, 275.
Von Schlabrendorf, Frederick the Great's authorization to, 279.

"Waggoners," the predecessors of "Drivers," 16.
Wagram, Battle of, 9.
Walcott, Lieutenant E. Y., 29, 35, 38.
Ward, Captain E. C., in command of 'C' Troop, 73; takes leave of his Troop, 74.
Wareham, 'C' Troop at, 28.
Warley, 'C' Troop at, 28.
War services of 'C' Troop, 298.
War services of 'D' Troop, 299.

Waterloo, Battle of, 68; review in Hyde Park on twenty-first anniversary of, 70.
Wauchope, Captain, 267.
Webber, Lieutenant W., 29, 33, 38, 40; wounded at Waterloo, 68.
Wellesley, note on the spelling of the name, 284.
Wellington, Duke of, letter from, in 1797, to General St. Leger, on the employment of Horse Artillery in India, 8, 282; despatched to the Peninsula with an English Army, 29; his reasons for reducing 'D' Troop, 68.
Wellington's Artillery in 1811, 22.
Wexford, atrocities of the rebels at, in 1798, 27.
Weymouth, 'C' Troop encamped at, 28.
Whinyates, Sir Edward, 55, 56; receives special praise from General Long for service at Ribera, 63; also from General Lallemand, 64, 65.
Willett, Capt., 75; proceeds to Varna, 81.
Wood, Colonel, his gift to Captain Evelegh, 47.
Woolwich, 'C' Troop formed at, 4.
Wurtz system of Artillery, 280.
Wyatt, Colonel, 38.
Wynn, Captain, death of, 103.

Zouaves, readiness for duty of the, 204.

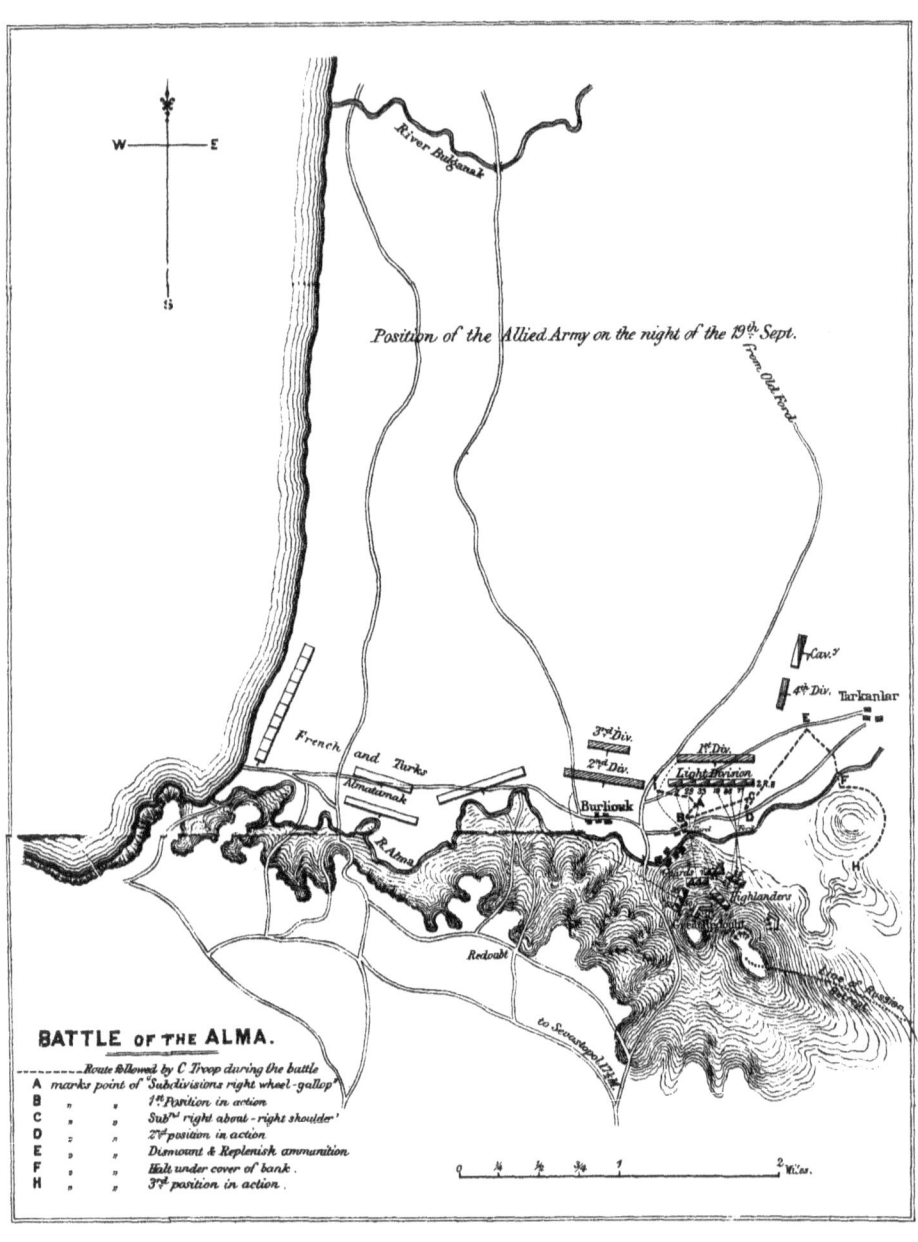

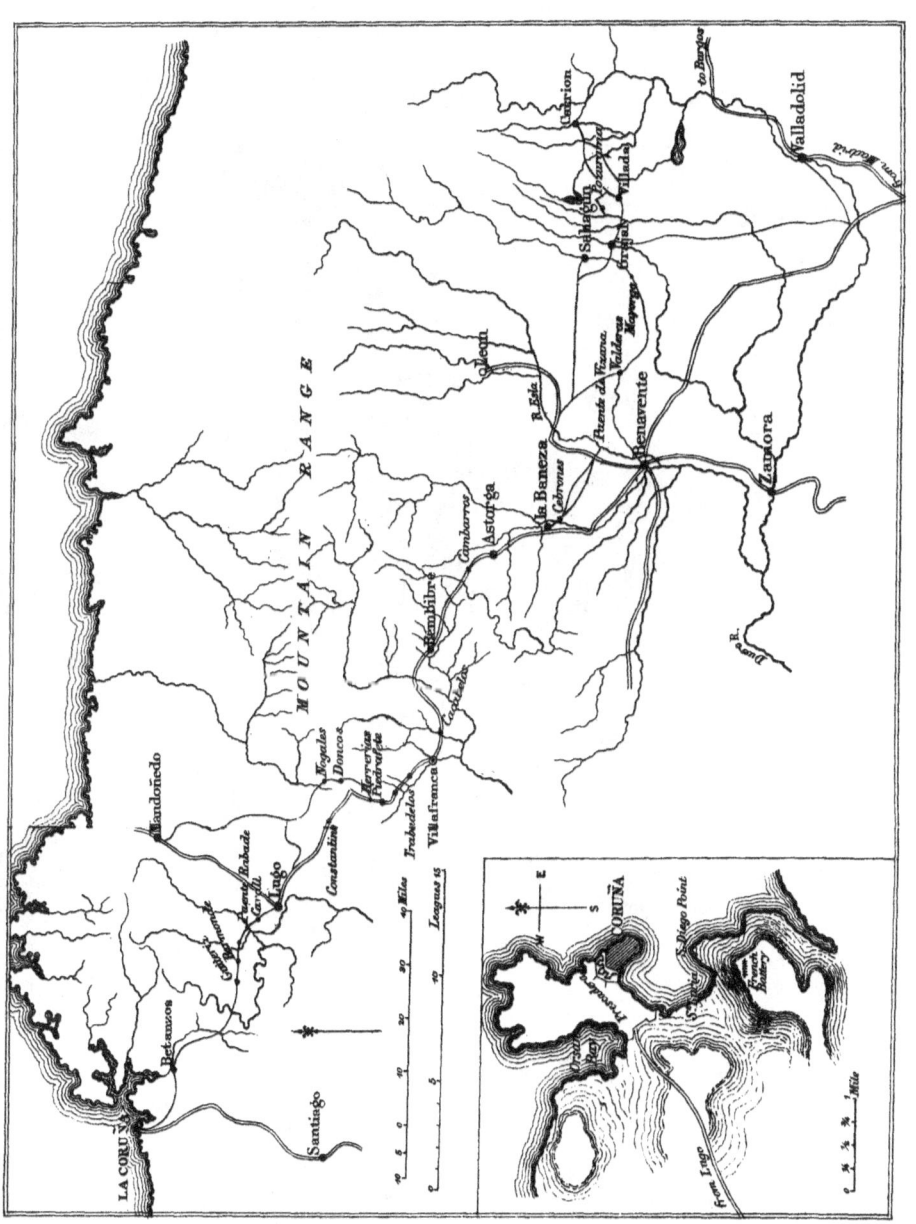